# Redirecting Radical Democracy

# REDIRECTING RADICAL DEMOCRACY

*From Antagonism to Alienation*

SOFIA ANCEAU HELANDER

EDINBURGH
University Press

Edinburgh University Press is one of the leading university presses in the UK. We publish academic books and journals in our selected subject areas across the humanities and social sciences, combining cutting-edge scholarship with high editorial and production values to produce academic works of lasting importance. For more information visit our website: edinburghuniversitypress.com

Edinburgh University Press Ltd
13 Infirmary Street
Edinburgh EH1 1LT

First published in hardback by Edinburgh University Press 2024

Typeset in 11/13pt Adobe Sabon LT Pro
by Cheshire Typesetting Ltd, Cuddington, Cheshire

A CIP record for this book is available from the British Library

ISBN 978 1 3995 2216 8 (hardback)
ISBN 978 1 3995 2217 5 (paperback)
ISBN 978 1 3995 2218 2 (webready PDF)
ISBN 978 1 3995 2215 1 (epub)

# Contents

# Tables

# Acknowledgements

Writing, being a solitary endeavour, is completely dependent on the companionships surrounding it. I am fortunate enough to have continuously received insightful comments and critique by numerous colleagues, family and friends, which made the process of writing this book genuinely inspiring and worthwhile.

The academic milieu at the Department of Government at Uppsala University has been important in shaping this book. Working in a place where we all do very different types of research is both rewarding and demanding. First and foremost, I wish to express my gratitude to Sofia Näsström for all the feedback and encouragement throughout the process, as well as for being a constant source of inspiration. I would like to express a special thanks to Bo Bengtsson and Alexandra Segerberg who have given me indispensable advice, as well as supportive and critical comments on various ideas and drafts. Many other colleagues in the Government department, and its guests, have also provided incisive comments on chapters of this book. I especially want to thank Katrin Uba, Jonas Hultin Rosenberg, Li Bennich-Björkman, Johan Tralau, Siri Sylvan, Gina Gustavsson, Ludvig Norman, Johanna Pettersson, Anthoula Malkopoulou, Benjamin Ask Popp-Madsen, Arda Gucler and Johan Wejryd. In addition, I thank the Johan och Jakob Söderbergs Foundation for generously providing me with the funding that allowed me to make some crucial final additions to the manuscript.

While writing this book, I had the privilege of visiting the Centre for Humanities and Social Change at Humboldt University, Berlin, the Department of Political Science at Columbia University in the City of New York, and the Centre for Social Movement Studies at Scuola Normale Superiore, Florence. I want to express my sincere gratitude to Rahel Jaeggi, Nadia Urbinati and Lorenzo Bosi for hosting me. I also want to thank Andrew Schaap for inviting me to the University of Exeter and everyone else at the workshop on precarity and democratic politics for their inspiration and sincere feedback. Moreover, I am indebted to the two anonymous reviewers at Edinburgh University Press for their stimulating observations, as well as the editors Beatriz Lopez and Ersev Ersoy for a smooth process.

Outside of these institutions, I am indebted to Sharon Rider, Mikael Carleheden and David Payne for enlightening criticism at a crucial stage in the project. I have also been fortunate to work and write in the company of some wonderful people and scholars. I am so greatful for Linus Westheuser, Karl Ekeman, Maya Ström, Hedvig Ördén, Nina Carlsson, Vincent Camus, Zohreh Khoban and Miriam Selén Gerson. All of you have shaped this project in so many ways.

Finally I want to thank my family. My wife's parents, Sandrine and Hubert, for sharing their kindness, good spirits and lovely (long!) lunches with me. Most especially, thanks to Tove, Hyben, My, Judith, Alice and Adèle. Beyond having you all – except little Adèle, of course – directly helping me with the book, you are each the loveliest mother, grandmother, great-grandmother, sisters, aunts, wife and daughter imaginable, and are the wonders of my life.

# From antagonism to alienation

Driven by a desire to leave the city where he grew up and the trajectory of low-paid jobs that seemed destined for him, Jacob moves to a larger city to pursue a business degree. However, he soon finds that the program and the traineeships are not leading anywhere. Despite this, Jacob has no choice but to stay. The program and the traineeships can, at least temporarily, hold off what seems like an inescapable future of unemployment or a string of low-income jobs.

Two years after earning a degree in media and communication, and having been among the top of her class, Samira cannot bring herself to care about her work any more. Working as a freelance journalist, she accepts every job she can get, even those that are unpaid – just to expand her network – or that go against her moral code. Her priorities are, primarily, the money and the experience. Moreover, she works extra hours at whatever temporary job she can get. She is always tired, unable to engage in either of her jobs.

Ever since the car factory shut down, Thomas has not managed to find another job. He has tried working at a warehouse in a nearby town, but the long commute, the low salary and the bad working conditions have made it logistically and physically impossible. Although the work at the car factory had been hard and the hours long, there had been the union, his friends and the respect between Thomas and his colleagues. Now, he no longer knows what job to apply for, and his motivation to do so is rapidly waning.

Emma cannot remember when she stopped caring about her work as a teacher. It could have been the new set of diagnostic tests she had to perform, the new managerial level she had to answer to, or the point at which the hours designated for her to plan new lessons were cut for the third time. At this point, however, she does not have much control over what she teaches or how she does it. People

1

keep saying that teaching is important, yet Emma feels increasingly disposable.

Jacob, Samira, Thomas and Emma all experience that their relations to their social world are inhibited in such a way that they also inhibit their relations to themselves. The professional path on which they had set out, as well as the social relations and forms of freedom associated with it, are lost. Jacob lingers in uncertainty, unable to enter the labour market. His expectation – that an education could lead to status and a new path in life – is thwarted. Samira can only get temporary jobs in the field that she is educated in; furthermore, the jobs she does get are not what she expected. Being a journalist does not, at least not for her, imply either status or professional integrity and freedom. Thomas is stuck in unemployment, unable to re-enter the labour market. He has lost the source of empowerment and bonds of solidarity that a job, albeit a hard one, had offered. And while Emma is still able to keep her job as a teacher, she sees her professional freedom gradually being undermined, leaving her unable to find herself in her work. Situations like those of Jacob, Samira, Thomas and Emma – where the subject's relation to the world is inhibited in such a way that her relationship to herself becomes dysfunctional – are examples of what I will call alienation.

As alienation grows increasingly widespread through processes of precarisation, we want people to address their grievances and to challenge the social processes that alienate them – and to do so in an open, democratic way, without falling into aggressively exclusionary politics that threatens to tear the political association apart. The purpose of this book is to ask what is needed for radical democratic theory to be able to address this problem. To remain politically relevant, I will argue, it has to satisfy two general criteria. On the one hand, it needs to be radical – to contain a dimension of social suffering, power and antagonism. It has to engage with the suffering that people experience in a way that encourages them to contest it. On the other hand, we want the theory to be open – to avoid what has been viewed as the authoritarian tendencies of alienation theory, including its determinism, human essentialism and idealisation of a final state of harmony beyond politics.

There are many different traditions of thinking democracy – liberal, republican, deliberative and agonistic, to name a few. Each of these would have its own response to the problem of alienation. Agonistic, what is also called radical, democracy is characterised by

2

its emphasis on transformative social struggle as well as its concern with avoiding what are seen as the authoritarian pitfalls of traditional socialism. It becomes relevant if we wish to address the problem of alienation in a way that is as radical as it is open. However, something important is missing in the theory. As I will show in this book, radical democracy is unable to address alienation. This, I argue, is not merely due to the historical conditions from which it emerges – marked by a turn away from traditional socialist concepts – but also due to a deeper tension in the theory itself. In its attempts to remain both radical and open, agonistic democracy comes to rely on a subject who is flexible, strong and conflict-seeking – perfectly suited to manoeuvering in situations of alienation. And in this, it fails to capture the situation of Jacob, Samira, Thomas and Emma, whose relations to their social worlds are inhibited in such a way that their relations to themselves become dysfunctional. In this book, therefore, I seek to reformulate the subject of radical democracy in order to theoretically address alienation in an open and radical way.

This Introduction begins by describing the social and political context of the inquiry – today's problem of alienation – and the research problem that guides it, that is, how to address alienation in an open and radical way within democratic theory. It goes on to discuss radical democracy's potential in responding to this problem, as well as the theoretical gap that prevents it from doing so. The Introduction ends with a note on the status of the argument, its significance, and a brief description of the chapters that follow.

## ALIENATION TODAY

Why is it important to study alienation today? Is alienation not just an essential part of the human condition, something that people have been experiencing throughout history? The most important manifestation of alienation today is precarity. And, according to many sociologists, what is particular about precarity today is how widespread and normalised it is. Precarity has in the last decade been subjected to intense academic and political debate. In its most narrow definition, precarity has been understood as a problem of unstable employment touching only society's most vulnerable groups, such as low-skilled routine workers (Savage et al. 2013, 12–15). In the broadest possible sense, precarity is conceptualised as a part of a general condition of vulnerability in which we all find ourselves (Butler 2006). Here,

3

I refer to precarity as a broad but social problem – encompassing a range of insecure and dependent situations linked to the dynamics of the labour market. Precarity, in my understanding, is neither a part of the general human condition nor something that only affects the most vulnerable people in society. Following the wider sociological literature on precarity, I will assume that precarity involves multiple processes of precarisation, affecting different strata of society (e.g. Bauman 2000; Berlant 2011; Lempiäinen 2015; Sennett 1998). For some people, precarity means decreased employment security, whereas for others it is primarily the work itself – its professional status, freedom and integrity – that is at risk. Often, these two processes are interlinked, in that processes of deprofessionalisation render employees more easily replaceable and their employment less secure.

Precarity has been captured in this general sense by a broad and influential literature on sociology and social theory (e.g. Bauman 2000; Berlant 2011, 192; Bourdieu et al. 1999; Della Porta 2015, 1; Sennett 1998). In his seminal work *Liquid Modernity*, Zygmunt Bauman describes precarity as 'the mark of the preliminary condition of . . . the livelihood, and particularly the most common sort of livelihood, that which is claimed on the ground of work and employment' (Bauman 2000, 161). According to Bauman, it encompasses an insecurity of position and entitlements, an uncertainty of future stability and a lack of safety concerning oneself, one's possessions and one's community – all of which are tied to one's work (Bauman 2000, 161). Bauman argues that what differentiates precarity from earlier forms of insecurity is how widespread it is. '[P]recariousness, instability, vulnerability is', he claims, 'the most widespread (as well as the most painfully felt) feature of contemporary life conditions' (Bauman 2000, 160). Influential sociologists Pierre Bourdieu and Richard Sennett make similar arguments. In 1997, Bourdieu published a paper titled 'Le precarité est aujourd'hui partout': today, precarity is everywhere. Precarity today is not only widespread but has, according to Sennett, grown so common that it can be described as a new state of normality. 'What's peculiar about uncertainty today', Sennett states, 'is that it exists without any looming historical disaster; instead it is woven into the everyday practices of a vigorous capitalism. Instability is meant to be normal' (Sennett 1998, 31). Our society is, in Bourdieu's words, an institutionalisation of 'generalised and permanent insecurity' (Bourdieu 1998, my translation).

Precarity is ingrained in all our institutions, and most of all in the labour market.

There are many explanations to precarisation. Scholars commonly associate it with wider processes, such as globalisation and technological development, in which both people and capital are able to move more freely and at a greater speed. These processes, sociologists suggest, are supported by the contemporary ideal of 'flexibilisation'. '"Flexibility"', Bauman asserts, 'is the catchword of the day' (Bauman 2000, 161). Both organisations and individuals are subjected to the imperative to move, reorganise, change – all in order not to lag behind. In the labour market, these processes manifest themselves as a destabilisation of both employment and professional life.

Precarisation of employment can be observed in the increase of fixed-term work and unemployment. The most insecure employments are found among routine workers – those bound to the assembly line or electronic, automated devices – who, requiring few particular skills, belong to the most replaceable elements of the economic system (Bauman 2000, 152). Routine workers are at the highest risk of losing their work as companies are outsourced or downsized. Other typical groups in this category include students and others who have yet to enter the labour market (Della Porta 2015, 4). The precarisation of young people can be most clearly observed in the growing gig economy; there, organisations hire independent workers for short-term commitments, such as for food delivery. It can also be observed in the increased movement between employments and workplaces. Sennett observes, for example, that a young, educated person could be expected to change jobs at least eleven times and change her entire skill base or profession at least three times (Sennett 1998, 22). While many young people may themselves prefer to 'be on the move', these drives are also part of the general cultural idea of 'flexibilisation'. Personal drives can, in Bourdieu's words, often be an attempt to make a 'virtue of necessity' (Bourdieu et al. 1999, 428).

Furthermore, while routine workers and students are at the highest risk of insecure unemployment, the experience of precarity can, according to Bauman and Sennett, affect everyone. In Bauman's words:

> No one may reasonably assume to be insured against the next round of 'downsizing', 'streamlining' or 'rationalizing', against erratic shifts of market demand and whimsical yet irresistible, indomitable pressures of

'competitiveness', 'productivity' and 'effectiveness' . . . No one can feel truly irreplaceable. (Bauman 2000, 161)

When some people are rendered insecure, it generates a general sense of insecurity.

However, the experience of precarity among employees with relatively stable contracts is not merely subjective. The flexible workplace is managed in such a way that each person's tasks are made increasingly simple, and each employee is rendered more easily replaceable (Sennett 1998, 72). Through processes of 'effectivisation' and 'flexibilisation', a variety of jobs are, according to Sennett, increasingly automatised and deskilled, which is followed by a decrease in status, salary, autonomy and work security. In many professional areas, scholars have witnessed an increasing automatisation (Collins 2013), a declining trust in experts (Collins 2013), the development of a freelance culture followed by a decline in full-time work (Srnicek 2017), and an increased need for retraining due to rapid technological progress (Kalleberg 2009; Smith 2010).

These processes – often described as 'precarisation' or 'deprofessionalisation' – affect a number of professions and semi-professions, including some, but not all, artisans, teachers, social workers, journalists, managers, academics and lawyers (Dominelli and Hoogvelt 1996; Haug 1972; Healy and Meagher 2004; Milner 2013; Posner 1992; Reed and Evans 1987). If professionals are defined by their capacity to use their knowledge to do things that are valued by, but appear difficult to, clients and society at large (Brante 2005, 9), deprofessionalisation means that professionals lose their status, autonomy and authority. As her tasks are increasingly automatised, the professional previously valued for her skills and knowledge becomes replaceable. The professional ethos, identities and social relations, often sustained by professional associations, are undermined (Haug 1975; Toren 1975).

Teachers are one of the professions most intensively affected by deprofessionalisation. Through standardised tests and pre-packaged curricula, they lose control over both the content and method of their teaching. This also means that their professional status is weakened. Teachers are increasingly viewed as service personnel, while students come to view themselves as customers (Filson 1988). Several manual semi-professions – including bakers and cobblers – have also been affected. Sennett observes, for example, how the work at a bakery he

6

had visited decades earlier had become almost completely automatised.[1] The work consists only in managing simple machinery, what he describes as 'simply pushing buttons in a windows-program' (Sennett 1998, 70). The people at the bakery are well aware of their deprofessionalisation, continuously saying 'the same thing in different words: I'm not really a baker' (Sennett 1998, 70). In the processes of deprofessionalisation, the value of professional expertise decreases. As their relations to their colleagues, to their clients and to their own professional identities are disrupted, professionals and semi-professionals lose their autonomy and are rendered increasingly precarious.

We have thus seen how the processes often described as 'precarisation' or 'deprofessionalisation' affect a wide range of social groups, leaving them in situations of insecurity and dependency. Given the purpose of this book, two aspects of these processes are particularly relevant. So far, I have primarily touched upon the first aspect: precarity as an inhibited social relation. The writings on precarisation and deprofessionalisation describe how many people experience a disruption in their relations to their social world, and, in particular, to their work. People's relations to their workplace, their colleagues and their professional community are severed. Furthermore, Sennett goes on to demonstrate that the destabilisation of work relations also results in a destabilisation of many other social ties, including relations to family, friends and local communities. Labour market precarisation and flexibilisation lead, for example, to people having to be ready to move to another town in order to find work, thus disrupting their neighbourhood ties. They also have to be ready to work at any time, which, again, disrupts commitments to family and friends (Sennett 1998, 28–30). Precarisation can thus inhibit the subject's relation not only to her work but also to her social world at large.

There is, however, a second aspect of the process of precarisation that is even more central to this study. Precarity scholars have captured how the inhibition of the precarious subject's social ties is followed by another, deeper form of inhibition: a dysfunction in the subject's relation to herself. Sennett describes this dysfunctional relation to the self as a 'corrosion of character' (Sennett 1998). He contends that precarisation, marked by the decreased possibility of long-term commitment, can disrupt the subject's relation to, and understanding of, her own will and behaviour: '"No long term"

7

disorients action over the long term, loosens bonds of trust . . . and divorces will from behaviour' (Sennett 1998, 31). Among his interviewees, Sennett observes not only a loss of 'interest in their work and the workplace' but also a 'fading of their wish to invest thought and moral energy in the future' (Sennett 1998, 152). The subject loses interest not only in the world around her but also in her own life. If our habits and routines allow us to navigate social practices and to maintain a sense of purpose, these capacities are lost in the process of precarisation. In Sennett's words, 'to imagine a life of momentary impulses . . . devoid of sustainable routines, a life without habits, is to imagine indeed a mindless existence' (Sennett 1998, 44). Similarly, Bauman observes, 'Work can no longer offer the secure axis around which to wrap and fix self-definitions, identities and life-projects. Neither can it be easily conceived of as . . . the ethical axis of individual life' (Bauman 2000, 139). As her social relations, including her identities, commitments and systems of meaning, corrode, so does the subject herself.

This is, according to Bauman, not merely a temporary, painful disruption; in a precarious world, it actually risks becoming so ingrained in the subject that it develops into a new form of subjectivity. For many people, this particular subjectivity quickly turns dysfunctional. Precarious subjects become habituated to powerlessness, disruptions and loss; to manage this, they develop what Bauman describes as the 'virtue of flexibility' (Bauman 2000, 155). In Bauman's words, they have to 'master the art of "labyrynthine [sic] living": acceptance of disorientation, readiness to live outside space and time, with vertigo and dizziness, with no inkling of the direction or the duration of travel they embark on' (Bauman 2000, 153). To be able to move quickly and with ease, people cannot be too rooted in their own identities, desires or moral commitments (Bauman 2000, 162; Tsianos and Papadopoulos 2006). They must be ready to let go, to disengage. The precarious labour market requires, Sennett writes, a 'particular strength of character – that of someone who has the confidence to dwell in disorder, someone who flourishes in the midst of dislocation' (Sennett 1998, 62). To stop caring becomes a survival skill; it makes possible the continuous movement and loss that a precarious society demands (Sennett 1998, 50).

However, although initially adopted as a strategy to navigate a precarious world, this form of disengaged subjectivity often becomes dysfunctional. In Sennett's view, contemporary ambiguity is a form of power that can only be wielded by a very few. For most people, it becomes disorienting and disempowering. As the precarious subject's frantic activity takes her nowhere, it becomes increasingly hard for her to make sense of her life in terms of a sustained narrative and to take command over her own actions (Sennett 1998, 117). However, although this lack of command can be experienced by almost anyone, it is, in Sennett's description, likely to be felt more intensely the further down in the precarious regime we get (Sennett 1998, 63). In Sennet's words, 'Less powerful individuals who try to exploit ambiguity wind up feeling exiles [sic]. Or, in moving, they lose their way' (Sennett 1998, 85). While precarious society obliges us to develop the ability to dwell, even flourish, in the state of disruption, only a few can meet these demands without losing their way and themselves.

These two aspects of the processes of precarisation – the inhibition of the subject's relation to the world and the dysfunction in her relationship to herself – indicate a deeper problem with which this study is concerned. I call this the problem of alienation. Alienation, broadly defined, is a social or psychological ill in which the subject's relation to an object is inhibited in such a way that her relationship to herself becomes dysfunctional. This, I have suggested, is precisely what scholars have observed in the precarious subject. As her social relations – and, in particular, her work relations – are disrupted, the precarious subject becomes unable not only to navigate specific social contexts but also to remain in command of herself.

## THE PROBLEM: ADDRESSING ALIENATION IN A RADICAL AND OPEN WAY

If we assume that many of the widespread processes of precarisation that we see today are, in fact, manifestations of alienation, this would pose a serious challenge to today's modern democracies. If people feel unable to contest, and struggle against, their alienation in a democratic way, we may see a significant portion of the population who, in practice, are standing outside of the democratic system, unable to raise their grievances, or who, in losing hope, revert to violent antagonisms that could threaten to tear the democratic political association apart.

In this book, I will assume that, in a healthy democracy, we would want to see alienated people mobilising against their alienation in

9

a way that is both radical – challenging existing power relations – and open – capable of harbouring a multiplicity of demands and responding to new claims.[2] However, while traditional concepts of alienation have been mobilised for radical social change, they have also been criticised for not being open enough.

In particular, the concept of alienation has been associated with three pitfalls. First, it has been accused of human essentialism, according to which the subject is predefined by a particular type of activity or way of life. In traditional socialism, for example, the human being is assumed to actualise herself primarily in and through her labour. Second, it has been claimed to imply determinism, the assumption that the subject's actions are entirely decided by the social structure and her position in it. Third, it has been associated with the ideal of a final state of harmony: the assumption that a stable state free of inner and social conflict is both possible and desirable. None of these assumptions is compatible with the idea of open political mobilisation, responsive to a plurality of emerging claims. Human essentialism and determinism imply that the subject's will and actions can be determined independently of the subject herself, suggesting that political movements do not have to listen to people's actual demands. The ideal of a final state of harmony suggests that once alienation has been overcome, we can reach a state beyond conflict and politics, a state in which democratic engagement and institutions are no longer needed.

In response to these problems, leading critical theorists have sought to revive the concept of alienation. This includes work by late Frankfurt school scholars such as Axel Honneth (2008), Hartmut Rosa (2010) and Rahel Jaeggi (2014). Among these, Jaeggi makes the most complex attempt at relieving the concept of its problematic baggage, which she describes as, 'on the one hand, its essentialism and its perfectionist orientation around a conception of the essence or nature of human beings . . .; on the other hand, the ideal of reconciliation – the ideal of a unity free of tension' (Jaeggi 2014, 2). However, as I will show later, in the attempts to open up the concept of alienation, the concern with its potential for political mobilisation falls out of focus – despite the fact that this potential was the reason why alienation was originally considered important within the left. When the mobilising qualities of the concept are no longer explicitly valued, the theory does not provide the analysis of unequal social power and antagonism that would make it conducive to thinking transformative social struggle and change.

10

Forming a theory of alienation that is both open – avoiding common pitfalls – and radical – maintaining a dimension of unequal power and antagonism – is thus not an easy task. Where would we expect such a theory to emerge – one that can conceptualise alienation in an open and radical way?

## RADICAL DEMOCRACY: THE STRONGEST ANSWER

In order to address the problem of alienation, I will turn to radical democracy, or, more specifically, to Chantal Mouffe's ideas, sometimes called the agonistic theory of democracy. Much like everyone else who studies political problems, I have to pick a particular lens through which to observe them (Shapiro, Smith, and Masoud 2004). Not only is radical democracy so politically influential today that it is in itself worth studying – with, for example, Mouffe personally working with the Spanish party Podemos and the French political leader Jean-Luc Mélenchon (Errejón and Mouffe 2016; Thomassen 2016). It should also have one of the potentially strongest answers to our problem: how to address alienation in a way that satisfies the criteria for an open and radical theory.

Radical democracy distinguishes itself from other democratic theories by its emphasis on the importance of passion, power, identities and deep disagreements in politics (Schaap 2009, 1). It stems from a strand within the democratic left that understands democracy as a space for open and radical struggle – a struggle that is plural, transformative and without any end point or conclusion. Democracy is, according to the radical democratic predecessor Claude Lefort, 'instituted and sustained by the dissolution of the markers of certainty' (Lefort 1988, 19). It opens up a space for continuous conflict and social transformation.

Among contemporary radical democrats, radicalism and openness are central to their understanding of democracy – although they commonly prioritise either the former (Laclau 2005; Rancière 2009) or the latter (Connolly 1995, 2002; Honig 1993). I will focus on Chantal Mouffe, whose work distinguishes itself by its equal emphasis on both radicalism and openness. Mouffe's work includes a strategic political project for the left, which she originally formulated alongside Ernesto Laclau, as well as a normative democratic theory, what she terms agonistic democracy. Laclau and Mouffe ([1985] 2001, 167) describe their strategy for political mobilisation as a

11

'radical and plural democracy'. It aims at being 'plural' in the sense that it binds together 'a multiplicity of heterogeneous demands in a way that maintains the internal differentiation of the group', and it is constructed in a way that is 'always susceptible to rearticulation' (Mouffe 2019, 62–3). At the same time, it is radical in the sense that 'the aim . . . is a profound transformation of the existing power relations' (Mouffe 2005a, 52; see also Mouffe 2019, 47). In short, the aim of Mouffe's radical democracy is to form an open and radical political association.

In asserting the need for an open and radical political practice, Mouffe also seeks to provide a theory of democracy that could be described as open and radical. Describing her approach as 'anti-essentialist', she emphasises that there is no essential human nature, no socially determined course of events, and no final state of harmony (Mouffe 2019, 87–9). At the same time, the theory seeks, according to Mouffe, to emphasise social power, suffering and antagonism. She criticises other radical democratic theories for not fully grasping the radical antagonistic dimension of politics (Mouffe 2013, 14). Society is, according to Mouffe, marked by power and divisions that, at any time, can erupt into antagonism (Mouffe 2019, 88). Antagonism, she argues, can never be fully eradicated, only tamed. For this reason, she claims, a central aim of modern democracies should be to maintain radical, transformative conflict, but also to transform it. Antagonism, a struggle between enemies seeking to destroy each other, should be transformed into agonism: the struggle between respected adversaries (Mouffe 2019, 91). In her model of agonistic democracy, Mouffe strives for both a theory and a practice that are open and radical.

Furthermore, given its own aims, agonistic democracy should be not only open and radical but also sufficiently equipped to theoretically accommodate alienation. The theory is, as I will argue, designed to address precisely those marginalised people whose social relations and identities have been inhibited.

Mouffe inscribes her radical democracy in a moment of disruption, the moment when previously shared commitments and identities fall into question and can no longer function (Mouffe 2005a, 5).[3] We are, Mouffe maintains, witnessing such a moment in Western democracies today: a moment when, 'under the pressure of political and socioeconomic transformations, the dominant hegemony is being destabilized by the multiplication of unsatisfied demands' (Mouffe 2019, 9). When the social world disintegrates – because of precarisation, globalisation and socioeconomic transformation – the power that holds us in place also disintegrates. Mouffe calls this power hegemony, defined as the 'point of confluence between objectivity and power' (Mouffe 2000b, 21). Hegemonic power establishes our common sense, what we, in a society or specific social milieu, share and take for granted. For radical democrats, today's disrupted social relations and identities come as no surprise. On the contrary, this is the moment radical democracy attempts to practically and theoretically address. We would thus expect radical democrats – focused on experiences of marginalisation and disrupted relations of identification – to be able to address alienation. But can they?

## WHAT IS MISSING? THE THEORETICAL GAP

Although experiences of social marginalisation are the focus of radical democracy, the theory has, its critics claim, become 'socially weightless', unable to address real instances of social suffering (McNay 2014, 40). In her influential volume *The Misguided Search for the Political* (2014), Lois McNay argues that thinkers such as Mouffe grant an 'absolute priority . . . to the supposedly necessary logic of the political over the inert realm of the social' and thus 'close[] off issues of empowerment that are crucial to an emancipatory account of agency' (McNay 2014, 25). In response, however, radical democrats maintain that the turn towards the political is itself a political intervention, driven by a deep concern for social subordination (Marchart 2018; Paipais 2017). The theory of the political suggests that even a society that appears to be just and harmonious is fraught with suffering and antagonism. By emphasising the political, then, we are encouraged to be attentive to these forms of suffering and find ways to address them.

This book shows that whereas radical democracy is indeed deeply concerned with social subordination, there is one particular form of social suffering that it cannot address: alienation. The theory cannot include Jacob, Samira, Thomas and Emma, who experience social disruption not as emancipating – inspiring radical resistance – but as deeply painful, disconnecting them from both their social relations and themselves. Why is that?

A central argument I make is that radical democracy cannot address the problem of alienation due to its underlying assumptions about the individual subject. The disappearance of the concept of

13

alienation can be traced back to the radical democratic turn of the left in the late twentieth century. With this turn, Karl Marx's concept of alienation, which the left had used during the post-war period to address disrupted expectations and social relations, became unviable (Keucheyan 2013, 35).

At the time, the concept of alienation was associated with what the radical democratic left considered to be the pitfalls of traditional socialism, the idea of an essential human nature, a deterministic course of history and a final conflict-free state. Having seen the violence and failures of the attempted socialist states, parts of the left feared that human essentialism and the ideal of a final state of harmony could breed authoritarianism and dangerous antagonism. In this vein, left-wing theorist Claude Lefort argued that

> [t]he image of society at one with itself delivered from social division and conflict, can be grasped only during the purge, where there is a separation between the enemies of the people and the People; or better yet during the enemy's extermination. (Lefort 1988, 84)

For that reason, radical democrats turned from a focus on the social – the struggle for freedom in social relations – to a focus on the political, that is, ineradicable power and antagonism. The aim was no longer to achieve social freedom, but to channel the antagonism that was seen as an unavoidable dimension of any social formation – and to do so in a democratically constructive way. With this move, the concept of alienation, associated with the idea of an unalienated state of harmony, free of inner and social contradictions, fell out of focus.

The inability of radical democracy to address alienation can thus partly be explained by the historical context and tradition from which it emerged, when the problem of antagonism seemed more acute than that of alienation. In addition, and even more importantly, I will explore the possibility that there is a deeper problem in the theory itself. I show that Mouffe defends an open and radical theory of democracy by relying on assumptions about the individual subject that renders it unable to address the problem of alienation.

While radical democrats emphasise how forms of individuality are central to democracy (Mouffe 2000b, 69), and some have tried to reformulate what a radical subjectivity (Norval 2004, 159), ethics (Critchley 2004) or ethos (Glynos 2003; Connolly 2004) should be, little critical attention has been paid to the ideas of the individual

14

subject that radical democratic theory has at its base. In this book, I show that Mouffe's theory, in its preoccupation with antagonism, falls back on three profound assumptions about the subject: that the subject is flexible, strong and conflict-seeking. The main weakness in the theory, then, is that it assumes the existence of a subject – an agonist – perfectly suited to straddle today's conditions of precarity and systemic disruptions. Radical democracy, therefore, excludes those who are alienated rather than empowered by said disruption, who cannot 'flourish in the midst of dislocation'. For this reason, it is unequipped to provide a theory of alienation and to accurately make sense of the practical challenges involved in mobilising alienated groups today.

The purpose of this book is to examine what it takes for radical democracy to address the problem of alienation while retaining its commitment to an open and radical theory and practice. It does so by putting radical democratic theory in dialogue with contemporary alienation theory, showing that the subject can indeed be reformulated to include the alienated – and, at the same time, remain potentially open and radical. This, however, will have implications for how we think radical democracy, both as a normative model and as a political strategy for social transformation. In this conception, radical democracy can no longer exclusively focus on taming antagonism by channelling 'the political', constitutive conflict through the political institutions. Instead, it becomes a form of democracy which also continuously interrogates its social conditions of existence, in order to maintain them. Resistance to alienation is conceived as both a condition for and a part of the radical democratic struggle.

## THE STATUS OF THE ARGUMENT

Although this study has practical implications and engages with some empirical literature, it is primarily theoretical. I study texts on radical democracy and alienation in order to reveal their underlying assumptions. Some of the work is also constructive, in that I examine how the theories of radical democracy and alienation can be reformulated to address alienation, and better live up to the criteria for a good theory – open and radical – criteria which are neither external nor fully internal to the theories that I analyse.

## *Open and radical in theory and practice*

The book addresses one of the democratic left's most central dilemmas: how to open up left theory and practice while retaining its emphasis on radical social transformation and change. This dilemma manifests itself clearly in the context of alienation. Alienation, we will see, is particularly difficult to address in a way that is both radical and open – theoretically, but also practically. In a study focused on alienation, it is thus important to make the dilemma between openness and radicalism explicit and to address the theoretical and practical challenges that it poses.

Table 0.1 shows how maintaining openness and radicalism is a dilemma that manifests itself in both left democratic theory and practice. While my focus is on theory, the meaning and value of an open and radical theory cannot be fully understood separately from the practical aims, which provide the normative horizon of the study. Before specifying the criteria for a successful theory, therefore, I will first outline what I mean by an open and radical practice.

It is within this normative horizon of open and radical mobilisation, as well as in the context of the history of democratic left theory, that I set up the criteria for a successful theory of alienation. Following many thinkers in a critical and radical democratic tradition (e.g. Marchart 2018, 12), I will assume that theories in themselves can be used politically and be read performatively. This means that a theory and the ontological assumptions on which it relies can be used in political practices as a source of inspiration or legitimacy. In emphasising contingency, spontaneity and plurality as a part of the political condition (Connolly 2002; Lefort 1988), theories tend to inspire inclusive and plural, rather than exclusionary, political mobilisation. At the same time, radical democrats seek to provide theories

Table 0.1 The theoretical and practical dilemma

|  | Open | Radical |
|---|---|---|
| **Practice** | Capable of harbouring a multiplicity of demands and to respond to new claims | Passionately challenging existing power relations |
| **Theory** | Retains a space for contingency, spontaneity and pluralism | Emphasises the need for social struggle and transformation |

that emphasise the need for social struggle and transformation – theories that lend themselves to transformative political mobilisation (e.g. Mouffe 2013). In this sense, the theory, too, should, in order to be fully radical democratic, be kept open and radical.

### Criteria for assessing whether the theory is open and radical

I use the notions of openness and radicalism in order to capture and separate two different sets of values that are continuously emphasised in left democratic theory and practice – whether it is radical democratic theory or the debate on alienation in critical theory (see Chapters 1 and 3, respectively). I assume that for the concept of alienation to be open, it should avoid the most criticised pitfalls of traditional socialism. These include the pitfalls of human essentialism, determinism and the ideal of a final state of harmony. The worry in the democratic left is that if these theoretical assumptions are taken seriously in political discourse, they could be used to legitimise authoritarian and exclusionary political practices.

Human essentialism means that the human being is predefined by a particular type of activity or a particular way of life. As we will see in Chapter 3, Marx's theory of alienation, for example, has been accused of essentialism for its assumption that what makes us distinctly human is our capacity to labour. According to Marx, it is only in her labour that the human being is able to fully realise herself (Marx and Engels 2000a, 42; Marx 1975a, 277). Marx's focus on labour is criticised for disregarding other important forms of human activity, in particular the speech and political action that goes on in the public realm, marked by plurality (Arendt 1998, 33). Beyond this, radical democratic and feminist critics hold that in emphasising one aspect of human life – such as labour, or even speech – other activities are downgraded. In elevating one aspect of life as distinctly human, essentialist theories risk being used to exclude marginalised groups, or to legitimise authoritarian restrictions on how people should live their lives (e.g. Honig 1993).

The second pitfall that an open theory should avoid is determinism, and, more specifically, the assumption that the subject's actions are determined by social structures and her position within them. As I focus primarily on this particular deterministic assumption, I will, throughout the text, refer to it simply as determinism. In general, determinism means that, given the way things are at a certain time,

17

the way things go thereafter is fixed by laws that function irrespective of time and place. In Marx's theory, for example, human behaviour and understanding, including our laws and politics, are decided by the economic structure.[4] One of the most criticised deterministic assumptions of traditional socialism is the assumption that the workers will eventually rise up and appropriate the means of production from the capitalists. The subject of radical social change is already given. The determinism of traditional socialism became increasingly criticised within the left as it became evident there was no large unified working class committed to overthrowing the capitalist system (Honneth 2017, 40). Deterministic theories fail to apprehend the need for a plural political movement, capable of responding to new claims.

Lastly, I will assume that an open theory should avoid the ideal of a final state of harmony: the assumption that a stable state free of conflict is possible and desirable. Such assumptions imply that once the right social configuration has been achieved, the subject, as well as society at large, will be in harmony with itself. There will be no more conflicting desires or claims. In this state, the subject is at peace with herself, others and her social world. Within traditional socialism, an important implication of the idea of harmony was that, in a socialist society, there would be no need for political engagement and democratic institutions. The greed, exploitation and antagonism that capitalism had produced would be replaced by feelings and bonds of solidarity. The traditional socialist ideal of a final conflict-free state thus became problematic for a democratic left concerned with maintaining a practice of continuous open engagement (Honneth 2017, 35–6).

According to the first criterion, an open theory can be said to avoid the pitfalls of human essentialism, determinism and the ideal of a final state of harmony. Such a theory opens up a space for contingency and spontaneity, as well as for multiple ideas of what makes human life meaningful.

However, if we are to remain within left discourse, a suitable concept of alienation cannot only be open but should also be radical. It should maintain the mobilising potential for which it was originally valued. A radical theory should be able to capture the social suffering that people experience in a context of social power and antagonism. For this second criterion to be fulfilled, the concept of alienation should, first, retain a dimension of social suffering. The suffering that a radical theory captures is social rather than psychological or existential – neither merely a subjective problem nor an unavoidable part of human existence. It requires social change to be overcome. Such suffering, naturally, can exist alongside other types of difficulties, better captured by psychological or existential theories. For our purposes, however, we are looking for a theory that is radical in that it lends itself to be mobilised for social struggle. It should, thus, be able capture precisely those instances of suffering that could be diminished by social struggle and change. Second, and even more importantly, it should be able to capture unequal social power relations, in which some people benefit from others' disadvantage. Third, and closely related to this, a radical theory should have dimension of antagonism. It should be able to capture social divisions. It captures situations in which we overcome our social suffering by struggling against those in power and transforming the social order.

This study thus proceeds from the starting point that we would like to see marginalised people today mobilising against their alienation, and have them do so in an open and radical way. For this reason, I assume we need to understand alienation in a way that avoids human essentialism, determinism and the ideal of a final state of harmony while at the same time retaining a dimension of social suffering, power and antagonism. These two criteria allow me to approach the problem of alienation in a left democratic context, while at the same time shedding light on one of the democratic left's central dilemmas.

### *What type of critique am I making?*

The criticism pursued in this book is not, and does not aim to be, either completely internal or external. External critique applies an external standard to a theory or practice and examines how well it lives up to it, while internal critique examines a theory purely on the basis of its own premises. A premise can in this context be both empirical and normative (Tralau 2012, 31), although the latter is often in focus (Stahl 2013, 6), and emphasis is primarily placed on consistency. With this being the case, external criticism risks being of little internal relevance; at the same time, a purely internal critique can become too limited and relativistic, especially in cases where the internal standards are low (Stahl 2013, 6).[5] Consequently, in this study, I aim to apply criteria that are germane to the theories

19

themselves, making this work relevant for both those committed to radical democracy and those who are interested in the left democratic debate on alienation. Throughout this book, I will try to show how the criteria of radicalism and openness are shared by the theoretical traditions that I criticise and reformulate. I also seek to show how my concern with addressing the problem of alienation should be shared by radical democrats, despite their dismissal of alienation as a concept.

At this point, however, a possible problem with the study must be squarely addressed. In this book I criticise radical democratic theory for not sufficiently addressing alienation. But why, one might ask, should radical democrats, concerned with the political, be interested in alienation – a problem that manifests mainly in the social and interpersonal realm? While the realm of the social is of central concern within social philosophy, radical democracy focuses on a more narrowly construed political realm, having grown out of a concern with the crisis of Marxist, liberal or social democratic movements. For this reason, one might assume that radical democrats are not particularly interested in the social.

This is precisely what has been suggested in a recent debate on the place of the social in radical democracy. In *The Misguided Search for the Political*, Lois McNay argues that Mouffe grants an 'absolute priority . . . to the supposedly necessary logic of the political over the inert realm of the social' and thus 'closes off issues of empowerment that are crucial to an emancipatory account of agency' (McNay 2014, 25). However, even if Mouffe herself has not responded to this criticism, the responses from other radical democrats have revealed a deep concern with the social. In *Thinking Antagonism* (2018), Oliver Marchart argues that the aim of abstract political ontologies is 'to rejuvenate political practice in order to open up spaces for, precisely, challenging patterns of subordination' (Marchart 2018, 12). On a similar note, Vassilios Paipais maintains that reflections on ontologies are themselves political. In contrast to Marchart, however, he agrees with McNay that radical democratic theory risks obscuring actual instances of social suffering. For Paipais, radical democratic theory should to a greater extent 'embrace the worldly condition, that of temporality and vulnerability' (Paipais 2017, 521, 203). In both of these responses, the emphasis on the political is suggested to be a strategy that ultimately aims at effecting social struggle and change. To claim, then, that social suffering, such as alienation, lies beyond radical democratic concerns does not appear to be a fair interpretation of radical democratic theory.

That being said, while addressing alienation should be internally relevant to radical democratic theory – given its concern with disruption and contesting social marginalisation – the empirical premise that alienation is an actual problem today is brought in from the outside. While testing a theory's empirical premises can be a form of internal criticism (Tralau 2012, 51), this is not necessarily the case. Alienation, being hard to prove, is a complex phenomenon, and the concept itself relies on contestable ontological assumptions rather than on empirical facts. For this reason, my critique of Mouffe's theory is not purely an internal criticism.

The same goes for my criticism of Rahel Jaeggi's alienation theory. Although the tradition from which her work stems, as well as indications in her own text, suggests that she seeks a theory that is both radical and open, Jaeggi's own emphasis is clearly on the latter. Had my main aim been to examine the theory's internal consistency, I, too, would have focused on the criterion of openness, instead of putting so much weight on a criterion that Jaeggi herself does not emphasise.

By setting up my own problem and evaluative criteria, I am able to examine theories in their most ambitious versions, given the broader traditions from which they stem. Instead of testing the theories themselves and seeking internal consistency, I can focus on the problem that guides this study: how to address alienation in an open and radical way. Furthermore, setting up my own criteria allows me to clearly spell out and examine the dilemma between openness and radicalism that would otherwise risk being overlooked, as the theories themselves focus more on one or the other. I thus study what we might call the sufficiency of the theory. For example, I argue that a theory that is unable to include the people it is supposed to address provides an insufficient basis for an open and radical political practice.

## SIGNIFICANCE AND CONTRIBUTION

Jacob, Samira, Thomas and Emma are caught in processes of precarisation that inhibit their social relations and their relations to themselves. In this book, I seek to address this problem – what I call the problem of alienation. The study offers a deeper understanding of

21

the challenges that alienation poses to democracies and democratic movements today.

In doing so, it engages with two literatures: radical democratic theory and critical theories on alienation. It seeks to contribute to the literature on radical democracy in three significant ways. First, it responds to the criticism of social weightlessness in a new manner. Rather than rejecting radical democracy (Laclau and Mouffe [1985] 2001; Mouffe 2005a, 2019) or its critics (McNay 2014), it seeks paths forwards by re-examining the link between the social and the political.

Second, the focus on the individual subject provides a new way of analysing radical democracy. While scholars in the field have begun to flesh out the type of subjectivity (Norval 2004, 159), ethics (Critchley 2004) and ethos (Glynos 2003; Connolly 2004) that would correspond to the radical democratic ideals, the underlying assumptions about the subject remain to be critically examined.

Third, the approach is innovative in its way of rethinking radical democracy by retrieving elements of the left-wing tradition from which it emerged – without, as some recent theorists have, giving in to the temptation to simply turn back to traditional socialist thinking (Dean 2016; Žižek 2001). By using and reconstructing key concepts from Marx, in particular the concept of alienation but also that of exploitation, it reconsiders radical democracy's relation to socialism. It provides a deeper understanding of how the concept of alienation was lost with the turn towards the political, as well as why and how it could be retrieved in a democratic way.

Furthermore, this book offers a new way of understanding not only radical democracy but also alienation. While recent debates on alienation have increasingly focused on opening up the concept – relieving it of its problematic baggage (Jaeggi 2014) and integrating it into a theory of democracy (Honneth 2017, 2014; Rosa 2019, 2010) – my aim is to also retain the mobilising antagonistic dimension for which it was first valued within the left.

In this, the project draws inspiration from recent work in critical theory that examines how democracy is threatened by reifying and alienating processes, and in particular Axel Honneth's recent work on freedom (2014) and socialism (2017). However, whereas Honneth starts in a reconstruction of social justice and freedom, I take my point of departure in the ideals of radical democracy, and its focus on antagonism and radical action.

The book thus brings together leading contemporary work in radical democratic theory and critical theory, in particular the work of Chantal Mouffe and Rahel Jaeggi. It analyses the relation between the concepts of 'lack', 'antagonism' and 'hegemony' in radical democratic theory along with the concept of 'alienation' in critical theory and the concept of 'disorientation' in cultural theory, and, in doing so, contributes to the revived debate on alienation.

## OUTLINE

The book is divided into three parts. The first part engages in a critique of radical democracy that could be relevant for anyone interested in the theory. The second part examines and aims to contribute to the ongoing debate on alienation. By bringing together the discussions on radical democracy and alienation in the third part, I show that there is a way to address alienation in an open and radical way.

The first and second parts can be read independently. Each of these begins with a chapter that places the problem in its historical context, followed by one or two chapters engaging in detail with one or two theories.

Chapter 1, 'From the Social to the Political: The Emergence and Disappearance of the Concept of Alienation', traces the emergence of radical democracy and the disappearance of the concept of alienation. It begins by examining the democratic turn of the left from 'the social' to 'the political'. In this, it follows a well-established discourse in left theory, represented with particular clarity in the work of Axel Honneth (2017). Going beyond this, however, I show that in the turn from the social to the political, a shift happened that has not been examined to the same extent: a shift in focus from alienation to antagonism. With the radical democratic turn from the social to the political, the concept of alienation was increasingly questioned and in time largely replaced by that of antagonism.

Chapter 2, 'Antagonism or Alienation?', critically examines the underlying assumptions about the subject that underpin Chantal Mouffe's work on radical and agonistic democracy. What is it that prevents Mouffe from including a theory of alienation, and why is that a problem? I argue that radical and agonistic democracy, two theories which, respectively, aim at the open and radical mobilisation of marginalised groups, should be especially suited to addressing marginalisation in the form of alienation. However, they cannot.

Mouffe's concepts of lack, antagonism and hegemony, although initially promising, cannot capture the problem of alienation. Instead, precisely in its exclusive focus on antagonism, Mouffe's work comes to rely on a conception of the subject that, under conditions of alienation, becomes insufficient. It assumes the subject to be naturally flexible, strong and conflict-seeking. The subject thus conceived is perfectly suited to 'flourish in the midst of dislocation', to straddle today's conditions of precarity. As a result, radical democracy comes to exclude those who experience marginalisation in the form of alienation. In order to rethink the subject, I thus turn to alienation theory.

Chapter 3, 'Alienation of the Knower, the Producer and the Actor', examines the internal debate on alienation and its underlying assumptions regarding the subject. It traces the concept from Georg Wilhelm Friedrich Hegel's alienated 'knower', via Karl Marx's alienated 'producer', to the alienated 'actor' captured by contemporary critical theory. The analysis shows that while Marx's concept of alienation is clearly radical, it has been criticised for being essentialist and thus not sufficiently open. Rahel Jaeggi's recent reconstruction of the concept of alienation, on the other hand, while being open, does not fully become the social and potentially radical theory that Jaeggi seeks. When opening up the conception of alienation (from alienated production to impaired appropriation) and its corresponding conception of the subject (from a producer to an actor), it loses its capacity to capture power and antagonism. For that reason, it cannot be mobilised for social change. The internal debate on alienation thus leaves us with a dilemma, suspending us between openness and radicalism.

Chapter 4, 'Towards an Open and Radical Concept of Alienation', aims at reconstructing a concept of alienation that is both open and radical. It does so by drawing on the work of Jaeggi's open theory and Marx's radical one – as well as Pierre Bourdieu's theories of domination and habitus as a link between the two. In the resulting reconstruction of the concept, the subject is alienated when she is dominated and disoriented. When she is dominated, others systematically appropriate social power at her expense; when disoriented, the subject's practical meaning- and sense-making is socially impaired. For the alienated subject, these two processes are interlinked, leaving her unable to appropriate her life and her world. Alienation, thus conceived, addresses the meaninglessness and powerlessness experienced by dominated groups in societies marked not only by inequality but also by disorder and dislocation.

Chapter 5, 'Alienation versus Acedia', examines the reconstructed concept of alienation, whether or not it lives up to the criteria of radicalism and openness, and how it differs from Jaeggi's concept of alienation from which it was developed. It argues that the reconstructed concept of alienation retains the openness of Jaeggi's theory, while at the same time radicalising it. In particular, it allows us to distinguish alienation, a form of domination deepened by disorientation, from what I, drawing on Walter Benjamin, call acedia – the unease experienced by the dominant when they become disoriented. While acedia captures only the experience of the dominant, alienation can be used to mobilise the dominated against the dominant in a radical social struggle.

Chapter 6, 'Reformulating Agonistic Democracy and Its Subject', returns to agonistic democratic theory in order to examine how its deep-seated assumptions about the subject should be reformulated to include the alienated. The reformulated subject is characterised by her activity of appropriation, an activity that involves division and conflict, but not the radical negativity that Mouffe calls antagonism. Having reformulated the subject in this way, the model of agonistic democracy is thus reshaped. The model remains agonistic in the sense that it regards conflict as ineradicable and central to democracy. However, it differs from Mouffe's agonistic pluralism in that the agon is not singular – stemming exclusively from the ontological condition of the political – but multi-scalar. It can no longer only focus on taming antagonism by channelling 'the political', constitutive conflict through the political institutions. Instead, it becomes a form of democracy which also continuously interrogates its social conditions of existence, in order to maintain them. Resistance to alienation is conceived as both a condition for and a part of the agonistic democratic struggle.

Chapter 7, 'Redirecting the Radical Democratic Strategy', examines new possible directions for radical democratic politics in light of the problem of alienation. Having reformulated the subject of radical democracy, a potential radical democratic strategy opens up: the possibility of uniting people (precarious youth, routine workers, professionals and semi-professionals) in a common struggle against alienation. At the same time, we are also in a better place to grasp the challenges that such a struggle would involve. Today, people from many different social milieus are precarised, and some of these are also alienated. The effort to unite these people risks turning alienating in and of itself, reproducing existing forms of domination and producing new forms of disorientation. The struggle against alienation therefore requires a complex set of strategies. For this, Mouffe's left populist movement – wherein the participants' relationships to each other only consist of a common, symbolic adversary – might no longer suffice. Calling for alienated people to act without constructing any new, empowering relations of appropriation risks turning into what Lauren Berlant (2011) calls 'cruel optimism', adding pressure to individuals who are already overburdened. For radical democracy to make itself relevant today, the chapter argues, it must reconsider some of its strategic choices, such as who to include, how to organise and what to demand.

The Conclusion, 'Antagonism and Alienation in the Process of Precarisation and Beyond', takes stock, asking what light it can shed on the present problem of alienation and the possibilities of democratic mobilisation against it. What can we see or do with this new way of thinking radical democracy and its subject that we could not see or do before? The Conclusion reiterates key insights from the previous chapter, discussing the practical implications for the democratic mobilisation against alienation as precarisation. Furthermore, it opens up the discussion to forms of intensified uncertainty today, which fall beyond the scope of the book – including climate alienation, pandemic isolation and migrants waiting to have their applications for citizenship approved. These issues deserve to be treated in their own right, where attention is paid to the specific forms of suffering and challenges that each involves. Such an engagement, I believe, could draw insights from the analysis and conceptual framework developed in this book.

## NOTES

1. It should be noted, however, that the automatisation of bakeries has not taken place without resistance, with smaller artisanal bakeries emerging in many cities.
2. This point of departure is a middle way between liberal democracy – prioritising pluralism and openness – and traditional socialism – emphasising transformative social struggle. From a liberal perspective, politics is important as a means to sustain individual freedom (Walzer

1989). However, politics should not mean that the majority can impose their particular views of the good on others. For some liberal theorists, this implies that the political agenda should, ideally, be limited to claims on which a rational consensus can, at least in theory, be reached, whereas issues of deep disagreement – such as religion – should be relegated to the private sphere (e.g. Rawls 1988; Kymlicka 1989). From a traditional socialist point of view, on the other hand, maintaining pluralism is secondary to social transformation. This view is reflected both in traditional socialist literature (for review, see Honneth 2017, 35–6), as well as in a more recent turn within the left towards Leninist ideas, calling for revolution (Žižek 2001; 2002, 177) and a stronger political party, capable of instituting transformative change (Dean 2016).

3. In Mouffe's words, 'I will inscribe my reflection in a particular conjecture . . . the populist moment we are currently witnessing in Western European countries' (Mouffe 2019, 9).

4. The economic structure, or what Marx calls the 'modes of production', consists of the forces of production (technology), and the relations of production (property, exchange and division of labour). Marx claims that '[i]n the social production of their life men enter into definite relations that are indispensable and independent of their will, relations of production which correspond to a definite stage of development of their material productive forces. The sum total of these relations of production constitutes the economic structure of society, the real foundation, on which rises a legal and political superstructure and to which correspond definite forms of social consciousness' (Marx 1972d, 4).

5. Stahl here discusses the critique of practice rather than of theory. However, the same argument applies in both cases.

# PART I

## Radical democracy

CHAPTER ONE

# From the social to the political: The emergence and disappearance of the concept of alienation

In this chapter, I examine the emergence and disappearance of the concept of alienation. I trace the democratic turn of the left from the economic and the social to the political. Here, I follow a well-established discourse in left theory, represented with particular clarity in the work of Axel Honneth (2017). Going beyond this, however, I show that in the turn from the social to the political, a shift happened that has not been examined to the same extent: a shift in focus from alienation to antagonism. With the radical democratic turn from the social to the political, the concept of alienation was increasingly questioned, and, eventually, largely replaced by that of antagonism.

The chapter falls into two parts. First, I examine how the concept of alienation emerged with the left's turn to the social. Second, I examine how, with the radical democratic turn to the political, the concept of alienation fell out of focus.

## THE TURN FROM THE ECONOMIC TO THE SOCIAL: THE EMERGENCE OF THE CONCEPT OF ALIENATION

The concept of alienation emerged as a central concept of the left in the post-war period, with the turn of the left from the economic – exploitation and struggles in the realm of industrial production – to the social – the struggle for freedom in a broader variety of intersubjective social relations. With the turn towards the social, the concept of alienation became central. It signified the corruption of social relations and the loss of social freedom.

In Western Marxism, the concept of alienation grew particularly important for the New Left. The term the 'New Left' refers to the various struggles marking a political cycle stretching from the end of the 1950s to the beginning of the 1970s. It was an expansion of the left struggle in response to imperialism and the emergence of the so-called new social movements, such as new feminist and ecologist movements. In particular, the New Left condemned the English and French policies towards Egypt, the Soviet invasion of Bucharest and the Vietnam War. It included various left-wing organisations, such as Maoists, Trotskyists and anarchists, as well as the new social movements, including feminists, pacifists, ecologists and LGBT rights activists (Keucheyan 2013, 7–8).

With the emergence of the New Left, both the aims and strategy of the left were reconceived. The left turned from the economic (exploitation and struggle in the realm of industrial production) to a wider concern with the social (the struggle for freedom in a broader variety of intersubjective social relations). For traditional socialists in the first half of the twentieth century, the aim was to seize the state and the means of production. The concept of exploitation – understood as the capitalist's extraction of surplus value from the worker – was central (Keucheyan 2013, 36). Inspired by Karl Marx's *Capital* and *The Communist Manifesto*, traditional socialists conceived of society as divided into the capitalists, who own the means of production, and the workers, who own nothing but their labour. In order to survive, to get food and shelter, the worker has no choice but to sell their labour to the capitalist. The capitalist buys labour and gains profit by exploiting the worker and extracting surplus value. This surplus consists, in its most simple version, of unpaid labour time (Marx 2000, 511–12). Eventually, the capitalists grow richer while the workers get poorer. In order to end exploitation, workers, according to the traditional socialists, had to appropriate the means of production. The strategy for doing so was understood in relation to the Russian revolutions in 1905 and 1917. Power was conceived as centred in the bourgeoisie – those owning the means of production – and in their main instrument of domination, the state (Keucheyan 2013, 38). So, in this view, the problem was exploitation and the solution was its eradication, via armed insurrection.

With the emergence of the New Left, the strategy, as well as the deeper aims of the struggle, was reconceived. The traditional socialist conception of power no longer seemed viable in the context of Western democracies in the post-war period. The communist parties, now integrated into the democratic states, were losing interest in armed insurrection (Keucheyan 2013, 38–9). Furthermore, the rise of new struggles of resistance revealed how power was not merely lodged in the central state and the sphere of production, but disseminated throughout a wide spectrum of social relations – including cultural institutions and the family.[1]

Beyond this shift in strategy, the deeper aims of the left, too, had shifted: from the economic to the social. In this vision, social relations and institutions are the aim of ethics, and, in particular, the realm of freedom: only in a society of solidarity can the individual be fully free and realise her deepest aspirations (Honneth 2017, 27). While an idea of social freedom had existed among the traditional socialists, such freedom was only to be realised in the realm of economic production. For the New Left, however, the vision was broader – including not only production but most of the important relations and institutions that make up a society: family relations, culture and politics. Ethics in social relations became the domain of study for a science that became increasingly influential: social philosophy. The social philosophers of the Frankfurt school emphasised in particular the possibility of freedom in social relations, but also the risk of its corruption. As we will see, American imperialism and the corrupting, alienating forces of consumer culture became key concerns. The turn from the economic to the social thus also meant a shift in focus from exploitation, a concept which remained too tied to the economic sphere, to alienation, understood as the corruption of freedom in social relations.

For the New Left, the traditional socialist concept of exploitation could no longer play a unifying and mobilising role. It remained too heavily associated with the economic sphere, and could not respond to the main problem that the left faced in the post-war period: its lack of an agent of transformative social change, a radical subject. Traditional socialists had assumed that the capitalist system itself generated the agent of its own demise: the workers. The exploited industrial workers would eventually be so impoverished that they would have no choice but to come together and overthrow the system (Honneth 2017, 40). In the post-war period, this seemed increasingly unlikely. The thinkers of the Frankfurt school were among the first to point out that the presumed radical subject was not actually there. There was no large unified working class committed to overthrowing the capitalist system (Honneth 2017, 40). The concept of exploitation – capturing the injustice suffered by the industrial worker – thus seemed unviable as a main mobilising concept.

The crisis of the subject thus spurred a search among left theorists for new sources of inspiration beyond the traditional socialist literature that focused on the exploitation of the workers. For this reason, many theorists turned from Marx's *Capital* to his early writings, such as the 1844 Paris Manuscripts, which were first published in the 1930s (Keucheyan 2013, 40). Here, Marx argued that human beings were marked by a certain type of social freedom – a freedom that could only be realised in a free, self-determinate, human community. In these writings, the concept of alienation was central. Alienation means the corruption of social relations and the loss of social freedom. Marx describes how the worker is alienated from the product of her labour as well as from her own activity, which had brought the product into being. As a result, the worker was alienated from himself, his own humanity and his fellow human beings (Marx 1975a, 272–8). Marx's writings on alienation inspired several left theorists at the time. Georg Lukács developed the concept of 'reification' – a variant of alienation – and critical theorists, such as Herbert Marcuse, used it to criticise the corrupting forces of modern consumer culture (e.g. Lukács 1972, 87; Marcuse 2005, 2013). Theorists thus expanded the concept's use, and the concept of alienation, in its various forms, became increasingly politically significant.

For the New Left, faced with the crisis of the subject, alienation became a central concept for political mobilisation. The concept of alienation played two main roles. First, the concept was used to address the growing sense of indifference and powerlessness that left historians and theorists have described as typical of the post-war period. For example, theorists Serge Mallet and Alain Touraine argue that the feeling of alienation among the post-war working class arose from the discrepancy between expectation and reality (see Keucheyan 2013, 35; Haber 2007). Following the end of the Second World War, urbanisation, intense economic growth and the improved availability of higher education had created a new class. For the educated working class, expectations were not matched by real social opportunities. As their lives and plans were disrupted, people no longer knew what to do with their lives, resulting in a sense of disorientation and powerlessness. The concept of alienation was used to address these experiences and to mobilise a social class that had not yet organised itself.

Second, alienation has been described by historians as a unifying concept, used to bring together different already existing anticapitalist struggles (see Keucheyan 2013, 36). While the industrial working class seemed less and less likely to function as the sole agent of transformative change, the struggles that traditional socialists had considered the 'secondary fronts' were growing increasingly important. These included, for example, the women's struggle against their unpaid labour in households, as well as the new social movements. The concept of alienation, with its broad domain of application, was introduced in the theoretical debate in order to reconnect these scattered struggles. Turning from the economic to the social therefore resulted in a shift in focus from exploitation to alienation.

## THE TURN FROM THE SOCIAL TO THE POLITICAL: THE DISAPPEARANCE OF THE CONCEPT OF ALIENATION

The influence of the concept of alienation gradually diminished with the radical democratic turn of the left. While, as we have seen, the traditional left focused on the economic (exploitation and struggle in the realm of industrial production) and the New Left focused on the social (the struggle for freedom in a broader variety of intersubjective social relations), the radical democratic left went further, discarding the idea of social freedom that, up until this point, had formed the basis of the left struggle. With this, I will argue, the concept of alienation was also abandoned – and largely replaced by that of antagonism.

### From the social to the political

The concept of social freedom was charged with what Honneth described 'the socio-theoretical burden', handed down from the traditional socialists that had first formulated it (Honneth 2017, 32). This theoretical burden became particularly apparent in Ernesto Laclau and Chantal Mouffe's seminal work *Hegemony and Socialist Strategy: Towards a Radical Democratic Politics* ([1985] 2001), in which they demonstrated how socialism throughout history had, in various ways, and in its quest to protect the ideas of unity and historical necessity on which the socialist project relied, concealed the facts of contingency and plurality. The aim of radical democrats became to dismantle these ideas, and, with this, the idea of social freedom (see Sim 2000, 13). For the radical democratic left, the social was no longer the realm of potential unity and freedom, but of power.

Power was, Mouffe asserted, 'constitutive of the social because the social could not exist without the power relations through which it is given shape' (Mouffe 2005a, 18). The social was, according to radical democrats, constituted by practices of power by which other alternatives were excluded. It was, in Mouffe's words, the 'temporary and precarious articulation of contingent practices' (Mouffe 2005a, 18). As such, it could, Mouffe claimed, always be contested.

Against the idea of the social, radical democrats sought to formulate another idea, which Mouffe calls 'the political'. 'The political', according to Mouffe, stresses the power and antagonism that mark all social relations. If 'the social' is the manifestation of ethical values in social relations, 'the political' is the irreducible possibility of challenging social constellations, including their ethical justifications. In this vein, radical democrat Jacques Rancière (1999, 2009) emphasises the moment in which a new, previously excluded identity appears, expressing an injustice that was previously unnameable. At any point, the excluded – the marginalised, the poor, the 'part that has no part' (Rancière 1999) – can rise up and challenge the social order from which they have been left out. This is, in the radical democratic view, a deeply political moment. As a particular response to a specific social context, 'politics, in its specificity, is rare. It is always local and occasional' (Rancière 1999, 139). Rather than emphasising universal ethical principles and their corruption, a focus on the political implies a focus on specific social relations and the particular forms of power that they involve.

How, then, can we understand the democratic left's turn from the social to the political? What historical events and intellectual currents was it associated with? While the New Left had faced several challenges, it was also fuelled by economic progress and a general atmosphere of hope. The radical democratic strand of the left, on the other hand, emerged from a defeatist mood. In 1985, Laclau and Mouffe wrote:

> from Budapest to Prague and the Polish coup d'état, from Kabul to the sequels of Communist victory in Vietnam and Cambodia, a question-mark has fallen more and more heavily over the whole way of conceiving both socialism and the roads that should lead to it. (Laclau and Mouffe [1985] 2001, xxi)

In the 1980s and 1990s, everything about socialism – from its ideas to its strategies – was internally questioned within the left.

The problems of the labour movement, left thinkers argued, were both moral and strategic. The newly created socialist states were collapsing and, as they collapsed, the violence which had sustained them was revealed. In the shadow of Stalinism, it was difficult to maintain the hope in socialism that had characterised both the traditional socialists and the New Left. In *The Hard Road to Renewal: Thatcherism and the Crisis of the Left*, published in 1988, left thinker Stuart Hall captured this sentiment within the left:

> the actuality of Stalinism and its aftermath has added the tragic dimension to the language of socialism: the stark possibility of failure. The socialist experiment can go wildly and disastrously wrong. It can produce a result which is both recognizable as 'socialism' and yet alien to everything intrinsic in our image of what socialism should be like. It can deliver consequences against which socialists may have to stand up and be counted. (Hall 1988, 184–5)

For many people on the left, the socialist project and its vision of social freedom seemed both unfeasible and undesirable. The fall of the Berlin wall marked an important turning point, signifying both the political and moral failure of the communist state.

This defeat of socialism went hand in hand with what seemed like the final victory of the right. The hegemony of social democracy and Keynesianism was broken, giving way to a new, right-wing common sense. There was, in Margaret Thatcher's words, 'no alternative'. Free market liberalism, rather than socialism, seemed to be the end of history. Within the left, the success of the right was interpreted as a failure of the left. While the left was waiting for the determinate course of history to unfold, the right was, in the words of Hall, waging 'an effective ideological crusade' (Hall 1988, 190). Hall describes how thinkers within the left came to attribute the success of the right to the fact that the right was 'not hung up on some low-flying materialism which tells them that, of course, ideas are wholly determined by material and economic conditions' (Hall 1988, 188). Thus, the left began to reconsider its strategy, learning from the example of the right that 'if you talk about it well enough, effectively and persuasively enough, you can touch people's understanding of how they live and work, and make a new kind of sense about what's wrong with society and what to do about it' (Hall 1988, 188). The left struggle, theorists began to argue, was not merely about material conditions; it was a struggle over how people talk and think.

While the ideas and strategies of the left were under increasing criticism, the main challenges that the New Left had faced still remained. In Razmig Keucheyan's words, 'The wall came down, the political movements suffered profound defeats, but the problems posed in the 1960s have survived underground and are re-emerging today, more burning than ever' (Keucheyan 2013, 7–8). The most pressing of these problems was still the crisis of the subject. In 1980, André Gorz's essay *Farewell to the Working Class* was published, arguing that the decline of the working class was irreversible. In a post-industrial society in which trade union rights were systematically undermined by the rising political right, a struggle driven by industrial workers seemed even less likely than in the 1960s (Sim 2000, 5). In the 1980s, the left had little hope, and no radical subject.

From this general air of defeatism, the radical democratic left emerged. Guided both by the strategic success of the right as well as by its own moral and strategic failure, the aim of the left became not only to revive but also to tame the left struggle. In response to the crisis of the subject, radical democrats sought, once again, to relocate the radical struggle and the subject of social transformation. This time, however, it did so with an intensified fear of left totalitarianism and a loss of faith in Marxist determinism and essentialism. The radical democratic left thus both continued on and broke from the path set out by the New Left. Altogether, it diverged in two main ways.

First, the radical democratic left abandoned the idea of the social – the struggle for freedom in intersubjective relations – that had guided the New Left. While the New Left had struggled for social freedom, radical democrats saw no end to the struggle. To them, there was no end point in which each individual could fulfil her deepest aspirations.

The radical democratic left thus went further than the New Left in rethinking the locus of power and struggle. For the radical democratic left, power was not only disseminated throughout a multiplicity of social institutions but a part of social life itself. It emerged already at the most basic levels of human interaction – and, in particular, in language. It could thus be found even in our way of talking and thinking. For Laclau and Mouffe, the concept of hegemony – the 'point of confluence between objectivity and power' (Mouffe 2000b, 21) – was central. Hegemony was conceived as the power involved in shaping objectivity and common sense – those things that we take for granted. In their argument, there was no single source of power and no given enemy that could be eradicated. The radical democratic left distinguished itself from the New Left by arguing that power could never be eradicated and that no final harmony could be achieved.

The emphasis on power as ineradicable was itself a response to Thatcherism. In Mouffe's words:

> Remember how many times Margaret Thatcher declared, 'There is no alternative'? Unfortunately many social democrats have accepted this view and believe that the only thing they can do is to manage this supposedly natural order of globalization in a more humane way. However, according to our approach, it is clear that every order is a political one, resulting from a hegemonic configuration of power relations. The present state of globalization, far from being 'natural', is the result of a neo-liberal hegemony, and it is structured through specific relations of power. This means that it can be challenged and transformed, and that alternatives are indeed available. (Mouffe 2013, 131–2)

By rethinking power, the radical democrats challenged the claim of the right that there would be no alternative to the unregulated market. There was, according to Mouffe, always an alternative: objectivity was power, and power could be contested.

At the same time, the concept of hegemony was also a response to the problems of the left. Having seen how totalitarian communism had been pursued in the name of reason, radical democrats feared that the idea of a final conflict-free state could be used to justify the annihilation of all opposition. Instead, they argued that the political struggle had no end point: power and antagonism could never be eradicated.

In making this argument, the radical democratic left not only continued the work of Marxists, such as Antonio Gramsci, but also drew on external theoretical sources – even those that stood in opposition to the assumptions and aims of socialism. Structuralism and post-structuralism, such as the work of Claude Lévi-Strauss, Jacques Derrida and Louis Althusser,[2] became influential – inspiring left thinkers such as Jacques Rancière, Michel Foucault, Gilles Deleuze, William Connolly, Ernesto Laclau and Chantal Mouffe (Keucheyan 2013, 42–6). Another, even more controversial, source of inspiration was the conservative jurist and previous Nazi, Carl Schmitt. Schmitt influenced the work of, for example, Giorgio Agamben, Antonio Negri, Étienne Balibar and Chantal Mouffe (Keucheyan 2013, 27; Monod 2016, 14). Mouffe drew on Schmitt's (2008) concept of 'the political' to argue that power and antagonism were ineradicable (Mouffe 2005b, vii), defining the political as 'the dimension of antagonism that is inherent in human relations' (Mouffe 2000b, 101).

By drawing on thinkers outside of the socialist tradition, radical democrats turned from the social to the political. The project of social freedom that had guided large parts of the left up until now was thus abandoned. The priority had shifted towards the political, to tame and maintain 'ineradicable' antagonism.

Second, the radical democrats continued to rethink the relation between the left-wing project and democracy. The left became radically democratic. In this view, democracy was valued in itself, not merely as a mean for social freedom. This implied a rethinking not only of the left but also of democracy. For radical democrats, democracy was defined by and valued for its ability to accommodate the political, that is, ineradicable power and antagonism. It opened up a space for the contingency and lack of unity that socialism had not been able to accommodate.

The turn to radical democracy can be traced back to the French left-wing group Socialisme ou Barbarie, formed in 1949. The group criticised the labour movements for freezing into highly bureaucratised and hierarchical forms. In seeing the development of the Soviet Union, they feared that the new societies created by socialist revolutions were becoming just as violent as Western capitalist society (Van der Linden 1997). Claude Lefort, one of the founders of the group, emphasised the value of democracy, which he understood as marked by uncertainty and plurality. Lefort described democracy as 'instituted and sustained by the dissolution of the markers of certainty'. Democracy, he argued, 'inaugurates a history in which people experience a fundamental indeterminacy as to the basis of power, law and knowledge, and as to the basis of relations between self and other at every level of social life' (Lefort 1988, 19). According to Lefort, democracy could open up a space for indeterminacy and conflict without an end point.

This idea of radical democracy had its main breakthrough in the public and intellectual debate in the time building up to and following the fall of the Berlin wall. As the authoritarianism of the Soviet state was increasingly revealed and criticised, the scepticism towards socialism – also within the left – was growing. Among radical democratic theories, the work of Laclau and Mouffe became particularly influential. Mouffe celebrated democracy for its 'refusal to suppress [conflict] by imposing an authoritarian order' (Mouffe 2000b, 204). Democratic institutions, Mouffe (2000b, 2005b) wrote, were crucial for channelling the political.

### From alienation to antagonism

With the radical democratic left's turn from the social to the political – from a struggle for social freedom to a never-ending democratic struggle – another important shift followed. As the idea of the social was increasingly criticised and eventually abandoned, so was the idea of alienation.

The criticism of the concepts of alienation appears already in the work of Claude Lefort and Louis Althusser – two of the main theorists that inspired the radical democratic turn. Both Lefort and Althusser connect their concerns with Marx's work and traditional Marxism precisely to the concept of alienation. These concerns are, in turn, reiterated in the work of more recent radical democratic thinkers, including that of Jacques Rancière and Michel Foucault, both former students of Althusser, as well as of Laclau. In this radical democratic literature, one can identify at least three pitfalls that came to be associated with the concept of alienation.

First, the concept of alienation was associated with determinism: the assumption that the subject's actions were determined by the social structures and her position within them. In particular, it became connected to the assumption that there was a given radical subject: the proletariat, which by necessity would rise up and overthrow the capitalist society.

Lefort described these essentialist assumptions as one of the reasons why he had begun to doubt Marx's theory of alienation that he himself had drawn on in his earlier work. While emphasising the importance of 'the position of the alien' in the mobilisation of radical resistance, Lefort remained critical of the way in which Marx's concept of alienation linked this position to that of the proletariat. In Lefort's words, 'the proletariat was alien; and it is because it was alien and at the same time the bearer of the productive forces, indeed itself the greatest productive force, that it was designated as the revolutionary class' (Lefort 1986, 133). These deterministic assumptions were, according to Lefort, neither desirable nor tenable. Paraphrasing Marx, he argues that 'it becomes impossible to make everything converge towards a unique revolutionary focus . . . to maintain . . . that

41

the bureaucracy trudges along to its own death as the mass of the dispossessed necessarily turns against it as a single force'; instead, 'the centres of conflict are', according to Lefort, as well as to the radical democratic theorists he inspired, 'multiple' (Lefort 1986, 133).

Even sharper in his criticism of Marx's theory of alienation and its arguably deterministic assumptions was Louis Althusser. In his work *For Marx* (2005), Althusser emphasised how Marx's idea of alienation contained in itself the inevitable development towards the revolution of the proletariat. 'The revolution', Althusser claimed, 'is the very practice of the logic immanent in alienation'[3] (Althusser 2005, 226). According to Althusser, the theory of alienation presupposed both a particular course of history and a particular subject supposed to enact it. It assumed that the working class, specifically, would act as a single, unified subject. In Althusser's words, the theory of alienation 'gives the proletariat the theory of what it is; in return, the proletariat gives it its armed force, a single unique force in which no one is allied except to himself' (Althusser 2005, 227). The concept of alienation presumed, Althusser meant, a given, unified subject of transformative social change.

According to Althusser's arguments, the concept of alienation thus came to rely on the type of deterministic assumptions that radical democrats had sought to disassociate themselves from. These arguments, in turn, influenced several post-structuralist and radical democratic theorists, including Laclau and Althusser's former students Jacques Rancière, Michel Foucault and Étienne Balibar. Laclau comes to reject determinism, asserting that '[f]or classical Marxism, the possibility of transcending capitalist society depends on the . . . emergence of a privileged agent of social change' (Laclau 1990, 41). This position, he argues, can be contrasted to his own, where 'the possibility of a democratic transformation of society depends on a proliferation of new subjects of change' (Laclau 1990, 41). For radical democrats emphasising that neither the direction nor the subject of change can be predetermined, the concept of alienation – associated with the assumptions of determinism – became problematic.

Second, the concept of alienation became associated with an essentialist conception of the human being that radical democrats rejected. Marx had argued in the Manuscripts that it was only in a free society that we could live fully human, unalienated lives (Marx 1975a, 276–7). In *For Marx*, Althusser rejected these ideas as essentialist:

The loss of man that produces history and man must presuppose a definite pre-existing essence. At the end of history, this man, having become
inhuman objectivity, has merely to re-grasp as subject his own essence
alienated in property, religion and the State to become total man, true
man. (Althusser 2005, 226)

Alienation – 'the loss of man' – presupposed, according to Althusser,
the existence of a 'true man'. '[T]he essence of man', he claimed, was
understood as 'the basis for history and politics' (Althusser 2005,
226). In Althusser's argument, Marx's theory of alienation in the
Manuscripts, as well as the alienation theories that it inspired, came
to rely on the assumption of a stable human essence.

According to Althusser, the theory of alienation and the human
essentialism on which it relied was problematic – an 'ideology that
would weigh down on real history and threaten to lead it into blind
alleys' (Althusser 2005, 230). Alienation and the theory of socialist
humanism could not function as a scientific theory and dismantle
the current order (Althusser 2005, 221). Rather, it blocked people
from understanding real human practices. In Althusser's words, 'It is
impossible to know anything about men except on the absolute precondition that the philosophical (theoretical) myth of man is reduced
to ashes'; to break with this essentialism becomes a 'precondition of
the (positive) knowledge of the human world itself, and of its practical transformation' (Althusser 2005, 229). In order to understand
real human practices and to enact transformative change, then, the
left had to break with the 'ideology' of alienation and 'the myth of
man'.

Althusser's ideas grew influential in the radical democratic literature. In Althusser's collaborative work *Reading Capital*, Jacques
Rancière argued, for example, that the young Marx's concept of
alienation in the Manuscripts remained trapped within the same
problems as the economic discourse that he sought to criticise. In
its focus on the subject and her essence, it failed to fully capture the
oppositional dynamic between labour and capital: it 'still remains
captive to the illusions of Wirklichkeit' (Rancière 1976, 370).

In his later work, which became central to the radical democratic
discourse, Rancière expanded on his criticism of the concept of alienation, including not only Marx's concept of social alienation but also
concepts of political alienation. For while radical democrats, as we
will see, are deeply concerned with the transferral of power from

43

the people to an instituted sovereign, they are sceptical towards the social contract literature which describes this as a form of 'alienation'. Rancière emphasises how the 'fable of alienation', such as Jean-Jacques Rousseau's theory of political alienation, relies on a 'fable of origin'. It presupposes an original human being, whose powers – in particular his freedom – have been alienated (Rancière 1999, 79). According to Rancière, the theory of political alienation 'sets out the distance of man from himself as the primary and final basis of the distance of the people from itself'. While such a distance opens up a space for political conflict, it at the same time closes it. Instead of focusing on politics in itself, it sets up the 'truth of politics' as something above it – a human essence to be obtained. In the theories of political alienation, 'the truth of politics is . . . located above politics as its essence or idea' (Rancière 1999, 82). While opening up a space of uncertainty, a gap, where politics can emerge, it thus at the same time masks it by basing it in a fable of a human essence.

The concept of alienation that had become influential within the New Left was thus, among radical democrats, associated with the problems of human essentialism. And since avoiding 'a positive and unified conception of human nature' became a central aim of the radical democratic theory, the concept of alienation was resolutely abandoned (Laclau and Mouffe [1985] 2001, 118).

Third, the concept of alienation became associated with the ideal of a final state of harmony. Lefort describes how in his earlier work, when he focused on alienation, and more specifically, the 'alienation of the proletariat from itself, this ultimate form of alienation', he had assumed that such alienation was a necessary step not only in the determinate course of history but also for it to achieve its end point – 'so that the need for an abolition of all social division, and not only of private property, would be fully affirmed'. 'Thus', Lefort argued, in thinking of alienation, 'the representation of a society delivered from division governed my thinking' (Lefort 1986, 294). Such ideas, according to Lefort, are risky, and the ultimate risk is totalitarianism. In Lefort's analysis, 'the representation of the People-as-One', an idea closely connected to that of harmony free from division, lays the foundation of totalitarianism. When no internal division is conceivable, the only division possible becomes that between inside and outside – the people and its enemy (Lefort 1986, 297). Such divisions, Lefort warns, breed violence and terror. In Lefort's words:

the constitution of the People-as-One requires the incessant production of enemies. It is not only necessary to convert, at the level of phantasy, real adversaries of the regime or real opponents into the figures of the evil Other: it is also necessary to invent them. However, this interpretation can be carried further. The campaigns of exclusion, persecution and, for quite awhile, terror reveal a new image of the social body. The enemy of the people is regarded as a parasite or a waste product to be eliminated. (Lefort 1986, 298)

Lefort argues that the idea of the unalienated people, free from internal division, consequently risks turning difference into violence, where those who are different are conceived as enemies to be eliminated.

The associations between the concept of alienation and the idealisation of harmony free from conflict and division is reiterated by several thinkers in the radical democratic literature. The associations became suspicious for radical democrats, for whom conflict and difference cannot be eradicated. In the words of Michel Foucault:

I have always been somewhat suspicious of the notion of liberation, because if it is not treated with precautions and within certain limits, one runs the risk of falling back on the idea that there exists a human nature or base that, as a consequence of certain historical, economic, and social processes, has been concealed, alienated, or imprisoned in and by mechanisms of repression. According to this hypothesis, all that is required is to break these repressive deadlocks and man will be reconciled with himself, rediscover his nature or regain contact with his origin, and reestablish a full and positive relationship with himself. (Foucault 1997, 282)

The notion of alienation was, in Foucault's argument associated with the idea of an unalienated state of 'liberation' and 'reconciliation' beyond difference and conflict. In her reading of Foucault's criticism of the concept of alienation, Rahel Jaeggi (2014) argues that 'Foucault not only attacks essentialist appeals to human nature; he also rejects the very idea of subjectivity that appears to underlie the critique of alienation ... the idea of a subject "beyond power"' (Jaeggi 2014, 31).

Similarly, Rancière emphasises the risks associated with the concept of alienation and the idea of reconciliation with which it became linked. It sets up the gap for political conflict as an 'absolute wrong', a wrong to be corrected through establishing a community at one with itself. As such, the 'political effectiveness of this ... gap has a name. That name is terror' (Rancière 1999, 81). An absolute wrong can only be rectified by forming a people at one with itself and its origin.[4]

The idea of a final state of harmony beyond conflict, one in which the human being is 'reconciled with himself', was therefore rejected by radical democrats. Power, conflict and difference could, radical democrats claimed, never be undone (e.g. Mouffe 2019, 87–8).

With the radical democratic turn from the social to the political – from a struggle for social freedom to a radical democratic struggle without an end point – the concept of alienation was abandoned. Yet the crisis of the subject that it responded to remained. A central aim for the radical democratic discourse became to find a way to understand the possibility for and subject of political resistance without succumbing to the aforementioned pitfalls. As we have seen, for the New Left, the concept of alienation had two roles to play in the formation of a radical political subject: to unify different movements and to address the experience of disrupted expectations prevalent in the post-war era. How did the radical democrats, lacking a concept of alienation, make sense of and respond to these problems?

With the turn to the political, the challenge of unifying different movements was reconceived. Radical democrats could no longer assume that different political movements shared a common core, such as a common human nature, the experience of alienation or the aspiration to social freedom. The challenge was no longer to find the unifying link between the movements but to construct it.

To construct a radical subject, Mouffe and Laclau argued, required the formulation of a New Left hegemony that could confront the hegemony of the right:

> If the task of radical democracy is indeed . . . to link together diverse democratic struggles, such a task requires the creation of new subject-positions that would allow the common articulation, for example, of antiracism, antisexism, and anticapitalism. These struggles do not spontaneously converge, and in order to establish democratic equivalences, a new 'common sense' is necessary, which would transform the identity of different groups so that the demands of each group could be articulated with those of others. (Mouffe 1989, 42)

With this new hegemony, or common sense, the various and sometimes contradictory demands of each group were to be reformulated so that they were recognised as equal – forming what Mouffe and

Laclau called a 'chain of equivalence'. When sharing a common sense, people with different ideas would be able to come together, forming a new radical political association. This formation did not require a specific, socially grounded theory, such as a theory of alienation; it was contingent.

For radical democrats, the construction of the subject was political, not only in the sense that it was contingent but also in the sense that it was antagonistic. It emerged, they claimed, through a political discourse that distinguishes between 'we' and 'they'. This insight was key to the radical democratic response to the crisis of the subject: to construct a collective subject one also had to construct an opponent. The radical collective subject – 'the people' – was constructed in relation to an opponent – 'the elite' or 'the oligarchs' (e.g. Mouffe 2019, 79). The antagonistic discourse was central to the radical democratic mobilising strategy. It was antagonism rather than alienation that would bring people together into a radical struggle.

Radical democrats thus found antagonism rather than alienation to be the response both to the crisis of the subject and to what seemed like the final victory of the right. By constructing themselves in opposition to something else, different struggles could be linked without having to rely on the shared prior experience of alienation. Political identities were to be created in the political struggle itself, in the antagonistic division between 'we' and 'they'.

For the New Left, however, the concept of alienation had not only been a way to link different struggles but also a response to another dimension of the crisis of the subject. It had been used to mobilise people who were suffering in the current order, but who had remained disengaged and disorganised. In particular, the post-war era had seen the rise of a new, unorganised social class: the educated working class whose expectation of social advancement had been thwarted. The concept of alienation had been used to address and mobilise this experience. Was the problem of social disruption still relevant in the late twentieth century, when the radical democratic left emerged? And how, in that case, did radical democracy address it?

The post-war period's problems of social disruption and impaired expectations were no longer central concerns for the left. Instead, the main focus lay on the seemingly unquestionable dominance of the right. The right had won the power over the discourse; the free, unregulated market had turned into an unquestionable fact. In this context, radical democracy developed a set of new concepts, designed to capture both the power of the right – such as 'hegemony' – as well as the potential for disruption and resistance – such as 'lack', 'dislocation' and 'antagonism'. While these concepts bore a certain resemblance to the New Left's concept of alienation – capturing disrupted social relations – they approached them in a different way. In a period when the left seemed defeated and Thatcher proclaimed, 'there is no alternative', an important function of the concepts of lack, antagonism and hegemony was to remind us that social disruption and change was possible. In Mouffe's words, the 'concept of an hegemonic configuration is crucial for envisaging how to act in politics. It reveals that you can always change things politically, that you can always intervene in the relations of power in order to transform them' (Mouffe 2013, 132).

In their emphasis on political power and subjectivity, the radical democratic concepts of lack, hegemony and antagonism are not simply similar to concepts of alienation in general, but they are similar to that of political alienation. They render how political collectives can challenge what could be described as alienated political power. In capturing the power constitutive of the social order and the potential for resistance, the concepts of lack, antagonism and hegemony, like the concept of political alienation, provide a way to open up what Rancière describes as the 'gap' or 'distance' of politics. They mark the distance between the people and the instituted sovereign to which they have transferred their power, as well as the distance of the people from itself, between those included and excluded in its formation. At the same time, they avoid what Rancière points out as the problem with the concept of alienation: the assumption that an 'absolute wrong' has been made and, ultimately, can be corrected. For radical democrats, antagonism is understood as an irresolvable problem but also, and more importantly, as an ineradicable potential for resistance.

In sum, with the radical democratic left's turn from the social – the struggle for freedom in social relations – to the political – ineradicable power and antagonism – the concept of alienation, in both its social and political conceptions, seemed to disappear. It was associated with what the radical democrats regarded as problematic assumptions to do with determinism, human essentialism and the pursuit of a final state of harmony. Instead, the concept of alienation was replaced by concepts such as hegemony, lack and, in particular, antagonism. These concepts partly came to play some of the roles that the concept of alienation previously had – to unify different movements and to capture experiences of disrupted expectations – and have even been understood by some radical democrats as new concepts of alienation (Laclau and Zac 1994, 14; Stavrakakis 2002). Yet it was not primarily in these capacities that antagonism and its related concepts were valued by the left. Even more importantly, they were formulated in response to the particular challenge that the left faced at the time: the seemingly unquestionable dominance of the right. In response to this, the concept of antagonism was used for two purposes: to reveal the power of the right over the discourse, and to emphasise that this power could be challenged.

In the next chapter, I will delve deeper into radical democratic theory and examine whether the theory – focused on lack, antagonism and hegemony – can still include alienation and respond to today's problem of systematic disruption and precarisation. As we will see, the historical context in which radical democracy emerged can only partly explain the absence of the problematisation of alienation.

## NOTES

1. Theorists thus developed new conceptions of power more suitable for advanced societies. Gramsci (1971) argued that power is not only located in institutions but disseminated throughout the social. In order to overthrow power, it does not suffice to struggle against state institutions. Fighting disseminated power requires a 'war of position'; culture must be conquered (see Keucheyan 2013, 40).
2. Althusser is also sometimes described as a Marxist or structural Marxist.
3. In Marx's alienation theory, Althusser argued, 'the proletariat will negate its own negation and take possession of itself in communism' (Althusser 2005, 226). Alienation is the 'negation' of the worker, and such a negation will amount to a 'negation of the negation' – a revolution where the proletariat appropriates the means of production and eventually overcomes their alienation.
4. 'Terror is the political *agir* that adopts as its *political* task the requirement of achieving community *arkhe*, its internalization and promotion of total awareness of it' (Rancière 1999, 81).

# CHAPTER TWO

# *Antagonism or alienation?*

What prevents Chantal Mouffe's radical democracy from including a theory of alienation – and why is that a problem? Radical democracy addresses itself particularly to marginalised people whose relations of identification have been disrupted and inhibited. The aim is to mobilise the marginalised – the poor, the excluded and the socially disadvantaged – in a radical yet open way, contesting existing power relations while remaining open towards new and diverse claims. This emphasis on marginalised people suggests that the theory of radical democracy should be particularly equipped to address experiences of alienation, the situation where the subject's relation to the world is inhibited in such a way that her relation to herself becomes dysfunctional. But does it have the theoretical resources to do so? In this chapter, I demonstrate how the exclusive concern with the problem of antagonism in Mouffe's theory of radical democracy prevents it from providing a theory of alienation, and, consequently, from grasping how experiences of alienation can hinder the open and radical mobilisation against marginalisation that it seeks.

The chapter separates into three parts. First, I identify the aims of the theory – open and radical mobilisation – as well as how the possible tension between these aims manifest themselves in the demands on the individual subject. Second, I examine whether radical democracy already has a theory of alienation, an argument that appears in particular in the psychoanalytic approaches to radical democracy (Laclau and Zac 1994, 14; Stavrakakis 2002). I show that, while the concept of antagonism has been taken to resemble that of alienation, antagonism, unlike alienation, is not a dysfunction in the subject's relation to herself. Third, I examine what prevents radical democracy from accommodating alienation. I argue that, in its exclusive concern with antagonism, radical democracy comes to rely on three basic assumptions about the subject: the subject as flexible, strong and conflict-seeking. However, while the subject thus conceived can, at least in theory, be both open and radical, she cannot be alienated; she is perfectly suited to straddle today's conditions of precarisation and alienation. I argue that in order to make itself relevant today, radical democracy should reformulate its conception of the subject to accommodate alienation.

## OPEN AND RADICAL: THE AIMS OF RADICAL DEMOCRACY

Before examining whether radical democracy can provide a theory of alienation, and why, given its own aims, it should, I will first examine what these aims are. Chantal Mouffe's radical democratic theory can be divided into three elements: a normative theory of democracy, a left-wing political strategy, and the theoretical assumptions upon which the aforementioned theory and strategy are based. These three elements are closely interlinked, especially with regards to its aim: an open and radical mobilisation against marginalisation.

### Theoretical approach

In order to understand Mouffe's normative and strategic arguments for open and radical mobilisation, we must first understand the theoretical assumptions on which it is based. As we will see, Mouffe seeks to provide a theory that is both open and radical, emphasising social suffering, power and antagonism while avoiding the pitfalls of human essentialism, determinism and the ideal of a final state of harmony.

Mouffe's theoretical approach is radical in the sense that it emphasises antagonism as distinctive of politics. There is, according to Mouffe, no politics – neither democratic nor undemocratic – without antagonism. Mouffe makes this argument by drawing on Carl Schmitt. '[O]ne of Schmitt's central insights', she claims, 'is his thesis that political identities consist in a certain type of we/they relation, the relation friend/enemy which can emerge out of very diverse forms of social relations' (Mouffe 2005a, 14). In this view, politics always involves an antagonistic dimension, a distinction between friend and enemy. According to Mouffe, power and antagonism are present in all societies. Every social order has a 'dimension of

51

radical negativity that manifests itself in the ever-present possibility of antagonism' (Mouffe 2019, 87). Inspired by Schmitt, Mouffe calls this condition of ineradicable antagonism 'the political'.

Every society and all relations of identification are, according to Mouffe, founded by a specific form of power, what she calls hegemony. Hegemony is the 'point of confluence between objectivity and power', the form of power that makes things appear as objective and unquestionable (Mouffe 2000b, 21). In Mouffe's theory, there is no natural objective order: 'What appears as the natural order is never the manifestation of a deeper objectivity that would be exterior to the practices that brought it into being' (Mouffe 2019, 88). Everything is contingent. Objectivity and rationality are merely a manifestation of hegemonic power.

The irreducible dimension of power of any social order means that any order harbours the risk of social antagonism. 'Things could always have been otherwise and every order is predicated on the exclusion of other possibilities', claims Mouffe, which means that '[e]very existing order is . . . susceptible to being challenged' (Mouffe 2019, 88). At any time, the power and exclusion on which the existing order is founded can be contested and antagonism – the struggle between 'we' and 'they' – can erupt. Mouffe's theory thus comes to emphasise both the exclusion and social suffering that every social order can give rise to, but also the ineradicable possibility of radical struggle and change.

With these theoretical assumptions, Mouffe not only seeks to radicalise the theory but also to, in my own terms, open it up by avoiding the common pitfalls. The first pitfall Mouffe seeks to avoid is, of course, the ideal of a final state of harmony. Since her early work with Ernesto Laclau, Mouffe has repeatedly argued that 'the myth of communism as a transparent and reconciled society – clearly implying the end of politics – had to be abandoned' (Mouffe 2019, 3). In Mouffe's theory, a final conflict-free state is neither possible nor desirable. Instead, she focuses on 'the ever-present possibility of antagonism', which 'impedes the full totalization of society and forecloses the possibility of a society beyond division and power' (Mouffe 2019, 87–8). As we will see, Mouffe's emphasis on ineradicable antagonism becomes crucial to support her normative and strategic emphasis on both open and radical political mobilisation.

Second, Mouffe seeks to avoid determinism – the assumption that the subject's actions are determined by the social structure and her position in it. A central argument in Mouffe's early work with Laclau is that the Marxist assumption 'that the workers' political struggle and economic struggle are unified by the concrete social agent – the working class – which conducts them both . . . is based on a fallacy' (Laclau and Mouffe [1985] 2001, 118). The subject of social change is, according to Mouffe, constructed by a plurality of discourses that can only be temporarily and 'partially fixed' (Mouffe 2019, 89). In practice, this means that a variety of discourses are collected around the same political symbol, such as a leader or a political slogan. Each of these constellations remains contingent and can be subject to rearticulation.

In emphasising the plurality and contingency of the subject, Mouffe seeks to open up the theory and move away from the determinism of traditional socialism. According to Mouffe, her theoretical approach consists in a plural and open-ended understanding of the subject of social change. The subject is 'multiple and contradictory', and its identity is 'always contingent, precarious, temporarily fixed' (Mouffe 2019, 88). There is no determinate subject of social change – such as the worker – and thus no determinate course of history – such as a predetermined transition from capitalism to communism.[1]

It should be noted that the category of the 'subject' varies throughout Mouffe's work. In her early work with Laclau, Mouffe describes the subject as a collective one, consisting of multiple 'struggles' or 'groups' of resistance. The aim is to 'link together diverse democratic struggles' (Mouffe 1993, 19; see also Laclau and Mouffe [1985] 2001, 183–4). In her later, strategic work, Mouffe increasingly describes the subject as discursively constructed: 'constituted by an ensemble of "discursive positions"'(Mouffe 2019, 88). The subject is, at that point, primarily conceived not as a collection of social groups but as a collection of discourses or demands. This can be read as another attempt to emphasise the constructed nature of the subject – consistent with Mouffe's view that 'every object is constituted as an object of discourse' – and therefore to avoid determinism (Laclau and Mouffe [1985] 2001, 107).

However, irrespective of whether the subject is collective or discursive, its construction still depends on individual subjects – their experiences and claims. Mouffe suggests that her conception of the discursive subject also has implications for the conception of the individual subject. In Mouffe's words:

this dialectic of non-fixity/fixation is possible only because fixity is not given before-hand, because no centre of subjectivity precedes the subject's identifications. For this reason, we have to conceive the history of the subject as the history of his/her identifications and there is no concealed identity to be rescued beyond the latter. (Mouffe 2019, 89)

In this passage, Mouffe refers to the subject as 'his/her', suggesting that she now refers to an individual rather than collective subject. Both the individual and collective subject are plural, undetermined and socially constructed. There is, according to Mouffe, no predefined subject of social change whose actions can be decided by the social structure and her position in it.

Third, with these assumptions about the subject, Mouffe seeks to avoid not only determinism but also human essentialism. Already in her early work with Laclau, Mouffe explicitly seeks to avoid a conception of the individual subject where '"Man" has the status of an essence – presumably a gift from heaven'; instead, she emphasises that '"human identity" involves . . . an ensemble of dispersed positions' (Laclau and Mouffe [1985] 2001, 117).[2] Laclau and Mouffe thus distinguish their theory from 'original forms of democratic thought . . . linked to a positive and unified conception of human nature' (Laclau and Mouffe [1985] 2001, 118). As human identity is conceived as plural, contingent and only partially fixed, human essentialism is, in Mouffe's view, avoided.

Mouffe thus seeks to formulate a theoretical approach that is open in the sense that it seeks to avoid the ideal of harmony (the assumption that a stable state free of inner and social conflict is possible and desirable), determinism (the assumption that the subject's action are determined by social structures and her position within them), as well as human essentialism (the assumption that the subject is predefined by a particular type of activity or way of life). Overall, then, we have seen that Mouffe seeks to construct her theories in both an open and radical way. And her open and radical theory is, we will also see, crucial to support her arguments for an open and radical political practice. In both her democratic theory and political strategy, Mouffe draws on her theoretical approach to emphasise the importance of open and radical mobilisation of marginalised groups.

## Democratic theory

Mouffe calls her normative model of democracy agonistic democracy. Its most explicit normative aim is to tame the antagonism that in Mouffe's theory is ineradicable. In Mouffe's words:

> Once we begin to acknowledge the dimension of 'the political' we begin to realise that one of the main challenges for pluralist liberal-democratic politics consists in trying to defuse the potential antagonism that exists in human relations so as to make human co-existence possible. (Mouffe 2019, 91)

Mouffe's theoretical approach and its emphasis on the political – ineradicable antagonism – is thus central to her normative argument. A democratic regime must, Mouffe argues, construct a division – a 'we/they distinction' – that is 'compatible with the recognition of pluralism' (Mouffe 2019, 91). The aim for a democratic association becomes to tame what she calls 'dangerous antagonism' or simply 'antagonism'[3] – 'the struggle between enemies' – into 'agonism' – 'the struggle between adversaries' (Mouffe 2019, 91). In agonistic politics, the adversary is 'not considered an enemy to be destroyed but an adversary whose existence is perceived as legitimate' (Mouffe 2019, 91). While we cannot eradicate antagonism, we can seek to channel it into forms that are compatible with a plural political association.

The model of democracy that Mouffe envisages is thus marked by a struggle that is both radical and open. Democratic politics depends on political actors radical enough to fight for power, but open enough not to fall into dangerous antagonism. The agonistic political mobilisation that Mouffe seeks can be described as 'open' in the sense that it avoids 'non-negotiable moral values or essentialist forms of identification' (Mouffe 2019, 93). Politics is practised with the recognition of the contingency of things and the impossibility of a final, objective resolution. The 'struggle between "right and left"', Mouffe argues, should not turn into a 'struggle between "right and wrong"' (Mouffe 2005a, 5). The political association is 'constituted on the basis of a particular we/they, and for that very reason it should be recognized as something contingent and open to contestation' (Mouffe 2013, 25). An open political association should be able to see the legitimacy of their opponents' claims, as well as the contingent and contestable nature of their own.

At the same time, the struggle must be radical. While Mouffe distances her approach from 'the Leninist tradition of total revolutionary break', it still values social struggle and transformation (Mouffe 2005a, 53). The aim of agonistic democracy is, in Mouffe's words, 'a profound transformation of the existing power relations and the establishment of a new hegemony'. 'This is', she claims, 'why it can properly be called radical' (Mouffe 2005a, 52).[4] Agonistic democracy involves a struggle for power.

Furthermore, for the struggle to remain radical, it needs to be passionate: 'it needs to have a real purchase on people's desires and fantasies' (Mouffe 2005a, 6). And, quoting Machiavelli, Mouffe argues that '[i]n each city are found these two different desires . . . the man of the people hates being ordered and oppressed by those greater than he. And the great like to order and oppress the people' (Mouffe 2005a, 7). In Mouffe's conception, democratic politics is not only open – capable of harbouring a plurality of demands while remaining open to new claims – but also radical, in that it passionately challenges existing power relations.

Agonistic democracy – aiming at openness and radicalism – requires people, and, in particular, marginalised people, to be ready to both listen and fight. At first sight, this may look incoherent. When involved in a passionate struggle, are you really ready to stop and listen? However, according to Mouffe, the aims of radicalism and openness do not fall into tension. In fact, radical struggle is, in the agonistic model of democracy, a central condition for taming antagonism and maintaining openness. Since antagonism is, in Mouffe's theory, ineradicable, the attempt to repress it will merely result in its transformation into new, more dangerous forms.

For this reason, Mouffe values liberal democratic institutions for their capacity to channel antagonism, for providing a 'battlefield on which hegemonic projects confront one another' (Mouffe 2019, 93).[5] However, Mouffe argues that in an 'increasingly "one-dimensional" world, in which any possibility of transformation of the relations of power has been erased, it is not surprising that right-wing populist parties are making significant inroads in several countries' (Mouffe 2000b, 7). When political parties move towards a 'consensus at the centre', antagonism tends to re-emerge in dangerously exclusionary forms.

Mouffe's theoretical assumption regarding ineradicable antagonism thus becomes central to her normative argument. It allows her to maintain that the core aims of agonistic democracy – openness and radicalism – do not fall into tension. Based on the assumption of ineradicable antagonism, openness and radicalism are not only compatible but mutually dependent. If democratic politics loses its radical dimension, it loses its ability to channel antagonism – resulting in the eruption of violently exclusionary politics. As we will see, Mouffe's strategic political project, too, aims at openness and radicalism. And here too, these aims remain compatible.

### Political strategy

Radical democracy first emerged as a left-wing political strategy. Together, Mouffe and her co-author Ernesto Laclau wrote *Hegemony and Socialist Strategy: Towards a Radical Democratic Politics* ([1985] 2001) . And in Mouffe's recent work, *For a Left Populism* (2018), the main argument remains the same: the left cannot rely on the assumption that there is a ready-made subject, such as the worker, who will be the sole agent of social transformation. In today's political context, marked by a plurality of different struggles – antiracist, antisexist and environmentalist – the left should instead be 'redefining of the socialist project in terms of a radicalization of democracy' (Mouffe 2019, 2). The strategic aims of the left should be to create a political association that remains open enough to include 'a multiplicity of struggles against different forms of domination' yet radical enough to challenge the current configuration of power (Mouffe 2019, 2). The aim becomes the open and radical mobilisation against marginalisation.

Mouffe refers to her political strategy as a 'radical and plural democracy' (Laclau and Mouffe [1985] 2001, 167; Mouffe 2019, 3). These terms, and radicalism in particular, take on several meanings in Mouffe's work.[6] For the sake of clarity, I will let them indicate the key characteristics of the radical democratic association as expressed by Mouffe. Radical democracy is radical in the sense that 'the aim . . . is a profound transformation of the existing power relations' (Mouffe 2005a, 52; see also Mouffe 2019, 47). A radical collective subject challenges the neoliberal hegemony and seeks to establish a new one. In order to form a new hegemony – defined as the 'point of confluence between objectivity and power' (Mouffe 2000b, 21) – 'frontiers need to be drawn and the moment of closure must be faced' (Mouffe 2013, 25). In the radical struggle for power and social change, the division between 'we' and 'they' is unavoidable.

In her updated political strategy – or what she also calls left populism – Mouffe argues that radical politics 'requires the construction of "a people" around a project that addressees the diverse forms of subordination around issues concerning exploitation, domination or discrimination' (Mouffe 2019, 61). The aim is for marginalised people to come together to challenge the diverse forms of subordination that they experience. For this, Mouffe suggests, a political strategy that seeks to oppose 'the people' against 'the oligarchs' could be effective (Mouffe 2019, 79). These categories, Mouffe argues, can be used to assemble people experiencing a wide range of grievances, such as indebtedness and environmental degradation (Mouffe 2019, 60).

Beyond being radical, Mouffe's radical democracy is also what she calls 'plural', or what I will describe as open. Radical democracy should, in Mouffe's vision, be capable of harbouring a multiplicity of demands and to respond to new claims. The aim of a radical and plural democracy is to 'link together diverse democratic struggles' (Mouffe 1993, 19; see also Laclau and Mouffe [1985] 2001, 183–4). Mouffe reiterates that

> [b]y reformulating the project of the left in terms of 'radical and plural democracy', we inscribed it in the wider field of the democratic revolution, indicating that multiple struggles for emancipation are founded on the plurality of social agents and their struggles. (Mouffe 2019, 3)

The radical struggle, Mouffe contends, 'was thereby extended rather than being concentrated in a "privileged agent" such as the working class' (Mouffe 2019, 3). The openness of radical democracy also means that it remains ready to respond to new claims. The radical democratic association brings together 'a multiplicity of heterogeneous demands in a way that maintains the internal differentiation of the group' and is constructed through a frontier that is 'always susceptible to rearticulation' (Mouffe 2019, 62–3). The radical democratic movement, Mouffe argues, should be ready to include new demands – even when they are expressed by opponents like right-wing populists. Rather than a 'demonization of the "enemies"', radical democrats should 'recognize the democratic nucleus at the origin of many of their demands' (Mouffe 2019, 22). Although political frontiers must be drawn for a radical democratic association to be formed, demands and groups should not be precluded.

Like her democratic theory, Mouffe's political strategy aims at a radical and open mobilisation of marginalised groups. And here too, the radicalism of the political association comes to depend on its openness. Pluralism is not only a part of the radical democratic movement, it is also required for such a movement to be able to pose a challenge to the current power configuration. 'There is no doubt', Mouffe claims, 'that under neoliberalism, the field of conflict has significantly widened' (Mouffe 2019, 60). This means that in order to successfully challenge the current order, 'more people than before could be recruited for a progressive alternative'. However, this alternative must also be more complex and able to harbour a greater plurality of demands (Mouffe 2019, 60). For radical movements to be successful in our present moment – to gather sufficient people and claims – they must also be open. Radicalism thus comes to depend on openness.

### Tensions in the subject?

As we have seen, Mouffe's theoretical approach, normative model of democracy and political strategy all seek to address marginalisation in a radical and open way. The aims of radicalism and openness are, in Mouffe's theory, closely interlinked. However, scholars have argued that the radical democratic aims not only depend on but also tend to fall into tension with one another (Rummens 2009; Thomassen 2016). Lasse Thomassen argues, for example, that 'the antagonistic division of society into two camps seems to preclude the development of agonistic, adversarial relations' (Thomassen 2016, 174). The struggle for hegemonic power – which poses a division between the people and the establishment – does not, according to Thomassen, seem entirely compatible with the idea that political opponents should not seek to eradicate one another. As I explained in the Introduction, part of my intention in keeping the two interlinked aims of radical democracy apart is to be able to explore this possible tension. However, rather than exploring the tension in the political association at large, I focus on how it manifests itself in the individual subject – and, more specifically, in a subject who find herself in a situation of alienation.

Mouffe's normative and strategic projects both rely on the possibility not only of a particular political association but also of a certain individual subject, an agonist, who establishes and sustains this association. An open and radical association depends on individual subjects who are ready to commit to a radical movement, but who, at the same time, can maintain a sufficient distance from their own commitments to listen to and respond to others. In short, it relies on a subject who can be radical and open, ready both to fight and to listen.

The agonist should be radical in the sense that she can passionately engage in a political struggle for power. For this, identification is key. In Mouffe's theory, political passions are spurred by relations of identification with a political slogan or a leader; it is in the construction of a 'we' and a 'they' that political passion is stirred. Without any specific object of identification, the subject would lack the passion and direction needed to challenge the hegemonic order. The individual subject's identification with the counter-hegemonic project must, in Mouffe's theory, be strong enough to inspire action, even in the face of the risks that come with challenging those in power from a position of marginalisation. The individual subject must consequently be radical enough to be able to form a strong connection to her object of identification.

At the same time, the subject should have enough distance from her commitments to remain capable of responding to new claims and to form plural associations with people of diverse opinions. Although political frontiers – such as that between 'the people' and 'the oligarchs' – should be drawn, the subject should not exclude anyone out of hand. She should be ready to include new claims, even when they are expressed by those who might, at first glance, seem to be her opponents (e.g. Mouffe 2019, 22).

The subject should thus be both radical and open, equally ready to fight and to listen. Initially, this may seem contradictory. As we have seen, it requires a subject who is passionate yet moderate, committed yet detached. Who is the radical democratic subject, the agonist, who can be both committed and detached? And can this subject still be alienated – experiencing an inhibition in her relation to the object in such a way that her relation to herself becomes dysfunctional? To answer these questions, I will turn back to and critically examine Mouffe's theoretical approach.

## A RADICAL DEMOCRATIC CONCEPT OF ALIENATION?

Can Chantal Mouffe's theory of radical democracy, given its theoretical assumptions, provide a theory of alienation? In order to answer this question, I will begin by re-examining Mouffe's theoretical approach, to see if, in fact, it already contains a concept of alienation – a concept that captures a situation wherein the subject's relation to the object is inhibited in such a way that her relation to herself also becomes dysfunctional. I will delve deeper into the theory of alienation and the assumptions on which it relies in Chapter 3. For the purposes of this chapter, however, it suffices to conclude that alienation, in its general definition, consists of at least three elements: (1) a dysfunctional social relation between subject and object, (2) a dysfunctional self-relation, and (3) a link between these two types of dysfunction.

To locate a radical democratic concept of alienation, I will focus on three concepts in the radical democratic arsenal: lack, antagonism and hegemony. These are all central to radical democracy, and can all, for different reasons, be connected to the concept of alienation. The concept of 'lack' or 'gap' is, in the radical democratic literature, occasionally referred to as 'alienation' (Laclau and Zac 1994, 14; Stavrakakis 2002); the concepts of antagonism and hegemony are, as we will see, structurally similar to these concepts. While the concept of lack is particularly prevalent in the psychoanalytical literature on alienation, the concepts of antagonism and hegemony stress primarily social and political relations, capturing how political collectives can challenge what can be described as estranged social and political power.

In the following discussion, I examine whether lack, antagonism or hegemony can function as a concept of alienation – covering the three elements listed above. I do so by studying not only Mouffe's work but also that of Ernesto Laclau. Mouffe and Laclau developed their conceptual framework together in their early co-authored work, and throughout both of their later writings, their theoretical approaches remain largely the same.[7] However, Laclau's conceptual discussions are more elaborate and, for this reason, I will draw on Laclau to clarify Mouffe's concepts.

### Lack

A possible concept of alienation is the concept that Mouffe and Laclau refer to as 'lack' or 'dislocation'. The concept is central to their theory of identity formation, which draws on the psychoanalytical theory of Jacques Lacan. Lacan and occasionally Laclau (Laclau and Zac 1994, 14) also refer to this lack as 'alienation'. Laclau describes lack

61

as a negative experience wherein something in both the subject's own identity and the society in which she lives seems to be missing. She experiences 'deprivation, dislocation, disorder' (Laclau 2004, 286). The concept of lack thus resembles that of alienation – whereby the subject's relation to the world is inhibited in such a way that her relation to herself becomes dysfunctional.

In order to understand the concept of lack, we must first understand the psychoanalytical theory of the subject on which it relies. For this reason, I will briefly introduce Lacan's theory of the subject, seeing as it is particularly relevant to Laclau and Mouffe. The self, in Lacan's conception, is constituted in relation to the external world. It is not until the subject sees herself in the other – the external world – that she can experience herself as a unified whole. According to Lacan, this experience of oneself as whole develops in what he calls the 'mirror-phase'. The 'mirror-phase' is the moment in an infant's development where she sees herself reflected in the external world – such as in a mirror – and begins to perceive herself as a self, as a subject. For Lacan, the external, social world in which we are primarily reflected is language.[8] He understands language as a symbolic order that exists prior to the subject. The self thus comes into existence through the subject's externalisation of itself through language.

However – and this is one of Lacan's central points – the process of externalisation is paradoxical and incomplete. The self that is externalised did not exist prior to its externalisation: there was no unified self to externalise. What is reflected – mirrored – in the external world cannot really be the subject herself. Furthermore, the external world in which the subject is reflected still remains, precisely, external. Although the reflection of the subject is a part of herself, it will also always differ from her: my image in the mirror is identical to me, but inverted. The self that is constituted in relation to her reflection is thus incomplete – and so is her reflection. The movement from the inner to the outer through which the subject is constituted always involves the production of lack – leaving the subject constitutively split or alienated. In Lacan's words, 'the human being has a special relation with his own image – a relation of gap, of alienating tension' (Lacan 1991, 323). The subject, in Lacan's conception, is constitutively split and alienated.

The conceptions of lack and of the subject as constitutively split become central to Mouffe and Laclau's theory of identity formation. In the words of the radical democratic Lacan scholar Yannis

Stavrakakis, 'by being essentially split and alienated' the subject 'becomes the *locus* of an impossible identity, the place where a whole politics of identification takes place' (Stavrakakis 2002, 13). In particular, it explains how the subject can be both open and radical, both committed and detached. According to Laclau, a condition for constituting a hegemony that consists of a plurality of claims is that these do not originally take on the form of positive political demands or programmes. Claims made in struggles against subordination are, according to Laclau, primarily negations (such as antiracism, antisexism and anticapitalism). The claims vary because they are based on different negative experiences. Laclau asserts that 'any struggle for justice starts off with an experience . . . lived originally in negative terms', as 'deprivation, dislocation, disorder' (Laclau 2004, 286). We experience a 'lack' of something, or a 'gap' in the social order. When experiencing a gap, Laclau argues, we want to fill it with something. We fill the gap by identifying with an object. The object is a symbol without any meaning of its own; it is 'empty' (Laclau 1996b, chap. 3). This explains how the subject can remain both passionately committed and open to a plurality of claims. Although people's experiences of lack differ, they can channel their indignation through the same symbol – a political leader or a slogan. When various negative experiences are brought together under a common symbolic roof – such as 'equality', 'the people' or 'the 99 per cent' – and mobilised against an equally symbolic adversary – 'the right', 'the elite' or 'the oligarchs' – a radical political association is formed.

This hegemonic relation of identification, then, enables openness. The new hegemony consists of little more than various negative experiences and the common symbol that unites them. The relations between people and their various claims are mediated by the leader or the slogan. Each person has her own relation to the common symbol – a relation consisting of the representation of her negative experience. As long as the negative experience, the lack, is reflected, the actual meaning of the object filling the gap – whether it is 'equality' or 'the people' – is up for grabs. The leader often plays an important role in giving the movement direction and fixing the meaning of the symbol (Errejón and Mouffe 2016, 108–17). Thomassen describes how the radical democratic strategy was used in practice by Podemos. The leader, Pablo Iglesias, expressed the indignation that Spanish people were already experiencing. People could identify with this and, therefore, came to identify with Podemos. The leader 'at once represent[s] an already existing indignation and makes that indignation present ("re-present[s]" it) in the media and within the political institutions' (Thomassen 2016, 166). Iglesias became the symbol under which various struggles of resistance could come together, and he came to play an important role in forming the actual political programme of the party.

Mouffe and Laclau's theory of identity formation explains how the agonist can remain both open and radical. It also relies on a set of assumptions about the agonist. She is assumed to have a particular experience – the experience of lack – and to react to this experience in a particular way – by strongly identifying with an object. The concept of lack – or what Lacan calls alienation – thus plays an important role in Mouffe's theory, allowing her demands on the subject to add up. However, what type of split between the subject and the social world, as well as between the subject and herself, does the concept of lack capture? Is it, as in the concept of alienation, a form of inhibition that renders the subject's relation to herself dysfunctional? For it to mark a relation that is dysfunctional, there must also be a possible scenario in which this relation is functional. Such a dysfunction could, for example, be a social ill (emerging in a certain social structure) or a psychological ill (stemming from the subject's mind and her particular way of relating to the world). Alienation can be conceived both as a social and a psychological ill – although in left theory, it is most often understood as the former. Let us therefore first examine whether the concept of lack captures a social ill.

For the concept of lack to capture a form of dysfunction that could be described as a social ill, it should appear only under particular historical and social conditions. There are indications in Mouffe and Laclau's work that the experience of lack is more intense in some situations than in others. Under conditions of intense destabilisation – in moments of what Laclau calls 'multiple dislocations' and Mouffe calls 'populist moments' – the experience of lack intensifies.

Laclau uses the concept of dislocation in two senses. First, it captures the constitutive lack of the subject. In Laclau's words, 'every identity is dislocated insofar as it depends on an outside which both denies that identity and provides its condition of possibility at the same time', and 'the location of the subject is that of dislocation' (Laclau 1990, 39, 41). Dislocation here has the same meaning as the concept of lack: the constitutive impossibility of the subject to be fully constituted.

Second, the concept of dislocation captures the situation of social destabilisation where the experience of constitutive lack is intensified. Laclau speaks, for example, of the 'dislocatory effects of emerging capitalism on the lives of workers'. Dislocatory effects include both 'the destruction of traditional communities . . . low wages and insecurity of work', as well as the workers' response to this, including strikes, the breaking of machines and organisation of trade unions (Laclau 1990, 39). While some societies are more stable and involve fewer dislocations, others give rise to a 'plurality of dislocation'. Contemporary 'disorganized capitalism' is, according to Laclau, an example of the latter (Laclau 1990, 59). For instance, beyond the contradictions in capitalism emphasised by traditional socialists, today's capitalism, is, Laclau argues, also destabilised by the decline of the nation state (Laclau 1990, 58–9). Similarly, Mouffe states that we are today witnessing what she calls a 'populist moment'. 'We can', Mouffe claims, 'speak of a "populist moment" when, under the pressure of political and socioeconomic transformations, the dominant hegemony is being destabilized by the multiplication of unsatisfied demands' (Mouffe 2019, 9). In contemporary capitalism, we are, Mouffe and Laclau claim, witnessing an acceleration of destabilising or 'dislocative' moments, which expose the structure of both the social world and the subject as constitutively dislocated or lacking.

Lack seems, therefore, to be experienced more intensely under some historical conditions than others. Does this mean that lack should be interpreted as a social ill? While dislocative or populist moments intensify the experience of lack, they do not themselves constitute it. In psychoanalytical and radical democratic theory, after all, the subject, as well as the social world of language, is always lacking. Recall that the process of externalisation, through which the subject and her social world are constituted, is paradoxical and incomplete – leaving the subject constitutively split. However, at certain historical junctures – at 'dislocative' or 'populist' moments – this ontological argument becomes particularly salient. At these moments, the primacy of the political reveals itself to us. Our exposure to the fundamental instability and contingency of both our social world and our own identities intensifies. With the radical democratic emphasis on ontological power and dislocation, social dislocations are given a certain meaning and importance: as moments where power is destabilised and ontological dislocation is exposed. Rather than impairing the subject's self-relation, these moments seem, if anything, to strengthen it. In Laclau's words, 'the more dislocated a structure is, the more the field of decisions not determined by it will expand . . . thereby leading to an increase in the role of the subject' (Laclau 1990, 39–40). And rather than blocking the subject, moments of dislocation enable counter-hegemonic action. At populist moments, we are, according to Mouffe, likely to see an intensification and pluralisation of political interventions. As the experience of lack intensifies in certain social structures, the subject is thus not impaired. The radical democratic concept of lack cannot capture a social ill.

Even more significantly, however, the concept of lack does not seem to capture any form of ill – neither social nor psychological. If we return to the deeper assumptions about the subject on which the concept of lack relies, we find that the concept of lack differs from that of alienation in one crucial respect. Unlike alienation, lack cannot be described as a dysfunction in the subject's self-relation. A dysfunction suggests the possibility of a relation that is functional; one that can, at least in theory, be overcome. A social ill could, for example, be overcome through social change, and a psychological one might be overcome through therapy. Overcoming alienation – establishing more functional relations to the world and the self – may be difficult, but it is not impossible. Lack, on the other hand, cannot be avoided. It is in lack, or dislocation, that the subject emerges: 'the location of the subject is that of dislocation'; 'the subject is', Laclau claims, 'the result of the impossibility of constituting the structure as such' (Laclau 1990, 41). In making lack constitutive of the subject, radical democrats cannot use it to distinguish a functioning relation to the world from an inhibited one – or a functioning self-relation from a dysfunctional one. The lacking subject can, like anyone, be both functioning and inhibited in her relations to the world and herself. Consequently, lack cannot work as a theory of alienation. It cannot capture the situation where the subject's relation to the world is inhibited in such a way that her relation to herself becomes dysfunctional.

Before, however, discarding the possibility of a radical democratic concept of alienation, I will turn to another – even more central – concept in radical democratic theory: the concept of antagonism. Can the concept of antagonism serve as a concept of alienation?

## Antagonism

Although the concept of antagonism may not initially seem to bear much resemblance to a concept of alienation, it may, in fact, be relevant. As we have seen, a concept of alienation should be able to distinguish between inhibited and functioning relations to the world and the self. In this regard, the concept of antagonism, which can be distinguished from that of agonism, seems more promising than that of lack.

The concept of antagonism, however, is closely related to that of lack. In fact, Laclau emphasises that the form of lack, or dislocation, that mainly interests him is 'a very specific dislocation: one that stems from the presence of antagonistic forces' (Laclau 1990, 40). The dislocation that marks the lacking subject is antagonism. This antagonism is, again in Mouffe's argument, ineradicable. Every time we form a relation of identification – when we see ourselves represented in an external object – we do so by distinguishing ourselves from something that we are not. Our self-relation is based on a relation of antagonism – the distinction between the 'I' and the 'other', or the 'we' and the 'they'. Irrespective of the mode in which antagonism emerges, it involves 'the formation of a "we" as opposed to a "they"'(Mouffe 2005a, 11) and 'points to a dimension of radical negativity' (Mouffe 2019, 88). Like 'lack', 'antagonism' is constitutive of both the subject herself and the external object on which she depends. In other words, the concept of antagonism relies on a conception of the subject as lacking. The subject, thus conceived, is radically negated by – or antagonistically related to – the outsides that constitute her.

So far, antagonism appears as something that resembles a concept of alienation: the subject is disconnected from herself in such a way that she is also disconnected from the outside world on which she depends. And, at the same time, like the concept of 'lack', 'antagonism' refers to a constitutive disconnection rather than a dysfunction in the subject's practical relations to herself and her social world. It does not mean that the subject is blocked from being herself or from living her life fully. Antagonism, like lack, is not a dysfunction but, again, constitutive of the subject herself. Lack is a part of the functioning of the subject. However, although very similar to the concept of lack, antagonism may be more apt for capturing the situation of alienation.

In Mouffe's democratic theory, the concept of antagonism takes on two different meanings. First, it is an ontological category as described above, and signifies ineradicable conflict. Second, it can signify one of two possible practical manifestations of ontological antagonism in society: antagonism – 'the struggle between enemies' – and agonism – 'the struggle between adversaries' (Mouffe 2019, 91). When antagonism is transformed into agonism, the other is 'not considered an enemy to be destroyed but an adversary whose existence is perceived as legitimate' (Mouffe 2019, 91). Consequently, although antagonism is ineradicable, it can take on different forms; it can be more or less functional. Whereas antagonism threatens to tear the political association apart, agonism is compatible with plural societies. Can the distinction between antagonism and agonism open up a space for a concept of alienation – where antagonism would imply an alienated relation and agonism would mean overcoming alienation?

Agonism, as opposed to antagonism, seems to represent a more functional relation to the world – or at least a less violent one. It allows us to live together in plural societies, without seeking to exclude one another with force. But does agonism, as opposed to antagonism, represent a more functional relation to the self? On the one hand, an agonistic relation to the world and to the self could, arguably, be interpreted as a more authentic relation. It may, as Mouffe, sometimes claims, involve a way of relating to the world and one's own commitments that is more in line with what, in Mouffe's argument, is the true, 'political' nature of things. In The Democratic Paradox, Mouffe describes the agonistic ethic as an 'ethics of psychoanalysis', which 'consists in dislocating the very idea of the good instead of proposing to reach harmony thanks to yet another conception of the good' (Mouffe 2000b, 138). It 'strives', she argues, 'to create among us a new form of bond, a bond that recognizes us as divided subject' (Mouffe 2000b, 139). In this view, an agonistic relation to the world means recognising oneself as well as the other as a divided, split subject – dependent upon another. While the antagonist seeks to eradicate the other on which she depends, the agonist accepts the other's existence. We may thus argue that the antagonist's relation to the external object and to herself is inhibited, while the agonist maintains a functional self-relation.

On the other hand, given my interpretation of agonism thus far, one could also argue the opposite: it is in her antagonistic attempts to eradicate the external object, the 'they', that the subject realises herself and her freedom. This is what allows her to occasionally break loose from the hegemonic order. In Laclau's words:

> the antagonizing force fulfils two crucial and contradictory roles at the same time. On the one hand, it 'blocks' the full constitution of the identity to which it is opposed and thus shows its contingency. On the other hand, given that this latter identity, like all identities, is merely relation and would therefore not be what it is outside the relationship with the force antagonizing it, the latter is also part of the conditions of existence of that identity. (Laclau 1990, 21)

The antagonistic dynamic is an important part of the subject's relation to herself. However, the antagonism that constitutes the subject does not seem to be inhibited in the agonistic subject. If one interprets the agonist as too peaceful, too keen on preserving the other on which she depends, she loses a part of the self-determining capacity – the element of contingency – that characterises her. If an agonistic relation is not also antagonistic in the ontological sense, it would not be fully functional.

For Mouffe's theory to add up, it seems as though I have to adjust my interpretation of her concept of agonism. Mouffe distinguishes agonism from what she calls the 'ethical' approach, which, according to her, 'has eliminated the antagonistic dimension'. This approach, Mouffe claims, 'implies the possibility of a plurality without antagonism. As if once we have been able to take responsibility for the other and to engage with its difference, violence and exclusion could disappear' (Mouffe 2000b, 134). To correctly interpret the concept of agonism, we must, it appears, recall that it should maintain the 'ineradicable' antagonistic dimension. Even in its agonistic forms, the ontological antagonism that constitutes the subject is maintained. Agonism, too, would then involve exclusion and harbour the risk of violence. We cannot, Mouffe claims, have a 'friend without an enemy, an agonism without antagonism' (Mouffe 2000b, 134). If we take these statements seriously, it seems that we should interpret Mouffe's concept of agonism as very similar to that of antagonism. How, then, should one understand Mouffe's distinction between agonism and antagonism?

Let us recall Mouffe's description of agonism as merely one possible manifestation of antagonism. Agonism should, alongside antagonism, be viewed as a specific expression of ontological antagonism. In her work on democratic theory, Mouffe argues that democratic, plural societies should attempt to channel antagonism as agonism – primarily by setting up an institutional framework that delimits, but never fully eradicates, the risk of violence. In this vein, Mouffe argues, for example, that 'when institutional channels do not exist for antagonism to be expressed in an agonistic way, they are likely to explode into violence' (Mouffe 2013, 122). In this interpretation, the agonistic relation to the world is not fundamentally different from the antagonistic one. It is merely temporarily and precariously tamed by institutions. Agonism is a politically and institutionally constructed expression of the ontological antagonism, and the innate possibility for resistance, that marks a functional subject.

In other words, the agonistic and antagonistic subjects' relations to the objects on which they depend remain structurally the same – and, for this reason, so do their self-relations. The subject's relations to herself and the world remain functional, irrespective of whether ontological antagonism is expressed as agonism or antagonism. The subject maintains her characteristic antagonistic relation to the outside that constitutes her, as well as her defining characteristic: that of being only partly determined by this outside. To tame antagonism is important for political purposes – for maintaining a peaceful political association – but not necessarily for the self-realisation of the subject. Irrespective of whether the antagonism through which she realises herself and her capacity for freedom is expressed through antagonism or agonism, it can, Mouffe contends, always be expressed. The concept of antagonism does not allow us to distinguish a functional self-relation from a dysfunctional one. For this reason, it cannot be considered a concept of alienation.

## Hegemony

Having seen that the radical democratic subject – the agonist – is not alienated at the moment during which social relations are destabilised, we can consider neither lack nor antagonism as concepts of alienation. But if instability and disconnection do not alienate the subject, how about their opposite: hegemonic power? Mouffe uses the concept of hegemony, alongside that of antagonism, in order to capture how political collectives can challenge what could be described as alienated social and political power. She defines hegemony as the form of power that establishes something as objective and unquestionable, as the 'point of confluence between objectivity and power' (Mouffe 2000b, 21). Recall that the subject seems to be particularly able to realise herself at the moment during which the current hegemonic power configuration breaks down. It is in these moments of 'dislocation' that the political nature of our social order is revealed. If the destabilisation of her social relations liberates the subject, one might argue that hegemonic power is what blocks her. Can hegemony thus function as a concept of alienation – capturing an inhibited social relation that also inhibits her self-relation?

I will not delve very deeply into this question as the problem with considering hegemony as a form of alienation is very similar to those already discussed in relation to the concepts of lack and antagonism. Hegemony is, alongside the concept of antagonism, one of the central concepts of radical democracy. And it is, like antagonism, constitutive of both social relations and the subject herself. Hegemonic power is, in Mouffe's opinion, also ineradicable. Mouffe states, 'Every social order is the temporary and precarious articulation of hegemonic practices whose aim is to establish order in a context of contingency' (Mouffe 2019, 88). Any society or identity is, in Mouffe's theory, based on power. It is power that makes us able to understand each other, to share a language and a common sense, and to navigate the world. Even resistance is a hegemonic – or what Mouffe calls a 'counter-hegemonic' – practice (Mouffe 2019, 88). Hegemony is constitutive of the subject's relation to the world, including the meaning she ascribes to things and the identities she takes on. It is a part of the paradoxical 'dialectic of non-fixity/fixation' that constitutes the social world and the subject (Mouffe 2019, 89). If hegemonic social relations could be described as impaired, then so could all social relations. As a result, hegemony can hardly be considered an inhibited or dysfunctional relation between the subject and her object of identification.

I have thus demonstrated that neither antagonism nor its closely related concepts of lack and hegemony can be considered concepts of alienation. And even more significantly, I have shown that radical democracy relies on a subject who is constitutively marked by lack, antagonism and hegemonic power. The subject, thus conceived, does not seem like she could experience any situation as alienating. If this is the case, radical democracy would not only lack a theory of alienation, it would be prevented from providing one. In order to find out if radical democracy can provide a theory of alienation, I will thus examine the subject, the agonist, on which the concept of antagonism, and its closely related concepts of lack and hegemony, relies. Primarily, I will analyse if it is theoretically possible for this subject to become alienated.

## THE AGONIST

Can the subject – the agonist – who is constituted by lack, antagonism and hegemonic power be inhibited in her relation to the world in such a way that her relation to herself becomes dysfunctional? In other words, can she be alienated? To answer this question, I will examine, first, what it means for this subject to have a functional self-relation and, second, whether this relation can be inhibited.

The subject's relation to herself is, as we have seen, paradoxical. She is both 'necessary' and 'contingent', both determined by her outside and never fully determined. But what does this mean in practice? We can begin to answer this question by taking a closer look at Mouffe and Laclau's writings on identity formation and left populist strategy. The antagonistic relation that marks the constitution of the subject manifests itself at two different moments. Together, these moments make up the 'dialectic of non-fixity/fixation' that constitutes the subject (Mouffe 2019, 89).

First, the subject is, most of the time, partially 'fixed', determined by hegemonic power. In the moment of hegemonic attachment, the subject and her actions are almost completely determined by the current social order. She acts, wills and understand things in the currently established way.

Second, at moments of 'non-fixity', social relations are destabilised and the subject is free to will and act. The subject will then have to make a decision in what Mouffe describes as a terrain of 'undecidability' (Mouffe 2013, 1–2).[9] There is no predetermined resolution to what the subject will be or how she will act. For example, radical democrats cannot, like traditional socialists would, assume that a ready-made radical subject, driven by necessity, will rise up and challenge the capitalist order. At moments of destabilisation, only the subject herself can decide how to act. The outside on which she has been conditioned does not determine her. Laclau sometimes describes this as 'impersonating God' (Laclau 1996a, 55). Relying only on herself, the subject decides in a terrain of 'undecidability' what she will do and what she will be. At this point, the subject can, if she chooses to, break with the current hegemony.

These God-like moments, however, are short-lived. In Mouffe's model, even resistance is a hegemonic project. Soon, the subject is either absorbed into a new relation of identification with a counter-hegemonic project or reabsorbed into the previous hegemonic construction. The subject is thus characterised by a conflictual dynamic to which there is no resolution. She oscillates between the moment of hegemonic fixation and the moment of destabilisation and decision. Neither of these moments can be considered as inhibiting, as they are constitutive of the subject.

Paradoxically, in a theory in which there is no escape from power, and in which every society and every subject is permeated by it, the subject also – and for this very reason – has an innate capacity for a remarkable freedom. Mouffe and Laclau come to rely on a subject who is both trapped in a social order from which she cannot escape and is never fully trapped. In Laclau's words, 'I am simply thrown up in my condition as a subject because I have not achieved constitution as an object' (Laclau 1990, 44). The never fully determined character of the subject is an important element of what constitutes the subject as a subject as opposed to an object. The subject is essentially marked by her capacity to will – to decide, among several alternatives, who she will be and what she will do – and to act or to change things. A dysfunctional subject would be one whose willing and acting are inhibited.

However, the paradoxical nature of the subject – both determined and never fully determined by the outside – leaves little room for a theory of alienation, that is, a theory of how the subject's relations to the world and herself are inhibited. The subject can, on the one hand, be trapped in the power of the current hegemony. But while one might think that such a power would block the subject from acting, it does not. This is one of Mouffe's key points. Hegemony is, in her conception, always based on antagonism and can, at any moment, be challenged. On the other hand, the subject can find herself in a moment of disruption. But while one might imagine that a deep disruption in the subject's world and identity could leave her disoriented and inhibited, it does not. Instead, disruption is, according to Mouffe and Laclau, the starting point of counter-hegemonic action (Laclau 2004, 286).

Thus, in its emphasis on lack, antagonism and hegemony, radical democratic theory comes to rely on a subject constituted by both necessity and contingency in such a way that it becomes difficult to conceive of anything that could genuinely inhibit her. She is so bound by power – determined by things outside of herself – yet so free – always lacking and thus never fully determined – that there is no real possibility for her to be too disconnected or too bound by existing commitments. In both scenarios, she will maintain her ability to will and act. The subject, it seems, cannot be alienated. In what follows, I will further develop this argument. I will show that the subject – the agonist – is marked by three particular characteristics that preclude alienation.

### Flexible, strong and conflict-seeking

I intend to make two arguments. First, as Laclau and Mouffe pull the concepts of lack, antagonism and hegemony into its centre, radical democracy comes to fall back on three main assumptions about the subject: the subject is flexible, strong and conflict-seeking. Second, I will establish how these assumptions also explain how the possible tension between the radical democratic demand on the subject to be both open and radical can – at least in theory – be resolved.

The agonist is assumed to be flexible in a specific sense: she can identify with any object that comes into view within a given situation, and any of these identities will, in their most relevant respects, fit her equally well. The antagonistic relation on which identity formation relies means that the agonist's identity is partly determined by her outside, but can, at the same time, never be fully determined. Or, in Lacanian language, the agonist can experience every object as lacking; she can both identify and break with any object. For this reason, she can remain open – able to share any object of identification with anyone and to respond to anyone's claims. When she experiences a lack in the social order, there are few limits to what it can be filled with. The concept of antagonism also means that there is always an alternative. Every order and identity is based on an option that is repressed.[10] There are, therefore, always alternatives between which we can choose; what choice we make is up to us (Mouffe 2013, 132).

The concept of antagonism means that the next object of identification, and its limitations, is determined not by dialectical progress, moral rules or social conditions but by individual decisions. The other is a radical negation of the subject herself; it is not internal to her. This means that there is no given resolution to the antagonism between the subject and her outside, no possibility of dialectical pro-

74

gress. In fact, there is no resolution at all. What will follow from the antagonistic dynamic between the subject and her outside, between 'we' and 'they', cannot be described as a process of problem-solving or conflict resolution. It is accidental, contingent. In Mouffe's words, 'bringing a conversation to a close is always a personal choice, a decision which cannot be simply presented as mere application of procedures and justified as the only move that we could make in those circumstances' (Mouffe 2000b, 75). We decide in a terrain of 'undecidability' (Mouffe 2013, 1–2). And '[t]o take a decision', Laclau asserts, 'is like impersonating God. It is like asserting that one does not have the means of being God, and one has, however, to proceed as if one were Him' (Laclau 1996a, 55). In the moment where our identities are put into question and their underlying antagonism rises to the surface, there is nothing to fall back on. It is all on us. The agonist has to, as Laclau writes, 'impersonate God' – to make decisions between available alternatives based on nothing but her own will.

Such a freedom and flexibility stems from the agonist's paradoxical, and antagonistic, relation to the world and to herself. In Laclau's words, 'I am condemned to be free, not because I have no structural identity as the existentialists assert, but because I have a failed structural identity' (Howarth 2015, 32). The agonist's failed structural identity – antagonistic and lacking – is the premise for her ability to will freely. For the agonist to be free to make decisions, she must be sufficiently disconnected from her given identities that they no longer appear to her as given; they cannot seem morally or socially objective. And because her structural identities fail, she is free: social and moral rules cannot bind her.

This constitutive failure of all social relations is not only what allows the subject to be flexible but also what enables her openness. The agonist always relates to herself and the world in a lacking way; she is always somewhat disconnected. For this reason, she can experience any identity or order as lacking, and, in response to this experience, she can choose to identify with any object. Her flexibility enables the agonist to be open, able to take on any identity and to share it with anyone.

To clarify, however, we must emphasise that what I have here described as a free and flexible subject should not be confused with what sometimes – and often by communitarian critics of social contract theories – has been called an 'individualist' or 'atomist' subject.

75

Atomism 'affirms', according to Charles Taylor, 'the self-sufficiency of man alone or, if you prefer, of the individual'. It opposes itself to the view of the human being as a social or political animal (Taylor 1985, 189).

As we have seen, Mouffe's conception of the subject differs significantly from the atomist one. Far from being self-sufficient, the subject is entirely relational. She is constituted antagonistically in relation to an other that is her radical negation. She is free to will and act, not because of her lack of specific social relations, but because social relations are always lacking. Laclau thus argues that the subject's contingency, her freedom, is not a 'head-on negation of necessity' but its 'subversion' (Laclau 1990, 27). The flexible subject is not completely atomist and self-sufficient. Rather, '[f]or antagonism to be able to *show* the contingent nature of an identity, that identity must be there in the first place' (Laclau 1990, 27, original emphasis). The implication of this is, in Laclau's view, that while the subject's paradoxical nature leaves her with the potential for free decision-making – to 'impersonate God' (Laclau 1996a, 55) – she always also finds herself in a 'limited and given situation in which objectivity is partially constituted and also partially threatened' (Laclau 1990, 27). It is precisely the social identity that we have, the outside that determine us, that opens up a space for the undeterminable. For Laclau, notions such as freedom or autonomy are, just like that of the subject, paradoxical: they refer 'to the locus of an insoluble tension'. Autonomy only gains a meaning in relation to something else, something that we are 'autonomous from' (Laclau 1990, 37). Freedom and autonomy should thus, like the subject of radical democracy, be understood as relational and paradoxical.[11]

Having made note of the limits of the agonist's flexibility – her dependence on social relations – we must also specify the limits to her relational qualities. Although the subject is relational, she is not social. She cannot realise herself and be free in social relations. All social relations are, in Mouffe's conception, based on power. The reason for the subject's freedom – her capacity to will and act – is the limit of the social. Because social relations always fail, the subject is always partially free. '[T]he subject is', as Laclau claims, 'the result of the impossibility of constituting the structure as such' (Laclau 1990, 41). The subject exists only because social relations always fail. Social relations are always lacking, and this lack opens up a space for the subject to be flexible. This is the specificity of the agonist. She is flexible but not atomist, relational but not social. And if this seems paradoxical, it is not surprising. Paradox – the relation of lack or antagonism – is what constitutes the agonist.

An important implication of the subject as flexible – as always only partially constituted and partially free – is, according to Laclau, that the subject's social relations are never more disrupted than what she can manage. 'The madness of the decision', Laclau claims, 'is, if you want, as all madness, a regulated one' (Laclau 1996a, 57). The agonist is never truly 'in the position of the absolute chooser who, faced with the contingency of all possible courses of action, would have no reason to choose' (Laclau 1990, 27). While the ago- nist may find herself in situations of deep disruption – when she is torn away from the relations on which she relies – she is not para- lysed. Laclau asserts that, in theory, the situation of undecidability could throw the subject into a paralysing situation, 'described by the existentialist', where 'a sovereign chooser, precisely because he is sovereign, does not have the ground of any choice'; however, he claims, this only occurs if too much 'is put into question at the same time' (Laclau 2004, 287). For the agonist, who always finds herself in a situation where undecidability is partly delimited, the moments of disruption do not paralyse her, nor do they inhibit her capacity to will and act. As the risk of paralysing disruption is dismissed, disrup- tion is instead conceived, if anything, as emancipatory. It tears the subject away from the structure that partially traps her, leaving her in a position to make free decisions. The subject, while far from being a self-sufficient, atomist individual, maintains an ineradicable poten- tial to will freely, to choose within the bounds of the situation she is in what to do and who to be. She maintains a capacity to reshape herself in the face of disruption: to remain flexible.

Beyond her flexibility, the agonist is also assumed to be strong. She does not rely on social objects to act, only on her own strength. For Mouffe and Laclau, loss is the moment of action. In Laclau's words, 'any struggle for justice starts off with an experience . . . lived originally in negative terms', as 'deprivation, dislocation, disorder' (Laclau 2004, 286). It is in the moment when we are torn away from the social object that we are committed to and identify with that we can act. Mouffe argues that in the current 'populist moment', when the social order is 'being destabilized by the multiplication of unsatisfied demands . . . the possibility arises of constructing a new subject of collective action . . . capable of reconfiguring a social order experienced as unjust' (Mouffe 2019, 11). Disruption and deprivation inspire radical action.

It should be noticed that Mouffe does not claim that the subject always will act when experiencing loss, only that she can – if she chooses to. Mouffe emphasises that her theoretical approach is 'crucial for envisaging how to act in politics'. 'You can', Mouffe claims, 'always change things politically. You can always intervene in relations of power in order to transform them' (Mouffe 2013, 132). Our irreducible capacity for radical action and change is one of the central messages of radical democracy. Laclau describes this stance as radical democracy's 'radical optimism' (Laclau 1990, 35). According to Laclau, the assumption of irreducible antagonism should not be a cause for pessimism, for 'if social relations are contingent it means they can be radically transformed through struggle' (Laclau 1990, 35–6). The unstable, contingent nature of our identities and our social world – where we are always on the verge of losing the things that we have and that define us – means that we can always act to change things.

The radical democratic emphasis on our capacity for action and change, is, as we saw in Chapter 1, inscribed in a particular historical context – a time when 'Margaret Thatcher declared, "There is no alternative"', and when 'many social democrats [had] accepted this view' (Mouffe 2013, 131). The assumed strength of the subject, her almost heroic ability to act in all situations, can be read as a message of hope delivered in a moment when the left seemed hopelessly defeated. In this context of defeat, it is not surprising that Mouffe does not discuss the opposite: the risk that loss, disruption and marginalisation, instead of inspiring radical political engagement, could result in a disabling sense of powerlessness.

When Mouffe's optimism wavers, it is not to warn against apathy and powerlessness but of the 'return of the political' (Mouffe 1993). Repressing struggle is risky, not because it could inhibit the subject but because it risks resulting in dangerous antagonism. In Mouffe's words, 'when channels are not available through which conflict could take "agonistic" form, those conflicts tend to emerge in the antagonistic mode' (Mouffe 2005a, 5). The attempt to repress the passions and engagement of the subject will not succeed. Even the most stabilised social order and sets of identities can eventually be politicised. The more resistance is repressed, the more dangerous and violent it will be when it erupts.

As we have seen, Mouffe reiterates both the irreducible possibility of struggle and the risk that this struggle – if repressed – will result in dangerous antagonism. Loss triggers radical action – agonistic or antagonistic. At the same time, the risk that deprivation will not inspire but impair passion and action remains unaddressed. This leaves radical democratic theory with a subject marked by a particular quality: she does not rely on social objects to act. She depends only on her own strength. Even in situations of deep deprivation, she can – if she chooses to – act to change things. But from where, then, does she draw her energy to act?

This question can be answered by a third assumption about the agonist: she is naturally conflict-seeking. Mouffe emphasises the 'predominant role of passions as moving forces of human conduct' (Mouffe 1993, 140) and as 'the driving force in the political field' (Mouffe 2013, 6). And the primary passion is antagonism. Although Mouffe recognises other passions in politics, such as bonds of love,[12] it is only antagonism – in the form of agonism or antagonism – that can mobilise people's affects and energise them into action. 'It is', Mouffe argues, 'only by restoring the agonistic character of democracy that it will be possible to mobilize affects' (Mouffe 2019, 85). To engage people, conflict is necessary. In Mouffe's words, 'To be able to mobilize passions . . . politics must have a partisan character' (Mouffe 2005a, 6). It must activate an antagonistic division, between 'we' and 'they', 'left' and 'right' or 'the people' and 'the oligarchs'. The exact forms that these divisions take vary throughout Mouffe's work, but they remain central (e.g. Mouffe 2005a, 6; 2019, 85). No conflict, no passion; no passion, no political action. Conflict is what energises the agonist.

It should be clarified that a subject driven by conflict itself is not the same as a subject driven by the desire to resolve conflict. Recall that Mouffe's subject is constituted through an antagonistic relation to an outside that radically negates her. In Mouffe's words, 'the perception of something other which constitutes its "exterior"' is 'a precondition for the existence of any identity' (Mouffe 2005a, 15). Antagonism is the agonist's deepest passion and most fundamental energising force – it is the force that constitutes her. For divisions to mobilise our passions, they must therefore tap into the deeper antagonism that constitutes us. It cannot be 'a mere difference of position' but should be 'envisaged in terms of a frontier, indicating the existence of an antagonism between respective position and the impossibility of a "centre position"' (Mouffe 2019, 84–5). Antagonism is, in Mouffe's theoretical approach, not 'mere difference'; it is radical negation. The antagonistic force that constitutes and drives the subject can have no 'centre position' or resolution (Mouffe 2019, 84–5). The agonist is, then, not essentially driven by the desire to find solutions to her particular problems or resolutions to the specific conflictual situations in which she finds herself. She is driven by conflict itself: the power struggle between 'we' and 'they'. Conflict is what awakens her passions and spurs her into action.

The subject's search for conflict explains how the agonist can be both open and radical. Due to her conflict-seeking, the agonist can, as the radical democratic strategy requires, identify with a symbol irrespective of its specific meaning; it suffices that the symbol is antagonistically related to an equally symbolic adversary. The mere distinction between 'the people' and 'the oligarchs' is enough to inspire action. Her conflict-seeking thus allows the agonist to share symbolic commitment with a plurality of people, whose experiences and demands differ. That same conflict-seeking also explains how the agonist can be simultaneously radical, acting passionately on decisions that lack ground in necessity, private motives or a sense of moral obligation. As long as she has an adversary against whom she can struggle, the agonist remains passionately committed.

### Open and radical – but never alienated

We have thus seen that radical democracy, with its focus on antagonism, as well as the related concepts of lack and hegemony, relies on three assumptions about the agonist: she is flexible, strong and conflict-seeking. These assumptions also leave radical democracy with a subject who can, at least in theory, be both open and radical. The flexible, strong and conflict-seeking subject should be able both to listen to a plurality of claims and to fight for transformative social change. But – while resolving the possible tension between the aims of radicalism and openness – can the subject, thus conceived, be alienated?

Radical democracy, I have established, presupposes a subject who realises herself in the activity of willing and acting. At the same time, the agonist's intrinsic characteristics – her flexibility, strength and propensity to seek conflict – mean that her capacity to will and act cannot be inhibited.

The first of the agonist's characteristics, her flexibility, means that her ability to will cannot be impaired. Even when she is disconnected from the world – when her identity and commitments are deeply disrupted – she is not paralysed. In fact, this capacity to remain engaged even as her affective attachments are inhibited is one of the agonist's defining features. For the flexible subject, the capacity to will freely stems not from her social relations but from their intrinsic tendency to break down. She can be free in any social order, because all social orders are precarious. A disruption in her relations of identification does not imply an inhibition in the subject's relation to herself. When her expectations are thwarted, the subject is flexible enough to merely shift her affective attachments to another object of identification.

The second of the agonist's defining features, her strength, leaves her with the ability to act under conditions of loss and deprivation. Rather than being disempowered by loss, deprivation is the starting point of radical action. The subject of radical democracy relies only on her own strength to act. An inhibition in the subject's relation to objects does not mean that her relation to herself becomes dysfunctional; instead, she maintains her capacity for action.

Lastly, the agonist's propensity to seek conflict is a condition for her flexibility and strength. It means that she can act and maintain a functional self-relation even as her relation to the social world is inhibited. Rather than being inspired by particular desires and commitments, the agonist is drawn to and energised by conflict. The abstract structure of antagonism – the distinction between 'we' and 'they' – activates her. The agonist – flexible, strong and conflict-seeking – does not rely on particular objects to will and act but is, in fact, spurred by negation.

Thus, given her intrinsic characteristics – her flexibility, strength and propensity to seek conflict – the agonist cannot be alienated. She can will even when her social relations are disrupted, and she does not depend on anything but herself to act. The subject's relation to the object cannot be inhibited in such a way that her relation to herself becomes dysfunctional. Although dislocation and deprivation may, in Laclau's words, initially be 'traumatic', such traumatic experiences are constitutive of the subject and a condition for her freedom (Laclau 1990, 44). In its focus on antagonism, radical democracy thus comes to rely on a subject who is flexible, strong and conflict-seeking enough to be both radical and open, but who, precisely for this reason, cannot be alienated.

## Why include the alienated?

I will go on to show that, for a theory concerned with the open and radical mobilisation of marginalised people, the conception of the subject as an agonist (flexible, strong and conflict-seeking) is, under current conditions of precarity, insufficient. While it theoretically resolves the possible tension between openness and radicalism, it leaves the theory unable to include those who are not empowered but deeply alienated by the social disruptions specific to our times.

Recall how contemporary, precarious society requires a 'particular strength of character – that of someone who has the confidence to dwell in disorder, someone who flourishes in the midst of dislocation' (Sennett 1998, 62). Since this is precisely what radical democracy requires of its subject, it cannot properly problematise and challenge these demands. Like the 'flexible subject' that the current social order demands, the agonist is perfectly suited to respond to the conditions of precarity and dislocation in the present.

In radical democratic theory, the agonist is perceived as marginalised – an 'underdog' (Laclau 2004, 297). Consequently, radical democracy should be able to theoretically accommodate and strategically mobilise precisely those who suffer from subordination and marginalisation. Radical democracy's presumed subject, however, does not suffer from disruption to the extent that she loses the energy to will and act. Due to its conception of the subject as an agonist, radical democracy is not theoretically equipped to make sense of the suffering that precarity can give rise to, or understand how the experience of precarity can block the open and radical engagement that the theory seeks.

This is precisely where radical democracy risks becoming 'socially weightless' (see McNay 2014, chap. 2). If the agonist, as I have shown, is assumed to be flexible, strong and conflict-seeking, we might be more likely to find her among people in power than among the marginalised and subordinated. Remember that, while people in higher positions can be spurred by disruption and dislocation, this disposition 'become more self-destructive among those who work lower down in the flexible regime' (Sennett 1998, 63). For precarious people with fewer opportunities to forge a new path in life, disruptions in their social relations are more likely to turn into a dysfunctional self-relation. In these cases, experiences of disruption and deprivation are not empowering but risk resulting in a loss of the passion and commitment that radical action requires.

Whether or not this is the case is an empirical question. Irrespective of the empirics, however, relaxing Mouffe's restrictive assumptions about the subject would widen the application of radical democratic theory and thus strengthen it. A theory that can only apply to people with the very particular qualities that Mouffe's theory assumes becomes a very narrow one – it suits only a few people in certain contexts. Not all reformulations of the subject would, however, necessarily have a wider application, and whether this is the case is difficult to judge.

But even more importantly, if we, beyond this, also take seriously the growing problem of alienation that the literature on precarity points towards, radical democracy would need to reformulate its subject to make itself relevant today. It would make the theory applicable not only to people who are flexible, strong and conflict-seeking but to those whose social relations are inhibited in such a way that their relation to themselves becomes dysfunctional: those people today who experience marginalisation in the form of alienation.

While radical democracy's 'radical optimism' may have been crucial in a time when Thatcher proclaimed that 'there is no alternative', the same optimism today risks being cruel rather than radical – intensifying the pressure on precarious people who are already overburdened.[13] As long as it falls back on a conception of the subject that cannot accommodate alienation, radical democracy is left unequipped to understand how alienation can block the realisation of its own aims.

## Conclusion

Radical democracy, aiming at the open and radical mobilisation of marginalised groups, should seek to address marginalisation in the form of alienation. However, it cannot. Its concepts of lack, antagonism and hegemony, although initially promising, cannot capture the problem of alienation. Instead, precisely in its exclusive focus on antagonism, radical democracy comes to rely on a conception of the subject that, under conditions of alienation, becomes insufficient. It assumes the subject to be an agonist: naturally flexible, strong and conflict-seeking. The subject thus conceived is perfectly suited to straddle today's conditions of precarity. As a result, radical democracy comes to exclude alienated groups and is unable to make sense of how today's problem of alienation could be blocking the open and radical struggle against social marginalisation that it strives for.

At the same time, we have seen that the conception of the subject as an agonist fulfils an important function in the theory by resolving the possible tension between its aims of open and radical engagement. The agonist's flexibility allows her to maintain enough distance to remain open, while her strength and natural propensity to seek conflict mean that she is, at the same time, always ready to commit to a radical struggle. Radical democracy is thus left with a challenge: it must find a subject who can, at least in theory, be both open and radical, but who is also capable of experiencing alienation. I will return to this challenge in the third and last part of the book. Before this, however, I will examine what a suitable subject – a subject who can be alienated – would look like. In search of such a subject, I turn to the literature on alienation.

## NOTES

1. Laclau clarifies this point further in his later work: 'For classical Marxism, the possibility of transcending capitalist society is dependent on . . . the emergence of a privileged agent of social change, while for us, the possibility of a democratic transformation of society depends on a proliferation of new subjects of change' (Laclau 1990, 41). The subject of change would have to be rethought, taking into consideration its plurality and indeterminacy.

2. It should be noted that, beyond this, human identity, in Laclau and Mouffe's conception, also involves the symbol – the 'nodal point' – around which the various positions gather and which temporarily binds them together (Laclau and Mouffe [1985] 2001, 117).

3. Mouffe uses the word 'antagonism' to denote both the form of conflict (the 'we/they distinction', that in her theoretical assumptions is ineradicable) as well as its more dangerous expression, that is, 'the struggle between enemies' (e.g. Mouffe 2019, 90–1).

4. Also in her later work, Mouffe maintains that 'what is at stake in agonistic politics is the very configuration of power relations that structure a social order' (Mouffe 2019, 92).

5. This, however, does not mean that the liberal democratic institutions are unpolitical and cannot be contested. In Mouffe's words, 'the ground on which hegemonic interventions occur is never neutral' (Mouffe

2019, 93). According to Mouffe, the liberal democratic battlefield is itself political.

6. In Laclau and Mouffe's work the term 'radical' is often used to refer to the lack of foundation and to open up the notion of pluralism: 'Pluralism is radical only to the extent that each term of this plurality of identities finds within itself the principle of its own validity, without this having to be sought in a transcendent or underlying positive ground for the hierarchy of meaning of them all and the source and guarantee of their legitimacy' (Laclau and Mouffe [1985] 2001, 167).

7. In her recent work, Mouffe asserts, for instance, that her 'reflection . . . is informed by a theoretical approach developed in *Hegemony and Socialist Strategy*, according to which two key concepts are needed to address the question of the political: "antagonism" and "hegemony"' (Mouffe 2019, 88).

8. In order to keep my reading of Lacan in line with the reading within the radical democratic tradition, I here draw on the radical democratic Lacan scholar Yannis Stavrakakis's summary of Lacan's theory of the subject (see Stavrakakis 2002, chap. 1). There are, however, many readings of Lacan's often enigmatic texts. Whereas most works on Lacan focus on language and the symbolic sphere, another reader of Lacan in the political context, Samo Tomšič (2019) also, interestingly, expands this reading of externalisation in Lacan to include labour. I have here, however, chosen to describe externalisation primarily as language, as this is not only the most common reading but also comes closer to that of Lacan.

9. Similarly, Laclau argues that the 'link between the blocking and simultaneous affirmation of an identity . . . introduces an element of radical undecidability into the structure of objectivity' (Laclau 1990, 21).

10. '[I]nstitution, as we have seen, is only possible through the repression of options that were equally open' (Laclau 1990, 34).

11. 'In the case of autonomy, it refers to the locus of an insoluble tension. If an entity was totally autonomous, it would mean that it was totally self-determined. But in that case the concept of autonomy would be completely redundant (what, exactly, would it be autonomous from?)' (Laclau 1990, 37).

12. However, in Mouffe's view, love too comes with the risk of antagonism. Quoting Freud, Mouffe states, 'It is always possible to bind together a considerable amount of people in love, so long as there are other people left over to receive the manifestation of their aggressiveness' (Mouffe 2013, 47).

13. Lauren Berlant captures precisely this burden of optimism under conditions of precarity in her book titled *Cruel Optimism* (2011).

# Part II

## *Alienation*

CHAPTER THREE

# Alienation of the knower, the producer and the actor

Alienation emerged in the eighteenth century with a view to capturing the fragmentation and distorted relation of the subject to herself and the world following the industrial revolution. The concept was, as we saw in Chapter 1, revived within the left to capture experiences of thwarted expectations in the post-war period. Throughout the concept's history, it has appeared in many different forms; in general, however, alienation can be defined as a social or psychological ill in which a subject and an object that belong together in a mutually constitutive relation are disconnected. In other words, the subject is alienated when her relation to the object is inhibited in such a way that her relation to herself becomes dysfunctional.

This definition of alienation was already briefly introduced in the Introduction and in Chapter 2. In this part of the book, however, I will delve more deeply into the concept and the underlying ideas on which it relies. On a deeper plane, there are three components to this definition. First, it involves a subject. The subject can be an individual, a group, humanity at large or 'the spirit' of the world. Second, alienation concerns an object. The object can be an inner drive, a thing, another person, a social institution or the world as whole. Third, the proper, assumed relation between subject and object is central to the concept of alienation. The subject and object belong together in a mutually constitutive relation; each is a part of the other. When the subject is alienated, this relation is inhibited. When thus alienated, the subject relates to a part of herself as something external. Referring to the alienated part of the subject as an object is thus both accurate and misleading. Although the alienated relation is a subject–object relation, it is not supposed to be. The object is supposed to be a part of the subject. The subject's self-relation takes on the distorted form of a subject–object

89

relation. Alienation can thus be understood as an inhibited, dysfunctional self-relation.

The concept of alienation was valued within the left for its capacity to locate seemingly individual experiences within social systems – to link the subjective and the objective. In alienation theory, the subject and the object form a mutually constitutive relation. This means that a dysfunctional social relation can also turn into a dysfunctional self-relation. For instance, Marx argues that the meaninglessness and powerlessness experienced by the worker in capitalist society is not merely a private experience but a systematic social problem. For that reason, the concept of alienation could be used by the left to mobilise people's seemingly private experiences of meaninglessness into a radical political struggle that served to challenge the social order.

However, the strength of the concept – its ability to connect the subjective and the objective – also becomes its main problem. Within the internal debate on alienation, the concept is criticised for not being open enough – for falling into the pitfalls of human essentialism, determinism and idealising a final state of harmony. At the same time, attempting to open up the concept risks constructing alienation as merely a subjective experience or a problem of understanding. Seen as such, the concept cannot be used for radical social criticism or struggle.

This tension – between the internal demands on the concept of alienation – also manifests itself in the subject. Following the analytical approach outlined in the Introduction, this chapter traces the development of the concept of alienation and its corresponding conception of the individual subject. The internal debate on alienation, I argue, amounts to a tension between openness and radicalism of the concept. The theory of alienation should remain both open – avoiding the pitfalls of human essentialism, determinism and idealising a final state of harmony – and radical – retaining a dimension of social suffering, power and antagonism. However, while open theories come to rely on an individual subject who engages with and impacts the world in a way that cannot be socially or essentially predetermined, radical theories assume a subject who is sufficiently socially grounded to experience social suffering, power and antagonism. These assumptions seem, at least in the literature on alienation, to be difficult to combine. Each conception of alienation and of the subject is left insufficient in one of these two respects.

90

In the following three chapters, I focus directly on alienation and the internal debate on the concept. In this chapter, I first trace the theory of alienation, from Georg Wilhelm Friedrich Hegel via Karl Marx to Rahel Jaeggi, and examine the conception of the subject on which they rely. Lastly, I discuss the two sets of theoretical criteria for the concept of alienation that the internal debate on alienation amounts to – openness and radicalism – as well as the difficulties so far in meeting both of these criteria. This discussion paves the way for my reconstruction of the concept in Chapters 4 and 5.

## Hegel's alienation of the knower

The left concept of alienation can be traced from Hegel via Marx to post-war critical theory.[1] Hegel, who was concerned with the modern experience of meaninglessness and lack of freedom, describes at least two sources of the modern subject's alienation.[2] First, modernity is marked by a principle of individuality. Whereas people in pre-modern society took social customs and rules as given, the modern individual starts questioning the authority of leaders and institutions. Having 'received the inner call to comprehend', she believes that she is not bound by anything that she herself does not understand as rational (Hegel 2011, 22). She takes herself to be the source of authority.[3] If formerly, Hegel argues in the *Phenomenology of Spirit*, '[t]he meaningful of all there is, hung on the thread of light by which it was linked to . . . heaven', this link has now been severed (Hegel 2013, 5 §8). The real world of particularities, the world in which we live, has lost its connection to the universal; it has lost its higher meaning. This loss took place in several phases, beginning with a loss of the actual world. The Enlightenment subject left this world of real sensuous experiences and came to understand the world through what Hegel calls 'pure insight' (Hegel 2013, 340 §557) or 'insubstantial reflection' (Hegel 2013, 4 §7): 'Instead of dwelling in this world's presence men looked beyond it, following this thread to an other-worldly presence' (Hegel 2013, 5 §8). In the present context, the subject has returned to the world, albeit to a meaningless one.[4] The present, empiricist subject with its 'sense . . . fast rooted in earthly things' fails to link the particular – actual social customs and institutions – to the universal – their higher meaning (Hegel 2013, 5 §8). '[L]ike a wanderer in the desert craving for a mere mouthful of water', the subject is left so 'impoverished' that it no longer even craves meaning in its full sense (Hegel 2013, 5 §8). Following the principle of individuality, the modern subject finds itself in a disenchanted world that seems chaotic and irrational.

Second, the modern principle of individuality not only implies that the individual is the sole source of authority, but she is also assumed to have interests that do not align with the good of society as a whole. Modern individuals have not only 'received the inner call to comprehend', but they have also received the call 'to preserve their subjective freedom in the realm of the substantial' (Hegel 2011, 22). The modern individual believes that there is a risk that her duties in society can get in the way of her own pursuit of freedom and happiness. There is, she believes, a conflict between her individual ends – such as happiness and freedom – and the ends of society as whole. The actual world – with its social institutions and practices – does not appear to be hospitable to her deepest aspirations to happiness and freedom. The subject is thus alienated. The world has lost its higher meaning, and it seems to stand in the way of individual freedom.

Hegel's theory of alienation not only diagnoses a modern pathology, it also prescribes a remedy. The opposite of modern alienation – the experience of the world as foreign and inhospitable – is reconciliation. Reconciliation means feeling at home in the world, or recognising it as hospitable to our deepest aspirations. In other words, the subject of reason comes to see that actual ethical social life (*Sittlichkeit*) shares its own rationality. Modern social institutions – the family, civil society and the state – come together into a coherent whole that actualises human happiness and freedom. The antidote to alienation is reconciliation through contemplation: knowing the world. We do this through religion, art and – in particular – through philosophy. Through philosophy, we come to recognise and delight in the rationality – 'the rose' – of our world:

> To recognize reason as the rose in the cross of the present; and thereby to delight in the present – this rational insight is the reconciliation with actuality which philosophy grants to those who have received the inner call to comprehend, to preserve their subjective freedom in the realm of the substantial, and at the same time to stand with their subjective freedom not in a particular and contingent situation, but in what has being in and for itself. (Hegel 2011, 22)

When reconciled, the subject of reason comes to see that ethical social life (*Sittlichkeit*) has the same rationality as the subject itself. We can overcome our alienation while, at the same time, preserving the modern principle of individuality. The individual will still feel 'the call to comprehend' and to seek her own 'subjective freedom'.[5] For Hegel, there is no turning back to our pre-modern comprehension of the world. Instead, modern people should come to see the world as a coherent whole in which each individual can realise her own freedom and happiness. And the means of doing so is, primarily, philosophical contemplation.

However, this contemplation should be distinguished from the abstract reason of the Enlightenment subject. It does not transcend this world and escape into ideal principles or worlds beyond our own: 'If reflection . . . regards the present as vain and looks beyond it in a spirit of superior knowledge, it finds itself in a vain position . . . It is itself mere vanity' (Hegel 2011, 20). Reflections that seek to transcend our actual world are not rational and will only alienate us further. In Hegel's famous words, 'What is rational is actual; and what is actual is rational', and 'since philosophy is exploration of the rational, it is for that very reason the comprehension of the present and the actual, not the setting up of a world beyond which exists God knows where' (Hegel 2011, 20). We can only contemplate the actual world from our own standpoint as human beings living in modern society.

For this reason, philosophy has certain historical preconditions. Only when the social order is rational can we come to understand it as such. According to Hegel, these conditions are in place in modern society. What is now needed is that it is 'comprehended as well, so that the content which is already rational in itself may also gain a rational form and thereby appear justified to free thinking' (Hegel 2011, 11). Overcoming alienation means comprehending and thus reconciling ourselves with our modern world – in seeing the world as a place hospitable to our deepest aspirations for freedom and happiness. If our questioning of the world has severed 'the thread of light by which it was linked to . . . heaven', our knowing it will restore the connection. The same modern self-consciousness that began to question social institutions – stripping the world of its higher meaning – can work itself out of its disenchantment – restoring the meaning of the world through reason. In the *Philosophy of Right*, Hegel seeks to do precisely this. His aim is to prove that our complex modern institutions – the family, the state and civil society – come together into a rational coherent whole that actualises and reproduces human freedom. When the subject comes to know the world in this way, we overcome our alienation.

What conception of the subject does Hegel's theory of alienation rely on? Hegel's subject is characterised by 'movement' or activity: 'Subject ... is in truth actual only in so far as it is the movement of positing itself, or is the mediation of its self-othering with itself' (Hegel 2013, 10). The subject is constituted by the activity of negation and assimilation; it continuously encounters objects that first appear alien, but that it assimilates in a second moment. The external object becomes an integrated part of the subject itself. In the *Phenomenology of Spirit*, this activity is also captured by the term 'knowing'.

Knowing is not merely intellectual but is also social – a form of life and a lived experience. In the social activity of knowing, the subject transforms itself and the world, superseding its previous state. The German word for superseding, *aufheben*, has a triple meaning: to nullify, to preserve and to elevate. When the subject is successful in its assimilation, it nullifies, preserves and elevates both the external object and itself.[6]

Alienation is, therefore, for Hegel, not only a critical concept but also an ontological condition of the subject that continuously encounters otherness – a form of alienation – and integrates this otherness into itself – thus overcoming alienation. Alienation spurs the development of the subject.[7] At the same time, the concept of alienation remains critical. The activity of the subject is interlinked with an idea of progress towards a point where our current form of alienation is overcome. In overcoming each form of alienation, the subject elevates itself and progresses. The progress of the subject is thus a condition for Hegel's alienation critique.

It should be noted that, for Hegel, the main focus is not the individual human being but what he calls 'spirit'. Spirit can be described as a self-conscious form of life – as a form of relation or activity. It has the structure of a subject as described above – marked by the relation, or activity, of negation, assimilation and elevation. Spirit is not external to but embedded in the world. Its activity of knowing is embedded in actual human beings living in a particular time and place.[8] Spirit emerges through history and develops in different stages that also depend on each other. In its higher stages, spirit is the movement of cultural, social and practical life and the conscious-ness it embodies. In this stage, spirit actualises itself in lived and embodied ethics (*Sittlichkeit*). Following the French Revolution, the world has taken a rational ethical form that serves the highest end of freedom. The modern social institutions, such as the modern family, civil society (the economy) and the state, actualise the end (that is, the freedom) of both spirit and the individual. However, as we have seen, spirit, as well as the individual human being, remains alien-ated. People in modern society cannot understand the rationality of modern life. Spirit in its highest stage – what Hegel calls 'absolute Spirit' – is the activity of contemplation by which alienation can finally be overcome.

If Hegel focuses on the subject as spirit, how should we under-stand the individual subject and her alienation? Human beings are, as we have seen, a part of spirit and the locus of spirit's activity. They are 'spiritual' subjects. When individual subjects lead fully actualised human lives, spirit is in its final stage of knowing. The individual subject is thus actualised when engaged in the activity of philosophical knowing, as well as in the social and political activity on which knowing is conditioned. Ethical life is the object of contem-plation. The individual subject lives life to the fullest, then, when she, alongside others, constitutes absolute spirit by assimilating otherness through contemplation. She is contemplative; she is a knower. The subject is characterised by her activity of contemplating the world through art, religion and, in particular, through philosophy.

Given Hegel's conception of contemplation, the knower can be described as reconciliatory and social. The activity of contemplation is, after all, one of reconciliation. By contemplating the world, the individual subject comes to comprehend the modern institutions as rational and hospitable to her own deepest aspirations. Her activity of knowing thus depends on the actual social world and real social relations. We can only comprehend our social world as rational if it actually is.

However, although Hegel's contemplative and reconciliatory sub-ject does not seek radical social transformation, she is not necessarily against any form of change. With only a few exceptions (e.g. Tunick 1994), most interpreters today understand Hegel's theory as compat-ible with social reform (e.g. Neuhouser 2009, 272–8; Patten 1999, 11–16; Pippin 1997, 106–9). Even though, according to Hegel, the modern institutions are rational in their basic features, this rationality has not necessarily been fully realised. Social change might still be needed. Such a change would not be radical – transforming institutions according to a new rationality – but reformist in its aim to realise the full potential of existing institutions. Hegel's knower is thus contemplative, social and reconciliatory. Her activity depends on the social world – its particular systems, practices and institutions – and while she can seek reformist change, she does not engage in radical struggle and antagonism. This emphasis on radical struggle we find, instead, in Marx's theory.

## MARX'S ALIENATION OF THE PRODUCER

Karl Marx develops his concept of alienation as a response to the economic and political writings of the time. In doing so, he both resists and retains Hegel's theory. Marx agrees with Hegel in that we are alienated in modern society; we experience the world as meaningless and inhospitable to our aspirations for freedom. However, according to Marx, modern alienation cannot be overcome by reconciliation. We are alienated not because we have come to see the world as irrational, but because it actually is. 'Hegel', he argues, 'adopts the standpoint of modern political economy . . . he sees only the positive and not the negative side of labour' (Marx 1975a, 386). Whereas both Hegel and the political economists of Marx's time emphasised the positive sides of industrial labour, Marx argues that labour in capitalist society is characterised by social divisions and alienation.

The differences between Hegel's and Marx's evaluations of the economic institutions have implications for what qualities of the subject are emphasised. According to Hegel, we overcome our alienation by contemplating the rational, systematic order of the world. For Marx, we must act to change our social world – and, in particular, the relations of production – to make it rational. The focus is no longer the subject's capacity to understand the world but her practical capacity to produce and recreate it. Marx thus positions himself against Hegel, arguing that '[t]he only labour which Hegel knows and recognises is abstractly mental labour' (Marx 1975a, 333). In this, Marx joins the mid-nineteenth-century left Hegelians who confronted Hegel's emphasis on theoretical knowing with the concept of praxis (Bernstein 1999, xv). Hegel, they argued, overemphasised the role of intellectual labour in social progress while downplaying the importance of practical activity and actual change. The subject is, in

Marx's conception, not a knower, but a producer. While still social, she is productive rather than contemplative, more prone to act to change things than to reconcile herself with them.

Marx sets out to reformulate Hegel's idea of alienation into a more radical concept, capable of challenging the economic writings and practices of that time as well as their underlying assumptions. He finds that modern political economy relies on the assumption of a greedy human nature. According to Marx, this assumption of a static human being, autonomous from society, is untenable. Instead, he argues, human greed emerges in alienated social relations. Marx's alienation critique is underpinned by a contrasting idea of the subject.

Again, the subject is not a knower but a producer. In the words of Marx and Engels, human beings begin 'to distinguish themselves from animals as soon as they begin to produce their means of subsistence' (Marx and Engels 2000a, 42). Marx emphasises that the subject realises herself in her practical engagement with the world – in encountering objects in nature and reshaping them. In this way, the subject makes the actual world human and thus meaningful. Marx describes how the human being realises herself and her freedom by practically actualising, 'objectifying', herself in the world:

> It is just in his work upon the objective world, therefore, that man really proves himself to be a species-being. This production is his active species-life. Through this production, nature appears as his work and his reality. The object of labour is, therefore, the objectification of man's species-life: for he duplicates himself not only, as in consciousness, intellectually, but also actively, in reality, and therefore he sees himself in a world that he has created. (Marx 1975a, 277)

By actively working on and transforming the world, the subject actualises herself and her freedom. In her labour, she externalises herself: she develops and demonstrates her human capacities. According to Marx, 'the particular human sensuous essential powers ... can find their objective realisation only in natural objects' (Marx 1975a, 304). The appropriated object becomes a manifestation of the subject's capacity and freedom. She is free, or self-sufficient, in a specific sense. Although she depends on objects, the objects on which she depends are also a part of her, products of her essential activity. In Marx's words, 'It is life-engendering life ... and free, conscious activity is man's species-character' (Marx 1975a, 276).

The producer's practical appropriation of the world is the practical equivalent to the knower's theoretical activity of negation and assimilation. When the alien object is assimilated into the subject, both the object and the subject change: they are nullified, preserved and elevated. In the labouring activity, the subject develops her capacities, senses and needs. Every object she encounters requires a specific set of capacities and senses to be appropriated. In constructing a house, for example, we need imagination, skills and physical strength. In order to make and appreciate music, we must develop our musical ear and our sense of beauty. Both subject and object are reshaped and realised in the labour process.

This labour process is a social relation and, for this reason, the subject, too, is social. Marx's producer is constituted through and realises herself specifically in certain social relations and processes. Production is a process of cooperation – and the object produced is not merely a thing but a social relation:

> We have seen that man does not lose himself in his object only when the object becomes for him a human object or objective man. This is possible only when the object becomes for him a social object, he himself for himself a social being, just as society becomes a being for him in this object. (Marx 1975a, 301)

In production, human beings work together in appropriating the objective world on which they work. At the same time, they also appropriate each other: 'man produces man – himself and the other man'; the object that the subject produces becomes both 'the direct manifestation of his individuality' and 'his own existence for the other man' (Marx 1975a, 297–8). In work, human beings mutually recognise each other in their freedom and productive capacity.

Marx's producer is thus, like Hegel's knower, active and social. The subject is marked by an activity of continuously reshaping the world and herself. When encountering otherness, the subject reforms it and makes it her own. This activity is social; it is not something that each subject can pursue autonomously. On the contrary, the subject's freedom and self-actualisation take place within and depend upon certain social relations and systems.

Having examined Marx's assumptions about the subject, we can begin to make sense of his criticism of the capitalist system as the root of the subject's alienation. Capitalism, Marx argues, functions as a corrupting force, distorting the relations of labour and the subject's productive activity. Unlike Hegel, Marx does not find modern social institutions to be rational at their core. Capitalist relations of production, Marx argues, are deeply alienating; they are not hospitable to human beings and their aspiration to freedom.

How, then, is the subject alienated in capitalist society? As we have seen, Marx's subject – the producer – constitutes herself and the world through her productive activity. The subject is thus alienated – her relations to herself and the world are inhibited – when her productive activity is inhibited. This is, according to Marx, precisely what happens in capitalist production. Marx describes four dimensions of alienated labour.

First, the worker is alienated from the product of her labour. In Marx's words, the worker is 'related to the product of his labour as to an alien object' (Marx 1975a, 272). In capitalism, marked by the division between labour and capital, the produced object does not belong to the producer. 'Under these economic conditions', Marx argues, 'this realisation of labour appears as loss of realisation for the workers; objectification as loss of the object and bondage to it; appropriation as estrangement, as alienation' (Marx 1975a, 272). The relation between the subject – the producer – and her objectified self – the product – is severed.

Recall that in his productive activity, the subject encounters an external object and transfers his own powers into it – thus objectifying himself – only to return to himself – by assimilating the object. In the process, both subject and object change and progress. In capitalism, this process is inhibited. The subject transfers her powers to the object but fails to return to herself. Instead of fully appropriating the object, she ends up nullifying herself. Having transferred her capacities to the object, the subject herself is left powerless. In Marx's words, 'The worker puts his life into the object; but now his life no longer belongs to him but to the object' (Marx 1975a, 272). The subject becomes increasingly impoverished and thing-like, while the object comes to have human powers. Among these human-like objects, money is, according to Marx, the most powerful. In modern capitalist society, all of the subject's powers – her skills, senses and imagination – can be bought. Money is 'regarded as omnipotent' (Marx 1975a, 323). In this society, we do not need individual capacities to produce, to make the world our own – we need money. Money is ascribed the productive capacities that human beings now lack. While unalienated labour establishes a connection between the subject and the objective world, alienated labour corrupts this relation. The worker is alienated from the product of her labour, thus failing to manifest herself in the world.

Second, the worker is alienated from his productive activity. Marx argues that 'in the very act of production' the worker is 'estranging himself from himself' (Marx 1975a, 274). Not only has the object become alien to him, but also his own activity. 'The worker therefore only feels himself outside his work, and in his work feels outside himself.' The worker's productive activity is not owned by the worker: labour 'is not his own, but someone else's' and 'in it he belongs, not to himself, but to another'; work is not 'voluntary' but 'coerced' (Marx 1975a, 274). The worker's productive activity is not his own, but alienated.

Furthermore, the worker experiences her productive activity as meaningless. Remember that in Marx's conception of the subject, productive activity is not 'merely a means to satisfy needs external to it'; it is her 'life activity' – the activity by which she sustains and actualises herself. Under capitalism, however, production becomes painful for the worker: 'in his work ... he does not affirm himself but denies himself, does not feel content but unhappy, does not develop freely his physical and mental energy but mortifies his body and ruins his mind' (Marx 1975a, 274). Alienated labour is meaningless and, in it, the worker herself is powerless.

Third, the subject is alienated from herself, from her human essence. Marx, drawing on Ludwig Feuerbach, calls this essence her 'species-being'. This dimension of alienation follows from the other two: 'In estranging from man (1) nature, and (2) himself, his own active functions, his life activity, estranged labour estranges the species from man' (Marx 1975a, 276). In alienated labour, the subject's labour turns into 'a means for his individual existence' (Marx 1975a, 277). The worker works only for her own survival, not for humanity at large. Her life is thus reduced to mere animal life, because while the 'animal only produces what it immediately needs for itself ... man produces universally' (Marx 1975a, 276). When the subject's essential productive activity is corrupted, she is also alienated from herself as a human being and from humanity at large.

Fourth, the subject is alienated from other subjects. Marx argues, 'An immediate consequence of the fact that man is estranged from the product of his labour, from his life activity, from his species-being is the estrangement of man from man' (Marx 1975a, 277). In unalienated labour, the workers cooperate, shaping the world together. They mutually recognise each other in their human capacities, identifying with and appropriating each other. When alienated, however, workers do not cooperate but compete. Their relationships to each other are corrupted. So is the worker's relationship to the capitalist, 'the person who does not produce'. As the worker creates a product that is alien to her, she also 'creates the domination of the person who does not produce over production and over the product'. The capitalist appears to the worker as someone 'who is alien, hostile, powerful, and independent of him' (Marx 1975a, 278). In alienated labour, the workers cannot identify with each other or with the capitalist. The subject is alienated from other subjects.

In Marx's writings, as in Hegel's, alienation is a situation of meaninglessness and powerlessness. The subject finds the world irrational and lacks the freedom to take command over her own life. However, Marx's theory adds a dimension of power and powerlessness that Hegel's theory lacks. There are at least two forms of powerlessness at work in what Marx describe as alienation. First, there is a dimension of powerlessness in Marx's theory similar to that of Hegel's: alienation is a corruption of the 'human powers' – our capacity to labour and create the world with others. The subject is powerless in the sense that she lacks the distinctive power as a subject to give shape and meaning to the world around her. The alienated subject thus lacks freedom in the form of self-sufficiency: the freedom to constitute herself in relation to a world which is also a part of herself. In capitalism, everyone's relations to the world and themselves are corrupted, and, consequently, everyone – both worker and capitalist – is powerless in this sense. They lack the specific power to mutually constitute themselves and their world. The subjects find themselves lacking power both over the world they inhabit and over themselves – not because someone else has power over them, but because the world around them does not seem hospitable to their deepest aspirations.

Second, in Marx's concept of alienation, we find a form of powerlessness that is not present in Hegel's theory. This powerlessness is experienced only by the worker. The worker is powerless due to her subordination to the capitalist. In order to sustain herself, she has no choice but to sell the only thing that she has: her labour. The capitalist thus comes to own the worker's labour. Ultimately, it is not the object that controls the worker but the capitalist. The worker lacks power because someone else has power over her. This unequal power dynamic is the source of the class antagonism – the conflict between labour and capital – inherent in Marx's concept of alienation.[9]

In Marx's theory, we thus overcome our alienation not by contemplation and reconciliation but by fighting. Like Hegel, Marx asserts that alienation is overcome by negation. We must negate and supersede our alienated state. However, while, for Hegel, negation is mainly a theoretical exercise, it is, in Marx's theory, primarily practical. Marx argues that although we can negate the current state of affairs in our minds, we can never truly move beyond it when living in a society characterised by alienating practical relations. In order to supersede our alienated consciousness, we must supersede alienation in practice. In his *Theses on Feuerbach*, Marx famously states, 'The philosophers have only interpreted the world, in various ways; the point is to change it' (Marx and Engels 2000c, 173). And change requires struggle – a class struggle between the workers and the capitalist. Only through struggle can the workers, in a first step, take hold of the means of production and then, eventually, abolish private property – superseding their alienation.[10] The labourer will struggle to appropriate the means of productions, and the capitalist will struggle to keep them. To overcome alienation, antagonism is unavoidable.

If Hegel claims that we should 'delight' in 'reason as the rose in the cross of the present', this would, for Marx, merely be to admire the decorations that disguise our chains. In order to be able to change the world, we must strip it of its enchantment. In Marx's words, 'Criticism has torn up the imaginary flowers from the chain not so that man shall wear the unadorned, bleak chain but so that he will shake off the chain and pluck the living flower' (Marx 1975b, 176). The solution to the problem of alienation is not reconciliation and reform but antagonism and revolution. While Hegel's knower is reconciliatory, Marx's producer is potentially revolutionary. She depends on resources, and, when deprived of these, she will fight. Marx thus conceptualises alienation in a way that is radical rather than reconciliatory. The social suffering that people experience is understood in a context of social antagonism and unequal power. Overcoming alienation comes to require a struggle for fundamental social transformation.

## THE ALIENATION OF THE ACTOR

The human being's capacity for free will and action becomes central to the twentieth-century post-war revival of alienation theory. Having experienced war and totalitarianism, theorists of the time emphasised not only man in his practical ability to act but also man in his ability to act freely. Freedom here takes on another meaning than for Hegel and Marx, in that it does not involve rationality and determinacy. Whereas Hegel and Marx had assumed that human development followed a certain predetermined, dialectical path, post-war thinkers emphasised the subject's capacity to act freely, in a way that cannot be predetermined by the social structure or her position in it. The claim is that human action does not rationally follow from the existing social configuration and its contradictions. Jean-Paul Sartre (2007) argues that our existence is our own – we are 'condemned to be free', to bear the burden of responsibility for our actions – and Martin Heidegger (2008) claims that the call of our conscience reminds us that our actions are always our own. To merely do 'as one does', to be generic, is to be alienated.[11]

In a similar vein, Hannah Arendt criticises Marx for failing to understand the highest form of human activity. The subject, she argues, is not a producer but an actor. In relying on a conception of the subject as a producer, Marx's alienation theory merely furthers our alienation. Alienation is, in Arendt's argument, a specific social ill of modernity whereby the human capacity to act is inhibited by the modern subject's incessant production (Arendt 1998, 305). While work builds and maintains a world fit for human use, action realises human freedom and affirms the reality of the world. In action, we actualise our capacity for freedom in the sense of starting something new: 'The fact that man is capable of action means that the unexpected can be expected from him, that he is able to perform what is infinitely improbable' (Arendt 1998, 177). When we act, we do not labour on objects. Action is 'the only activity that goes on directly between men without the intermediary of things or matter' (Arendt 1998, 7). Whereas work is mediated by objects – we consume or we build – action takes place through unmediated human interaction, and especially through speech. Marx, Arendt claims, has reversed the order between human activities. It is action, not work, that we should prioritise.

Contemporary critical theorists attempting to revive the concept of alienation, including Axel Honneth (1996, 2008), Hartmut Rosa (2010, 2019) and Rahel Jaeggi (2014), take Arendt's line of criticism seriously. They also take into consideration a wide spectrum of radical democratic and feminist criticism that can be directed primarily against Marx but also, to some extent, against Arendt. Beyond its supposed determinism, two other aspects of Marx's theory have provoked criticism. First, Marx is criticised for idealising a final state of harmony. According to the critics, Marx's theory comes to assume the possibility of a communist society marked by harmony and solidarity. This assumption becomes problematic for critical theorists valuing democracy. Once a final conflict-free state has been reached, politics and democratic institutions would no longer be needed (e.g. Honneth 2017, 35–6). Furthermore, both Arendt and Marx have been accused of human essentialism (e.g. Honig 1993). The criticism holds that in emphasising one aspect of human life, such as labour or speech, other activities are downgraded, in particular activities such as care and housework that are predominantly practised by women. In elevating one aspect of life as distinctly human, the theory risks excluding marginalised groups or legitimising authoritarian restrictions on how people should live their lives.

Among contemporary alienation theorists, Rahel Jaeggi stands out in her explicit ambition to avoid the pitfalls of determinism, human essentialism and idealising a final state of harmony. Jaeggi identifies primarily two problems with the concept of alienation as it had been formulated in previous theories: 'on the one hand, its essentialism and its perfectionist orientation around a conception of the essence or nature of human beings . . .; on the other hand, the ideal of reconciliation – the ideal of a unity free of tension' (Jaeggi 2014, 2). By drawing on resources from both Marx and Heidegger, Jaeggi seeks to construct a social and critical theory of alienation that avoids these potential pitfalls.

In Jaeggi's conceptualisation, alienation is generally understood as a deficient relation to the world and to the self – 'a relation of relationlessness' (Jaeggi 2014, 1). In her work on alienation, Jaeggi (2014), like Marx did with Hegel's concept of alienation, both resists and retains aspects of Marx's theory. She avoids Marx's emphasis on labour and production as specifically human activities, and focuses on another, more abstract concept in Marx's theory: appropriation. In line with Marx's conceptualisation of alienation as an inhibition of the worker's 'appropriation of the human essence' (Marx 1975a, 296), the concept of appropriation is central. Jaeggi defines alienation as 'an impairment of acts of appropriation' (Jaeggi 2014, 36), where appropriation is defined in the following way:

> The concept of appropriation refers to a comprehensive conception of practical relations to the self and world. It includes a broadly understood capacity of knowing and dealing with oneself: having access to or command over oneself and the world. This can be explicated as the capacity to make the life one leads, or what one *wills* and *does*, one's own; as the capacity to identify with oneself and with what one does; in other words, as the ability to realize oneself in what one does. (Jaeggi 2014, 37)

The concept of appropriation, and that of alienation, is marked by four features. First, appropriation is a relation. The relation of appropriation is a practical relation by which we make the world our own. When this relation is inhibited, we become alienated. Second, the object to be appropriated – to establish a relation of appropriation with – is both the self and the world: 'someone is alienated when she cannot relate to herself and (thereby) to her own preconditions, that is, when she cannot appropriate them as her own' (Jaeggi 2014, 37). Third, Jaeggi, like Marx, assumes that the subject actualises herself in her practical engagement with the world; 'we cannot be separated from how we express ourselves' (Jaeggi 2014, 165). When this activity of appropriation is inhibited, the subject can no longer find meaning in what she does and experience herself as in command over herself. Fourth, the subject's activity of appropriation is open; it does not progress in a predetermined manner. To Jaeggi, appropriation is an 'experimental' activity; it is open-ended and never-ending (Jaeggi 2014, 153).

Jaeggi's description of the human being as constituted through her activity of appropriation brings to the forefront an element that arguably was present already in Hegel's and Marx's theories: the subject as active, as continuously constituting and reconstituting herself. How can we make sense of the subject's activity of appropriation and its impairment – alienation – in practice?

Jaeggi specifies four dimensions of alienation, each representing a way in which appropriation can be inhibited. The first dimension of alienation is the 'interruption of the process of appropriating one's own actions' (Jaeggi 2014, 65). The alienated subject cannot conceive of herself as a responsible subject with the capacity to act. She experiences herself as powerless. This form of alienation could also be described as reification. Jaeggi gives the example of a bohemian academic who has a baby and, as a natural next step, moves with his family to the suburb where he starts living an orderly suburban life. This all seems to have happened by itself, beyond his control. He is not, he feels, in charge of his own actions.

Second, Jaeggi describes alienation as an interruption of the process of appropriating one's roles, resulting in *inauthenticity*. For Jaeggi, social roles are not in themselves alienating; they are 'constitutive for the development of individuality' (Jaeggi 2014, 69). Throughout our lives, we take on different roles that we then bring with us in our various endeavours. For Jaeggi, 'the problem is not that we play a role but how we play it' (Jaeggi 2014, 92). We take on roles successfully by making them our own, by appropriating them. When we fail to articulate ourselves in our roles, however, we become alienated. Inspired by Georg Simmel, Jaeggi compares successful role-appropriation to an actor in a theatre creatively interpreting a role: she takes it up and plays it in her own way (Jaeggi 2014, 96). Jaeggi contrasts this to 'the ambitious junior editor, who has his hair cut, buys himself a suit that fits just a little too well, and begins to imitate his boss's mannerisms' (Jaeggi 2014, 69). In its conformity, the role appears like a mask. The junior editor has lost himself; he is alienated.

Third, alienation is an interruption of the process of appropriating oneself. It inhibits the alienated subject's *self-accessibility* and inner mobility. Her 'self-conception does not "function"'; she does not have herself under her own command (Jaeggi 2014, 126). Jaeggi gives the example of a feminist who perceive herself as independent but has an intense desire to be protected. She experiences this desire as alien to herself, incompatible with her feminist identity. Jaeggi describes the woman's alienation as a lack of inner immobility, an inability to integrate new impulses. This emphasis on integration, Jaeggi argues, does not presume the possibility of inner harmony. Rather, alienation in this sense could mean a failure to enter into the process of inner conflict. The alienated subject holds on to norms and previous self-images in a way that leaves her unable to respond to new experiences, emotions and thoughts. She is rigid, blocked from ways of understanding and acting that do not fall within the boundaries of her previous self-conception.

Fourth, alienation is an interruption of the process of appropriating the world. The alienated subject is *indifferent*: 'The world as

106

a whole has submerged – without apparent cause – into the haze of indifference and become unreal' (Jaeggi 2014, 132). When her appropriation of the world is impeded, she loses her connection with the world around her and with her own life. She is alienated from both the world and herself. Jaeggi exemplifies this with an academic who ceases to care about his work. If someone criticises his arguments, he no longer has the desire to defend them. He cannot understand why he ever cared and his old concerns are not replaced by new ones.

Alienation as indifference can be understood as a failure to identify with something one is supposed to identify with. When I identify with someone or something, 'I tie my fate to that of the other person or thing in such a way that its fate is constitutive for my identity' (Jaeggi 2014, 138). If the soccer club I identify with does well, I am not merely pleased; I am proud. The success of the soccer club is also a success for me. In Jaeggi's understanding, the self is constituted through its different identifications. When I fail to identify with something I am supposed to identify with, I fail to identify with myself. Since we are always already immersed in the world, the loss of identification does not result in a loss of our relation to the world. Rather, it results in a dysfunctional relation, a relation of relationlessness. We fail to form relations of identification and thus to make affective attachments.

In Jaeggi's theory, alienation is a blockage to our social freedom (Jaeggi 2014, 35–6). We are alienated when we are either so disconnected from or so consumed by the social world that we cannot find ourselves in it. In practice, alienation manifests itself as powerlessness, inauthenticity, inner immobility or indifference. The concept of alienation, Jaeggi argues, allows us to understand the individual subject's indifference and powerlessness as a blockage to social freedom.

In focusing on the activity of appropriation and its blockages, Jaeggi's alienation theory comes to rely on an individual subject who is neither a knower nor a producer. Rather than being characterised by contemplation or production, she constitutes herself in the activity of problem-solving. Her relationship to herself and to the world is formed in an activity in which she continuously encounters problems and resolves them. She is an actor in the sense that her problem-solving is experimental and open-ended; its outcome cannot be predetermined. Does Jaeggi's concept of alienation thus avoid the pitfalls of previous alienation theories?

First, in relying on a subject characterised by her problem-solving, Jaeggi's concept overcomes the pitfall of human essentialism – but not mainly for the reasons that she gives herself. Human essentialism can be described as the elevation of a particular activity or way of life as distinctly human. Jaeggi argues that her concept avoids this essentialism because it emphasises the 'how' rather than the 'what' of willing:

> I must have my will at my command if it is to count as my own. This criterion is, in the first place, formal: it concerns the How, not the What, of willing. That is, I need not will anything in particular; rather, I must be able to will what I will in a free or self-determined manner. (Jaeggi 2014, 34)

In being tied to the 'how' rather than the 'what' of willing and acting, successful appropriation does not require that we will for anything particular. For this reason, Jaeggi's concept of alienation does not give a perfectionist account of the good life.

However, Jaeggi's emphasis on the 'how' rather than the 'what' of willing is not enough to defend her theory against the criticism of human essentialism. Following her line of argument, we could, for example, maintain that Marx's theory, too, escapes the pitfall of human essentialism. Marx, one could argue, focuses more on the 'how' than the 'what' of production. In this view, Marx's theory would not be essentialist merely because it predefines the subject as essentially characterised by her production. This only becomes a problem if the theory also determines what she should produce. If, on the other hand, an essentialist theory is a theory in which a particular activity or way of life, such as labour, is conceived as distinctly human, Jaeggi's defence does not hold. Does the theory of alienation as impaired appropriation fall into the pitfall of human essentialism in this conception?

Beyond its focus on human activities rather than their aims, there is another aspect of Jaeggi's alienation theory that plays a more crucial role in avoiding human essentialism. Rather than defining the subject and her way of relating to the world by a particular activity – such as labour – Jaeggi focuses on the general structure of human activity. The subject is, in Jaeggi's theory, defined by her activity of appropriation or problem-solving – a form of activity by which the human being and the world is continuously and mutually constituted. The activity of problem-solving is something that can be practised in many ways and in many spheres of life – by contemplating, producing, speaking, or taking care of each other. It is general rather than particular.

Jaeggi's reconstruction of Marx's theory of alienation is thus a move away from labour to appropriation, from particularity to abstraction. Jaeggi escapes essentialism by decoupling the particular from the abstract, existential dimension of Marx's theory. While keeping the general theory of the subject, she discards the emphasis on the particular activity of labour. By abstracting the core structure of Marx's and Hegel's subject – the structure where the subject encounters and assimilates otherness – Jaeggi arrives at a conception that avoids essentialism.

Although Jaeggi's theory still makes some assumptions about how the subject and the world around her are constituted, it avoids a central problem associated with human essentialism. By focusing on the 'how' rather than the 'what' of willing and acting, it cannot easily be used to legitimate an authoritarian imposition of the good on people. Furthermore, it does not exclude social groups by downgrading some spheres of human life into mere animal functions. It does not prioritise a particular sphere of activity – such as the realm of economic production – while excluding others – such as the realm of reproduction.

Second, Jaeggi's concept of alienation escapes the pitfall of determinism, the assumption that the subject's actions can be predetermined by the social structures and her position in them. The subject on which Jaeggi's theory relies is characterised by the activity of appropriation – experimental problem-solving. This activity remains open-ended and its results cannot be predetermined. In the process of appropriation, the subject, as well as the objective world with which she engages, changes in an unpredictable way. Determinism is thus precluded. The subject's actions and their consequences cannot be predicted based on the social structure or her position in them. Instead, she experiments to find solutions to the problems she encounters. These problems do not have a single given resolution. What the subject's course of action will be, and what it will result in, remains contingent.

Third, Jaeggi's theory avoids the ideal of a final state of harmony – the assumption that a stable state free of inner and social conflict is possible and desirable. Jaeggi convincingly argues that overcoming alienation does not mean the end of conflict: 'The openness of the

109

process of appropriation and its experimental character imply that overcoming alienation need not be described as a "coming to oneself" or as reconciliation but can be conceived of instead as an open-ended and never-ending process' (Jaeggi 2014, 153). Since appropriation is an ongoing activity without any harmonious end point, overcoming alienation – impaired appropriation – does not imply harmony. Rather, it involves problems and conflicts. Appropriation means problem-solving, and there is no problem-solving without problems. Although alienation – a dysfunctional relation – presupposes the possibility of a functional relation, such a relation does not have to be harmonious.

Jaeggi's theory of alienation can, therefore, in my terms, be described as open – avoiding the pitfalls of human essentialism, determinism and idealising a final state of harmony. It relies on a subject who engages with and affects the world in a way that cannot be predetermined or finalised. We cannot decide beforehand what type of practices the subject will find meaningful or what the result of her engagement will be. She can be a knower, a producer or a political actor; and her knowing, production and acting remain open-ended. There is no single human way of life and no predetermined path for human action and history to follow. Furthermore, the subject's activity does not presuppose harmony; it always involves problems and conflicts.

In relying on a conception of the subject as an actor and problem-solver, Jaeggi thus opens up the concept of alienation and relieves it of some of its heaviest baggage. But what are the implications of this? Does the theory still retain the radicalism of Marx's theory – its dimension of social suffering, power and antagonism? An important manoeuvre in opening up, and avoiding essentialism, is the decoupling of the particular and the universal. The subject is no longer primarily a producer; she can engage with the world in many different ways. However, as the human activity of labour is abstracted, alienation – understood as impaired human activity – risks losing its grounding in particular social relations.

Despite her explicit intentions to conceptualise alienation as a blockage to social freedom, and although the subtitle of the original German version of *Alienation* is 'A Contemporary Problem of Social Philosophy', Jaeggi's theory of alienation does not amount to a social theory or a social critique (Jaeggi 2014, 153). As the translator Frederick Neuhouser points out in his introduction to the book,

110

the lack of a critical social theory might not be surprising given that 'completing this task would require (at least) a separate book-length treatment of its own' (Neuhouser 2014, xv). The absence of a social critique could be due to a lack of space, but it could also be due to the theory itself. Does Jaeggi's open concept of alienation lack the conceptual resources to criticise society and to capture experiences of social suffering?

Consider Jaeggi's example of the woman struggling with an inner conflict between her feminist identity and her desire to be protected. The woman's dilemma might, on the one hand, be one of social suffering – emerging, for example, from the tension between conflicting social norms. On the other hand, the inner conflict experienced by the woman could also be psychological – arising from an inner, personal conflict that can be resolved through contemplation. By contemplating this dilemma, the woman might find that being a feminist and desiring protection does not necessarily fall into conflict. While we know that the woman's appropriation is impaired, we do not know how and where this impairment is located. Alienation could reside in the individual, in the social system – or somewhere in between. However, beyond the abstract concept of appropriation, Jaeggi leaves us with few theoretical resources to link the individual experience of alienation to particular social processes.

Jaeggi's book on alienation comes the closest to specifying a link between the subject and the social when Jaeggi describes her alienation critique as an 'immanent critique' of the subject or of a 'form of life'. Here, she clarifies that

> [o]n the level of relations to the material and social world and its institutions, alienation critique points out discrepancies between the claims of modern ideals of freedom and their actual realization or, in other words, discrepancies between the ideal of control or command and actual impotence with respect to (self-created) relations. (Jaeggi 2014, 41)

This gives some guidance as to where alienation as a social problem is located: somewhere in the discrepancy between modern ideals and their realisation. However, these discrepancies remain unexamined; the analysis remains focused on the individual subject rather than on social institutions. In Jaeggi's words, 'while I considered the cases of alienation presented here from the perspective of how the subject is constituted, the corresponding analysis and evaluation – of how institutions are constituted – remains to be carried out' (Jaeggi 2014, 220).

It is instead in her latest book, *Critique of Forms of Life* (2018), that Jaeggi develops her critique – or rather, her method of critique – of modern institutions. The focus of the book is not the individual subject and her alienation but 'the cultural and social reproduction of human life' – what Jaeggi calls 'forms of life' (Jaeggi 2018, 20). The form of life shares a similar structure with the individual subject described earlier. It is marked by problem-solving, or what Jaeggi, in this context, calls 'learning-processes' (Jaeggi 2018, chap. 7). While in *Alienation*, Jaeggi phenomenologically examines the individual subject's experience of impaired appropriation, in *Forms of Life*, she examines how a social form of life can be blocked in its learning-process. Learning-processes can, according to Jaeggi, be blocked, and alienation is one possible blockage, alongside, for example, ideology (Jaeggi 2018, 351, 454). However, in these later writings, Jaeggi does not speak of alienation as an individual experience; instead, it concerns the 'alienated character of a form of life' (Jaeggi 2018, 48). Still, Jaeggi's writings on forms of life could give us some hints about the social conditions for the subject's appropriation and alienation.

In *Critique of Forms of Life*, there is a brief discussion on the relationship between collective and individual learning. According to Jaeggi, forms of life learn through individual action. At the same time, individual actions are also conditioned on forms of life and their learning.[12] We can thus assume that blockages in the learning-processes of a form of life can also imply some impairment of the participating subjects' problem-solving. However, central questions with regards to the relation between the individual subject and the social processes in which she is involved remain to be answered; for example, can an individual subject become alienated in a functional form of life? The link between the individual subject and the form of life is never systematically examined.

Although we know that the individual relates to the social world through her appropriation, the process of appropriation remains abstract and its conditions unspecified. For this reason, the extent to which the individual subject's alienation can be understood as a social form of suffering – experienced in certain social processes but not in others – remains to be clarified. Jaeggi's theory of alienation would thus have to be further developed for it to be radical in the sense that it would retain a dimension of social suffering.

This leads us to another, closely related question. For the theory of alienation to retain the radicalism of Marx's theory, it should be able not only to capture social suffering but also to locate it in relations of power and antagonism. Recall that, according to Marx, the problem with Hegel's theory is that it does not recognise alienation as a problem in the basic structure of society. Instead, alienation becomes a problem of understanding. The theory encourages us to reconcile ourselves with the world as it is. This call for reconciliation is, according to Marx, misplaced in capitalist society, which, he argues, is deeply irrational and fraught by power and division. We should, Marx claims, not try to reconcile ourselves with the world, but struggle to radically change it. Can Jaeggi's concept of alienation, in relying on a problem-solving subject, retain a dimension of unequal social power and antagonism?

As we have seen, Jaeggi recognises the ideal of 'reconciliation' as one of the problematic aspects of traditional theories of alienation. Here, however, the problem with the ideal of reconciliation is that it involves an assumption of a final state of harmony. Jaeggi's concern is, therefore, with the theory's openness rather than its radicalism. But while Jaeggi's concept escapes the pitfall of idealising harmony, can it avoid the ideal of reconciliation for which Marx criticised Hegel – and maintain a dimension of unequal power and antagonism?

Recall that there are two forms of power at work in Marx's alienation theory, where the second constitutes its antagonistic dimension. The first form of power is aimless and anonymous. This form of power is perceived both by Marx's producer and Jaeggi's problem-solving actor. For example, Jaeggi's previously bohemian man is, like Marx's producer, caught up in a process that he cannot control. No one else seems to be exercising power over him; he feels overwhelmed by a world that seemingly lies beyond his control. In Marx's theory, this anonymous power is the capitalist system and its central objects – such as money. To some extent, the power of these objects overwhelms both the worker and the capitalist.

Marx's worker, however, is also submitted to a second, more conflictual form of power that is not included in Jaeggi's theory. Although mediated by the capitalist system, this power has both an agent and a purpose. The worker is submitted to the power of the capitalist. In order to sustain herself, the worker has no choice but to sell the only thing that she has: her labour. The capitalist thus comes to own the worker's labour. This unequal power dynamic is the source of class antagonism – the conflict between labour and capital – inherent in Marx's concept of alienation. To overcome her alienation, the worker must struggle against the capitalist to appropriate the means of production and her own human powers.

Jaeggi's theory of alienation lacks this dimension of antagonism. In seeking to distinguish her theory from the concepts of 'coercion' and 'manipulation', Jaeggi also comes to separate her concept of alienation from the form of unequal power emphasised by Marx (Jaeggi 2014, 51). For Jaeggi, coercion and manipulation include any situation in which the subject acts in a particular way because of her lack of other options. A subject who, like Marx's worker, lacks real options and must submit to the power of the capitalist is, in Jaeggi's conception, 'coerced' or 'manipulated', not alienated.

For Jaeggi, the alienated subject is powerless not because she lacks real options – but because she lacks awareness of the options that she actually has. In Jaeggi's words, the alienated subject 'experiences a process that she can in principle influence (or should be able to influence) as beyond her influence – or that something that can in fact be decided on appears to her as if it could not be'. Jaeggi argues, for example, that the alienation of the bohemian man can be 'traced back to a lack of awareness of the possibilities of action that are open to him' (Jaeggi 2014, 57). Alienation is, then, in Jaeggi's conception, not a lack of real options but a lack of awareness. It does not include unequal power relations, in which some people exploit others' dependency and lack of options.

Who, then, is the subject that Jaeggi's theory of alienation addresses itself to? Who can be alienated – and who cannot? Even when alienated – powerless – Jaeggi's subject has options. From this follow two possible assumptions about the relation between the subject and social resources. Either Jaeggi's subject is not dependent on social resources for acting, or she has not been deprived of the resources she needs in order to act. In other words, in so far as the subject needs resources to act – to appropriate the world and herself – she is already in possession of them. Jaeggi's subject is, in this sense, strong: she does not rely on social objects from which she can be deprived. For this reason, the previously bohemian man who now leads a conventional life can be seen as a typical example of alienation in Jaeggi's conception while Marx's worker cannot.

Jaeggi's strong subject differs from Marx's producer, and, for this reason, so do her strategies for overcoming alienation. Marx's producer depends on social resources; and, if deprived of these, she will struggle. Jaeggi, however, not only avoids Marx's deterministic link between deprivation and struggle, she avoids the problem of deprivation altogether. Overcoming alienation does not, for Jaeggi, necessarily involve reconciliation through contemplation, but, because it does not retain a conception of unequal power and antagonism, neither does it involve a struggle against those in power. Although Jaeggi emphasises that 'the concept of alienation posits a connection between indifference and domination', the concept of domination is limited to the agentless domination of a world that 'appear[s] to take on a life of [its] own' (Jaeggi 2014, 24). Jaeggi's theory of alienation comes to lack a dimension of unequal power and antagonism.

We have thus seen that Jaeggi's concept of alienation relies on a conception of the subject as problem-solving and strong. She continuously encounters and resolves problems in an open-ended, experimental way; and she cannot be deprived of the social resources she needs for doing so. The openness of the subject allows us to avoid the pitfalls of essentialism and determinism. The subject is not defined by any essential activity, such as labour, and the results of her actions cannot be predetermined. However, while Jaeggi's theory of alienation is open, it does not fully retain the radical mobilising potential of Marx's concept. It does not indicate that the suffering that the alienated subject experiences has a social basis or grounding in antagonistic relations of power – thus giving us fewer reasons to believe that alienation could be overcome through radical struggle.

## OPEN AND RADICAL?

The internal debate on alienation leaves us with a problem that reflects the general dilemma of the democratic left seeking to escape the authoritarian tendencies of the late twentieth-century left (see Chapter 1) while maintaining its emphasis on social struggle and change. On the one hand, the democratic left wants a concept of alienation that is open – avoiding human essentialism, determinism and the ideal of harmony. An open concept is less prone to become exclusionary or to fail to capture the subject's freedom and responsibility. On the other hand, the concept should be sufficiently radical in the sense that it retains a dimension of social suffering, unequal power and antagonism. In the left tradition, the concept of alienation has been valued for its capacity to locate seemingly private experiences of indifference and powerlessness in social practices and to mobilise them for political struggle. At the same time, the aims of openness and radicalism seem difficult to reconcile.

This becomes particularly evident when we examine how they manifest themselves in the subject. While an open theory relies on a subject who engages with and impacts the world in a way that cannot be predetermined, a radical theory relies on a conception of the subject as sufficiently socially grounded to be able to experience specific forms of social suffering, power and antagonism.

This amounts to a dilemma both in alienation theory and of the democratic left in general that I have described as a dilemma between radicalism and openness. Before setting out to resolve this dilemma, which will be the focus of the next chapter, I want to say a few words on how my formulation of it can be problematised.

The dilemma I have presented can also be described as contradiction internal to the contemporary conception of 'radicalism' or 'radicalisation'. In the left and democratic discourse, radicalisation is often used synonymously with openness. To radicalise a theory means to de-essentialise it – stripping it of its social foundations. This is also how Jaeggi describes her own move from Marx's concept of alienation, which, in her words, 'involves rehabilitating what is alien in the model of appropriation and radicalizing that model in the direction of a nonessentialist conception of appropriation' (Jaeggi 2014, 39). In the left discourse, radicalism not only has maintained its traditional meaning – to fundamentally challenge the social system of power – but has also gained a new meaning – to challenge it in an open way. A radical theory, in this understanding, avoids essentialism, determinism and the ideal of harmony.

In my analysis of the left democratic literature on alienation, I have chosen to separate these two meanings of radicalism into two concepts – radicalism and openness. This allows me to shed light on the tension in the left democratic discourse and attempt to resolve it.

## CONCLUSION

The concept of alienation – generally defined as a social, political or psychological ill in which the subject's relation to the object is inhibited in such a way that her relation to herself becomes dysfunctional – can be used to make sense of experiences of meaninglessness, powerlessness and thwarted expectations. Within the left, it has served as a tool for social criticism and radical political mobilisation. However,

116

it has also, within the internal discourse, been subjected to intense criticism. In particular, it is accused of not being open enough, and succumbing to the pitfalls of traditional socialism.

Having traced the concept of alienation from Hegel's alienated knower to Marx's alienated producer, I examined the contemporary alienation debate, which seeks to open up the concept. Rahel Jaeggi defines alienation as impaired appropriation. In focusing on the activity of appropriation and its blockages, Jaeggi's alienation theory comes to rely on an individual subject who is neither a knower nor a producer but an actor and a problem-solver. With these ideas about the subject, Jaeggi's theory of alienation escapes the common pitfalls discussed previously in the text.

However, in the revived debate on alienation, something has been lost – most importantly the social grounding and antagonistic dimension of the concept. When relying on this conception of the subject, the theory of alienation cannot easily be mobilised for radical social struggle. Can the concept of alienation as impaired appropriation be radicalised while remaining open? This will be the subject of the next chapter.

## NOTES

1. Although Hegel does not himself use the term 'Alienation' (*Entfremdung*) to name the general form of divisions in modern society that his work diagnoses, it is, to quote Hegel scholar Michael Hardimon, 'clear – and uncontroversial – that Hegel's social philosophy is meant, among other things, as a response to the problem that is now standardly called alienation' (Hardimon 1994, 2; see also Hegel 2005, 5–8).
2. There are several, quite different, ways of interpreting Hegel. My reading here largely follows what can be described as a combination of a historicist and civic humanist reading of Hegel. In the historicist reading, the progress of spirit, and the institutions and practices in society, represents a resolution of the contradictions in the previous articulations of meaning (e.g. Pinkard 1994; Pippin 1997). In the civic humanist reading, the progress of social institutions and practices can be understood as a process of human self-actualisation (e.g. Patten 1999). This reading can, according to its proponent Alan Patten, be combined with historicist elements (Patten 1999, 10). On the other hand, my interpretation can be distinguished from Charles Taylor's (2005) influential metaphysical reading of Hegel. In this view, the progress of spirit is understood as a process of God's self-realisation (Taylor 2005; for review, see Patten 1999, 8–40).

117

3. This form of individuality should be distinguished from its previous form – which interpreters have associated with ancient Greece (Pinkard 1994, 138) – where 'individuality has the meaning of *self-consciousness* in general, not of a particular, contingent consciousness' (Hegel 2013, 267 §447). This individual constructs himself in his social role and finds certainty 'in the nation as a whole' (Hegel 2013, 267 §447). As this form of community falls apart, meaning becomes 'soulless and dead . . . alive only in the *single* individual *qua* single' (Hegel 2013, 289 §475).

4. 'Spirit has now got beyond the substantial life it formerly led in the element of thought, that it is beyond the immediacy of faith, beyond the satisfaction and security of the certainty that consciousness then had, of its reconciliation with the essential being, and of that being's universal presence both within and without. It has not only gone beyond all this into the other extreme of an insubstantial reflection of itself into itself, but beyond that too' (Hegel 2013, 4 §7).

5. For a further discussion on the reconciliation between the modern subject of reason and the world see, for example, Hardimon 1994, 136.

6. Through this activity, the subject supersedes its previous states. Since the object is both other and a part of the subject itself, everything the subject does to the object it also does to itself. The object of the subject is both itself and its object. On the dual object of the subject (self-consciousness), see Hegel 2013, 111 §§178–80.

7. In Hegel's words, 'the spirit which comprehends this comprehension anew and which – and this amounts to the same thing – returns into itself from its alienation, is the spirit at a stage higher than that at which it stood in its earlier [phase of] comprehension' (Hegel 2011, 372 §343).

8. Hegel's concept of spirit has been interpreted in a variety of different ways. Spirit is here understood as a form of relation or activity – or a form of life (Hegel 2005, 4–5; Pinkard 1994, 9). For instance, Pinkard describes spirit as 'not a metaphysical entity but a fundamental *relation* among persons that mediates their *self-consciousness*, a way in which people reflect on what they have come to take as authoritative for themselves' (Pinkard 1994, 9). This socially and historically embedded interpretation can be distinguished from a metaphysical reading, in which spirit is understood as a metaphysical entity, a greater mind, of which particular human minds are part (Inwood 1983; Taylor 2005).

9. It should be noted that in order to understand Marx's concept of alienation, I have drawn on both his early writings in the Manuscripts and his later writings on alienation in *Capital*. Such a reading presumes that Marx's early writings can fruitfully be read alongside his later. This interpretation is compatible with both the Marxist humanist reading

118

(e.g. Korsch 2012; Lukács 1972), which assumes a continuity between Marx's earlier and later work, as well as the readings emphasising that there *are* contradictions in Marx's works but that these run through his entire oeuvre (e.g. Balibar 2007). However, my reading of Marx can be distinguished from that which holds that Marx's writings on alienation in the Manuscripts fundamentally contradict and remain incompatible with his later writings. This position is, as we saw in Chapter 1, most clearly represented by Louis Althusser in *For Marx* (2005).

10. 'Communism as the positive transcendence of private property, as human self-estrangement, and therefore as the real appropriation of the human essence' (Marx 1975a, 296). Note that 'transcendence' in this passage has also been translated as 'supersession'.

11. Heidegger describes this as a 'falling' into 'the "they"' (*das Man*), where the subject 'compares itself with everything' and thus 'drifts along towards an alienation' (Heidegger 2008, 222).

12. 'The bearers of the change described are neither a macrosubject nor the individual subjects alone; an ensemble of practices, which is simultaneously the result and the condition of individual action, undergoes a change through the mediation of the subjects. Then individuals (or collectives) change social practices, whose transformation in turn exerts effects back on individual possibilities of experiencing and learning' (Jaeggi 2018, 283).

## CHAPTER FOUR

# *Towards an open and radical concept of alienation*

In the previous chapter, we saw that the concept of alienation has served as a tool for social criticism and political mobilisation. However, it has also been subjected to intense internal criticism. In particular, it has been associated with the main pitfalls of traditional socialism: determinism, the assumption that the subject's actions are decided by the social structure and her position in it; human essentialism, according to which the subject is predefined by a particular type of activity or way of life; and the ideal of a final state of harmony, the assumption that a stable state free of inner and social conflict is possible and desirable.

At the same time, while the traditional concept of alienation seems to lack the openness that a democratic left seeks, the attempts to avoid these pitfalls have resulted in a loss of the concept's radical, mobilising potential – where the suffering of the subject can be understood in a context of unequal power and social antagonism. Can we find a concept of alienation that is open – neither essentialist, deterministic nor idealising a final state of harmony – yet radical – retaining a dimension of social suffering, power and antagonism?

## RECONSTRUCTING THE CONCEPT OF ALIENATION: RESOURCES AND CHALLENGES

Before beginning the work on reconstructing the concept of alienation, I would like to recall the dilemma in the discourse on alienation that I seek to resolve – the problem of finding a concept that is both radical and open – and discuss the resources I plan to draw on in order to resolve it – the work of Karl Marx, Rahel Jaeggi and Pierre Bourdieu.

When tracing the internal debate on alienation in Chapter 3, we saw that while Karl Marx's concept of alienation is radical, it is not sufficiently open; in particular, it maintains a narrow focus on production as both essentially defining of the subject and determinate of her behaviour.

In her reconstruction of Marx's theory, Rahel Jaeggi opens up the concept of alienation and the conception of the subject to which it corresponds. In Jaeggi's theory, the subject is not reduced to a producer but defined by her appropriation – an activity of open-ended problem-solving, in which the subject and the social world mutually constitute one another. When this activity is impaired, so is the subject's relation to the world and to herself; she is alienated. Jaeggi thus relieves the concept of alienation of some of its heaviest baggage and enables others to re-engage with the concept. However, in this revived alienation debate, something significant has been lost – most importantly, the social grounding of the concept as well as its antagonistic dimension. The concept has lost elements of its radical potential.

To recover the radicalism of the concept of alienation, two components of Marx's theory need to be retrieved. First, alienation has to be established as a form of social suffering – as a distinctly social rather than merely subjective problem. While Jaeggi establishes that the subject relates to the social world through her appropriation, the activity of appropriation is abstract and its conditions undefined. For this reason, the problem of alienation – impaired appropriation – is not located within any specific social processes or systems. This makes it difficult to make use of the theory of alienation to formulate a concrete social criticism. To radicalise the concept, the relation between the subject and the social world, and the impairment of this relation, should be specified.

Second, in order to radicalise the concept of alienation as impaired appropriation, it does not merely suffice to socially ground it; we also need to rethink it. It should be reconstructed to capture unequal social power and antagonism. This involves including contemporary situations of social subordination. Jaeggi distinguishes the problem of alienation from those of coercion and manipulation by specifying that it only applies to those who have actual options but lack awareness of them. Alienation thus becomes a problem of awareness rather than of social power and resources. For this reason, it cannot be used to criticise some of the more severe forms of marginalisation.

121

To radicalise the concept of alienation, we would need to bring back the elements from Marx's concept that locate alienation in relations of power and antagonism and include those who are subordinated in these relations.

In this chapter, I seek to radicalise the concept of alienation as impaired appropriation while still maintaining its openness. I do so by drawing on conceptual resources from Karl Marx and Pierre Bourdieu. While Marx's theory of alienation is radical, its emphasis on industrial labour and capital makes it prone to economic reductionism and human essentialism. Bourdieu's work is helpful in enlarging Marx's theory while maintaining its capacity for social criticism.

While Jaeggi makes no explicit references to Bourdieu, they share theoretical roots; both are influenced by the work of Marx and Heidegger, which may be why they exhibit some compatibility. Moreover, they complement each other. While Jaeggi provides theories for the corruption of the subject (Jaeggi 2014) and of the social world (Jaeggi 2018), Bourdieu examines primarily the link between the two. In particular, he provides a theory for the link between the subject and central social institutions, such as the state, the education system and the economic system. In this, Bourdieu's writing distinguishes itself from other theories of power, such as Ernesto Laclau and Chantal Mouffe's ([1985] 2001) theory of hegemony or Philip Pettit's (1999) theory of domination, where power is located in language and individual subjects, respectively.

By reading Jaeggi with Marx and Bourdieu, I reconstruct alienation in a new way – as simultaneous domination and disorientation. In this, I contribute to an emerging literature seeking to maintain the openness of contemporary alienation theories (e.g. Jaeggi 2014; Rosa 2010) while drawing on Marx and Bourdieu to bring back and open up central elements of the social – such as social dispossession (dépossession) (Haber 2007, 2013), social cleavages (Bialakowsky 2019) and domination (Medearis 2015). By weaving social power and antagonism into the dynamics of alienation, these approaches to alienation distinguish themselves by their potential to be mobilised for social criticism and change. Social power and domination are here understood either as dependent upon (Bialakowsky 2019) or as an inseparable aspect of (Medearis 2015) alienation.

My contribution to this literature lies in maintaining the link found in the classical theories of alienation, between impaired social relations and an impaired self-relation. While John Medearis's work provides the most elaborate conception of alienated social structures and forces, it does not provide a theory of the alienated subject. In this chapter, I seek to contribute to the debate on alienation by fleshing out the link between the social world and the subject. I show that the concept of appropriation – central to both Jaeggi's and Marx's theories of alienation – can, if read alongside Bourdieu's theory of habitus, serve as such a link. This amounts to a theory of alienation where I combine Bourdieu's concept of domination with his notion of uprootedness, or what I call disorientation. By bringing these theories together, we are able to make sense of the impaired self-relation experienced by dominated subjects in social processes of precarisation.

## APPROPRIATION: A CONCEPTUAL CLARIFICATION

My reconstruction of the concept of alienation takes the theories of Rahel Jaeggi and Karl Marx as its point of departure. I will show that both of these philosophers formulate their theories of alienation in relation to the concept of appropriation – alienation can, in both theories, in general terms be defined as impaired appropriation. However, at the same time, we have seen that Jaeggi's and Marx's theories of alienation differ significantly from one another: the former is open, the latter is radical. In my attempt to reconstruct the concept of alienation in a way that is both open and radical, I will begin with the concept of appropriation. How do Jaeggi's and Marx's understandings of appropriation differ? And what do these differences say about their different concepts of alienation?

In Jaeggi's theory, the notion of appropriation is unmistakably central. Jaeggi defines alienation as 'an impairment of acts of appropriation' (Jaeggi 2014, 36). Here, appropriation means an activity of experimental problem-solving in which both the subject and object are mutually constituted. In Jaeggi's conception, appropriating the world means understanding it, in a practical sense – an understanding that allows the subject to navigate the world in her own way (Jaeggi 2014, 37). To overcome alienation is thus primarily an endeavour of understanding, although of the practical kind. One must understand oneself and the world in the sense that one manages 'to make the life one leads' (Jaeggi 2014, 37).

Although less explicit, Marx's concept of alienation can also be read as an impairment of the worker's 'appropriation of the human essence' (Marx 1975a, 296). Appropriation can be used to describe the continuous activity that marks the subject in Marx's work. Recall from Chapter 3 how Marx assumes that the subject is constituted in a continuous process whereby she encounters an alien object, enters into it and returns to herself. According to Marx, this process primarily takes place in production. In his early work, Marx emphasises that the 'worker by his labour appropriates the external world' (Marx 1975a, 273) – an idea that he returns to in *Capital*:

> The work process resolved as above into its simple elementary factors is human action with a view to the production of use-values, appropriation of natural substances to human requirements; it is the necessary condition for effecting exchanges of matter between man and nature; it is the everlasting nature-imposed condition of human existence; and therefore is independent of every social phase of that existence, or rather common to every such phase. (Marx 2000, 497)

The appropriation of nature, Marx argues, is a part of the human condition. In the process of appropriation, nature is made fit for human use. Moreover, in this process, the labourer develops her skills, senses, needs and imagination. Appropriation is conceived as an activity of mutual constitution, in which both the subject and object are constituted. Here, we can begin to see how alienation, in Marx's theory, can be defined as impaired appropriation. When the activity of appropriation is impaired, the subject's relation to the world is inhibited in such a way that her relationship to herself becomes dysfunctional: she cannot develop her human capacities.

Unsurprisingly, Jaeggi is not the only philosopher to reconstruct Marx's concept of alienation in relation to the concept of appropriation. In the literature on Marx's concept of alienation and the human subject, two of the most comprehensive accounts – those of Erich Fromm (Fromm and Marx 2017) and Bertell Ollman (1976) – both emphasise the human subject in her productive capacity. Ollman describes this productive activity as a version of a more general process of appropriation, which he defines as 'the realization of some or other of man's powers' (Ollman 1976, 86). It captures 'the interaction between man's senses and nature' (Ollman 1976, 86). In appropriating the world, the subject externalises herself, manifesting herself in the world. And when this activity is impaired, the subject is left alienated. The idea of appropriation is thus central not only to Jaeggi's but also to Marx's theory of alienation. But how, then, does

Marx's concept of appropriation – and thus of alienation – differ from Jaeggi's?

The concept of appropriation appears both in Marx's early writings on alienation and in his texts on exploitation. It is in the latter that it appears in its more antagonistic dimension. When the capitalist exploits the worker, she appropriates the worker's labour. This implies that, in Marx's conception, one person's appropriation can impair another's. In this way, the relation of appropriation turns antagonistic. Appropriation, in this conflictual dimension, is not discussed by Jaeggi. None of her practical examples of alienation involve situations in which one subject's appropriation is blocked by another's appropriation. In order to identify the antagonistic dimension of Marx's concept of appropriation, I will examine the concept and its different components more closely, drawing on Ollman's reconstruction of Marx's theory.

Ollman reconstructs Marx's concept of appropriation according to three intertwined dimensions: perception, orientation and appropriation. *Perception* is the moment when the subject encounters the object, the 'immediate contact with nature man achieves through his senses' (Ollman 1976, 85). *Orientation* is the meaning that the subject finds in the object. It 'has to do with how we perceive things, and particularly what we understand of their purposes. It establishes patterns, assigns places and worth, and, consequently, involves setting up an entire framework for our action *vis à vis* the rest of the world' (Ollman 1976, 85). Orientation, then, is the subject's practical understanding of the object. It is the process in which the subject understands what the object is worth and how to use it. In orientation, the subject orients herself – her senses, skills and imagination – towards the object.

Lastly, the notion of 'appropriation' denotes both the entire process of appropriation, including perception and orientation, as well as a specific moment in this process, the moment of *constructive use*. To appropriate is, in this sense, 'to utilize constructively' (Ollman 1976, 89). In the process of constructive use, subjects 'use nature they come into contact with for their own end' (Ollman 1976, 86). In constructive use, the subject derives value from the process of production and the object produced. In Ollman's words, 'perception is the individual's immediate contact with nature; orientation how he understands this contact'; and what I will call constructive use, 'the use he makes of it' (Ollman 1976, 97).

As Ollman notes, the three dimensions of appropriation – perception, orientation and constructive use – cannot be fully separated from each other. In Ollman's words, 'To be able to distinguish between these processes, I have broken a unity which really cannot be broken in this way, for each process is included in the other' (Ollman 1976, 86). The difficulty in distinguishing between Ollman's categories stems from the fact that, for Marx, appropriation in these three dimensions remains inseparable, interactive and often simultaneous.

Ollman's division of the concept of alienation is merely analytical. However, for the purpose of identifying the conflictual element of Marx's concept of appropriation, it can be helpful. Focusing on the last two dimensions – orientation and constructive use – we can understand how Marx's and Jaeggi's concepts of appropriation, as well as of alienation, differ, and why Marx's is more conflictual.

Whereas Marx understands appropriation both as orientation and constructive use, focusing primarily on the latter, Jaeggi understands appropriation mainly as orientation. Consequently, alienation in Jaeggi's conception can be described as impaired orientation – what I will call disorientation. Marx's concept of alienation, on the other hand, has another dimension – what I will call domination. In the next section, I will further develop what I mean by domination, and why I have chosen to call it so. For now, however, domination, in general terms, simply means impaired constructive use. As we will see, this emphasis on domination as a dimension of alienation makes Marx's concept more conflictual, in that it comes to imply unequal social power and division.

When we are disoriented, our way of making meaning is impaired – the world around us, and our own engagement with it, no longer makes sense. When, on the other hand, the subject is dominated, something – or rather, someone – hinders her from appropriating the value of her own activity, from acquiring new social capacities and resources. In Marx's theory, the capitalist exploits the worker by appropriating the product of her labour and thus the value of her activity. For this reason, the worker, as she labours, grows increasingly poor, both economically and spiritually. Her appropriation in terms of constructive use is inhibited. She does not develop her capacities in her labour, and she does not own the social product that she produces.

Impaired appropriation as impaired constructive use is highly antagonistic. In Marx's theory, it stems from the division between capital and labour. In capitalist society, the worker, who owns nothing but her labour power, produces; and the capitalist, who monopolises the capital that is needed for production, appropriates the value of the worker's productive activity. With the social division between capital and labour, the relation of appropriation is thus corrupted, taking the form of competition and exploitation. One subject's appropriation impairs the other's. In Marx's words, 'Under these economic conditions this realization of labour appears as loss of realization for the workers; . . . appropriation as estrangement, as alienation' (Marx 1975a, 272). As the capitalist appropriates the worker's labour, the worker's appropriation is impaired, leaving her alienated.

Alienation involves a corrupted, antagonistic relation between labour and capital. And overcoming alienation becomes a matter of reappropriation – of struggle. For the worker to appropriate herself, her human essence, she must reappropriate the means of production from the capitalist who has monopolised them. In Marx's words, 'The appropriation of a totality of instruments of production is . . . the development of a totality of capacities in the individuals themselves' (Marx and Engels 2000a, 192). This can be described as a reappropriation since, in Marx's conception, '[c]apital is among other things also an instrument of production, also past, objectified labour' (Marx 1986, 23). To overcome her alienation, the worker must, in a first step, reappropriate the product of her labour, taking it back from the capitalist.[1] Until the division between labour and capital has been overcome, appropriation will remain a corrupt, exploiting practice, wherein the capitalist takes from the labourer. Marx's concept of alienation, due mostly to its dimension of impaired constructive use, is thus highly antagonistic – involving divisions between social groups, unequal power relations and radical struggle.

Alienation as impaired appropriation becomes more antagonistic depending on which dimension of appropriation is emphasised: orientation or constructive use. As opposed to orientation, constructive use depends on resources that – in certain social systems – are monopolised. However, we should also recall that, in Marx's theory, these two dimensions of appropriation are inseparable. Meaning and constructive use are, for Marx, necessarily connected in a particular way. In Marx's writings, the main form of constructive use is production, and, according to him, the economic structure of production determines people's behaviour and understanding.[2] Because of this deterministic assumption, there is, in Marx's theory, a necessary

127

connection between what I have called domination and disorientation. This is a form of determinism that Jaeggi's theory, focusing primarily on disorientation, breaks with. Here, the relation between the objective and the subjective – between our orientation and our constructive use – is detached and they cannot determine one another.

The aim in this chapter is to socially ground, and add an antagonistic dimension to, the concept of alienation as impaired appropriation – while at the same time maintaining the openness of Jaeggi's theory. This means both reconsidering and bringing together the two dimensions of alienation as impaired appropriation. And it means doing so without linking them by necessity. I will argue, however, that when they do occur together, it amounts to a specific type of social suffering. It is this form of suffering – of disorientation deepened by domination – that I seek to capture with the concept of alienation.

In the following discussion, I will seek to open up and radicalise alienation in its two dimensions: domination and disorientation. I will begin by examining how Marx's concept of alienation can be conceptually linked – via exploitation – to Bourdieu's concept of domination.

## IMPAIRED APPROPRIATION AS DOMINATION

In order to radicalise the concept of alienation as impaired appropriation, we need to bring back a dimension of unequal power and antagonism. As we have seen, this means that impaired appropriation cannot merely be understood as a blockage in our understanding of the situation, but should also be conceived as impaired constructive use. As we have seen, this type of impaired appropriation is in focus in Marx's writings on exploitation. Here, appropriation becomes a highly conflictual activity. The capitalist's appropriation blocks the appropriation of the worker – leaving the worker unable to make constructive use of her time and capacities. A possible way of radicalising the concept of alienation as impaired appropriation is thus to link it to that of exploitation. At the same time, for the theory of alienation to also remain open, we must avoid the singular focus on industrial production that distinguishes Marx's theory of exploitation.

In order to bring back an adversarial dimension of social power into the concept of alienation, I will, therefore, first turn to Marx's theory of exploitation and examine how it is linked to his concept of alienation. I will then draw on Bourdieu's theory of domination to enlarge the concept of exploitation beyond the process of industrial production. The concept of domination, I show, is structurally similar to that of exploitation, but more expansive. When dominated, the subject's time and engagement, in several areas of life, is deprived of its value – leaving her unable to make constructive use of her own time.

## Exploitation is intrinsic to alienation

In his writings on exploitation, Marx makes explicit the unequal power relation between worker and capitalist that, I will show, underlies his theory of alienation.[3] Like alienation, exploitation has its basis in the relation of labour. Capital is, for Marx, an abstract concept marking a particular social relation: the monopoly over the means of subsistence. This amounts to a power relation between two social groups – workers and capitalists. The relation of capital renders the workers – those who do not own the means of subsistence – vulnerable to exploitation. While the concept of exploitation denotes specifically the relation between capital and labour, the concept of alienation captures primarily the worker's relations to the world, other workers and herself. The theories of alienation and exploitation are thus, I argue, complementary. Before discussing how it is integrated in the theory of alienation, I will introduce the theory of exploitation.

Marx's theory of exploitation begins with the observation that, in capitalist society, the capitalist has a monopoly over the means of production and thus over the means of subsistence. The worker, on the other hand, is assumed to lack the means of subsistence; she depends on the capitalist for food and shelter. According to Marx, 'The capitalist system presupposes the complete separation of the labourers from all property in the means by which they can realize their labour' (Marx 1972a, 432). In the shift from feudalism to capitalism, Marx claims, the producers went from being serfs – owned by one person – to being labourers – owned by the capitalist class. Lacking the means of production, and thus the means of subsistence, the workers have no choice but to sell their labour to the capitalists. They cannot choose whether to sell their labour or not – only which capitalist to work for.[4] This relation between capitalist and worker sets the condition for exploitation.

REDIRECTING RADICAL DEMOCRACY

The time and activity of the worker – her labour – is turned into a commodity – labour power. The worker gives her labour power and the capitalist pays. At the same time, the capitalist depends on the worker. The capitalist makes profit out of labour by appropriating surplus value, the amount of labour exceeding the reproduction of labour. This appropriation of surplus value is the social process and relation that Marx calls exploitation (Marx 2000, 512).

In the simplest version of Marx's theory, the surplus value that the capitalists appropriate, and, consequently, the profit that they make, stems from unpaid labour time. To maximise profit, Marx argues, the capitalists decrease the workers' wages over time. The wages are pressed down until they merely cover the cost for reproducing labour – the cost of food, shelter and necessary training. By pushing down the workers' wages to the minimum, the capitalists take out a surplus value, which is then transferred on the market into monetary profit. During a part of the working day, the labourer thus produces the amount of value necessary to cover the means of subsistence. The rest of the day, however, she produces surplus value – value that she does not gain herself but that goes to the capitalist:

> During the second period of the labour process, that in which his labour is no longer necessary labour, the workman, it is true, labours, expends labour power; but his labour, being no longer necessary labour, he creates no value for himself. He creates surplus value which, for the capitalist, has all the charms of a creation out of nothing. (Marx 2000, 511)

The surplus value that the worker creates when she works beyond what is necessary to sustain herself is appropriated by the capitalist and, as a result, is of no constructive use to the worker. Another way of looking at exploitation is, thus, this impaired use of time. In Marx's words, 'The rate of surplus value is . . . an exact expression for the degree of exploitation of labour power by capital, or of the labourer by the capitalist' (Marx 2000, 512). Exploitation is the capitalist's appropriation of surplus value. Although surplus value, in practical terms, is the basis of profit, it is, ultimately, an abstract social relation. In the process of exploitation, the capitalist accumulates capital, or, in other words, monopoly over the means of subsistence – a power that can then be yielded to further exploit the worker.

Alienation and exploitation are closely conceptually linked. I will show that alienation, in each of its four dimensions introduced in

Chapter 3, is based on exploitation. In the first dimension of alienation, the labourer is alienated from the product of her labour. The worker invests herself in the product she produces, but the product appears as something alien to her. For this reason, Marx argues that the 'worker becomes all the poorer the more wealth he produces' (Marx 1975a, 271). At the same time, the object – the product – grows increasingly powerful. Fundamentally, however, the relation between the worker and the object is based on another relation: the relation of exploitation between worker and capitalist.

According to Marx, the power of the object over the worker must ultimately stem from a subject:

> If the product of labour does not belong to the worker, if it confronts him as an alien power, then this can only be because it belongs to some other man than the worker. If the worker's activity is a torment to him, to another it must give satisfaction and pleasure. Not the gods, not nature, but only man himself can be this alien power over man. (Marx 1975a, 278)

For Marx, alienation is no subjectless power. Ultimately, the subject's subordination to the object stems from a human power relation, the relation of exploitation. The labourer is alienated because she does not own the product of her labour, which has been appropriated by the capitalist. The power to which the worker is subjected is neither anonymous nor aimless. The worker is alienated and powerless in relation to the objective world because her labour is owned by the capitalist who benefits at her expense. The relation of alienation is a relation of exploitation.

In the second dimension of alienation, the worker is alienated from her labour – her time and activity. Recall from Chapter 3 that the worker is alienated from her labour both in the sense that her labour is not her own and that she cannot find meaning in it (see Marx 1975a, 274). As we will see, alienation in both of these senses ultimately stems from another relation – the relation of exploitation between labour and capital.

The worker does not own her labour, because it is appropriated and controlled by the capitalist. When the capitalist exploits the labourer, appropriating surplus value, what the capitalist *actually* appropriates is the labourer's life activity. Surplus value is extracted through prolonged, unpaid work hours, and technological innovation aimed at increasing productivity.[5] This means that, because of

131

long working hours and little free time, the labourer does not own her time. Moreover, she does not own her activity, which is fragmented and automatised due to new machines and forms of organisation. The capitalist's appropriation of surplus value thus alienates the worker from her labour:

> within the capitalist system all methods for raising the social productiveness of labour are brought about at the cost of the individual labourer; all means for the development of production transform themselves into means of domination over, and exploitation of, the producers; they mutilate the labourer into a fragment of a man, degrade him to the level of an appendage of a machine, destroy every remnant of charm in his work and turn it into a hated toil; they estrange from him the intellectual potentialities of the labour process in the same proportion as science is incorporated in it as an independent power; they distort the conditions under which he works, subject him during the labour process to a despotism the more hateful for its meanness; they transform his lifetime into working time, and drag his wife and child beneath the wheels of the Juggernaut of capital. (Marx 1972a, 430)

In the process of exploitation, the capitalist appropriates the worker's life and labour, 'estranging' her from it. As the capitalist exploits the worker, the worker's time and activity lose their meaning and value for the worker. It is no longer an affirmation of the worker herself; she does not get to put her capacities and engagement into it. At the same time, the worker's own capacities and possibilities do not develop, thus locking her in a situation of subordination and alienation.

In the third dimension of alienation, the worker is alienated from herself – her 'species being'. Marx derives this dimension from the other two (Marx 1975a, 276). For this reason, one can assume that this dimension of alienation, too, stems from the relation of exploitation. To understand why, however, we must recall how Marx's subject relates to and realises herself.

For Marx, the subject is a producer, distinguished by her specifically human labour. While animals work for food and shelter – the means of subsistence – humans labour for all of humanity. In alienated labour – wage labour – however, the subject works only to sustain herself, leaving her alienated from herself and her own humanity (Marx 1975a, 276). And, as we have seen, the reason that the worker produces only for herself is exploitation – the capitalist's appropriation of surplus value. All the value of the labour, beyond that which is necessary for the worker to sustain herself, is appropriated by the capitalist. Because of exploitation, the worker works not for humanity at large but merely to sustain herself. She is alienated from her species being.

Fourth, the subject is alienated from other subjects. This dimension of alienation follows from the three other dimensions (Marx 1975a, 277). As their activity of labour is corrupted, subjects can no longer recognise each other in their specifically human productive capacity. The relations between subjects are thus inhibited; the relation between worker and capitalist is corrupted by unequal power, and the bonds of solidarity between workers are broken. Both these types of dysfunctional relations stem from exploitation. By exploiting workers, capitalists appropriate and accumulate capital. In the competition between capitalists, the capitalists thus grow richer and fewer, while the workers grow poorer and more numerous (Marx 1972b, 216). The workers are thus forced to compete with each other by selling their labour power even more cheaply. This competition means that the bonds of solidarity between workers are broken, alienating them from each other.

We have thus seen how the relation of exploitation between capital and labour – wherein the capitalists appropriate surplus value from the workers – inhibits and alienates the subject. It is because of the capitalist's appropriation of surplus value that the labourer is unable to form relations of appropriation to the world, to her labour, to other people and to herself as a human being.

In the theory of both exploitation and alienation, appropriation thus takes on a conflictual meaning, whereby one subject's appropriation impairs another's. This conflictual meaning of appropriation constitutes the antagonistic dimension of alienation as impaired appropriation. The subject is alienated because someone else is benefiting at her expense. For Marx, the antagonism between labour and capital is the source of exploitation and, in prolongation, of alienation.

If the theory of alienation captures why the workers initially do not resist – because of the broken bonds of solidarity – the theory of exploitation explicates why, eventually, they will. In the process of exploitation, the capitalists become fewer and richer while the workers are increasingly impoverished – to the point where they must revolt to survive. In the competition for profit among capitalists, some will lose; they go bankrupt and are forced to sell their labour as workers. Marx describes how 'a mass of petty industrialists and small rentiers are hurled down into its ranks and have nothing better to do than urgently stretch out their arms alongside those of the workers'; and thus, he argues, 'the forest of uplifted arms demanding work becomes ever thicker, while the arms themselves become ever thinner' (Marx 1972b, 216). Eventually the situation for the impoverished workers becomes unsustainable – resulting in crisis and revolt. In Marx's words, 'the antagonism between the proletariat and the bourgeoisie is a struggle of class against class, a struggle which carried to its highest expression is a total revolution' (Marx 1972c, 219). In Marx's theory, exploitation results in class antagonism and, eventually, in revolution.

Linking the concept of alienation to that of exploitation thus radicalises it, adding a dimension of unequal social power and antagonism. It captures how one group's appropriation can systematically be impaired by the appropriation of another. At the same time, however, it is also precisely this link that pushes Marx's theory of alienation towards the three pitfalls that the democratic left sought to avoid. First, a concept of alienation connected to that of exploitation – which exclusively emphasises industrial production – risks becoming essentialist, defining the subject by her productive activity. Second, the emphasis in the theory of exploitation on the unavoidable impoverishment of the working class, the necessary development of class antagonism and the eventual revolution of the proletariat makes it prone to determinism. The subject's actions are assumed to be determined by the social structure and her position in it. Third, the link between alienation and capitalist exploitation suggests that once capitalism has been abolished and the distinction between capital and labour is dissolved, we can reach a final state of harmony in which antagonism is replaced by bonds of solidarity. In order to radicalise the concept of alienation, linking it to that exploitation, we must find a way to broaden the latter beyond its narrow focus on industrial production.

## From exploitation to domination

For the theory of alienation to be linked to that of exploitation while simultaneously remaining open, the concept of exploitation should be opened up for contingencies and a wider spectrum of social relations than merely those of production. To find a way to enlarge the concept of exploitation, I will turn to the concept of domination.

While the literature on the relations between domination and exploitation is limited, the two concepts are commonly considered to be closely related, with exploitation defined as a form of domination (e.g. Bellamy 2007, 151; Vrousalis 2013).[6] There are several different theories of domination – with Philip Pettit's republican theory and Pierre Bourdieu's sociological theory being among the most influential. For my purposes – to enlarge the concept of exploitation while maintaining its radicalism – Bourdieu's concept should be particularly suitable. There are three main reasons for this.

First, Bourdieu's theory of domination retains the antagonistic dimension of Marx's theory, in which power is agent-driven and intentional – rather than, for example, in Jaeggi's conception of domination, aimless and agentless.

Second, Bourdieu's concept of domination captures a form of power that, like exploitation, is located in and mediated by social institutions. In its emphasis on institutional mediation, it differs from Pettit's theory of domination. In his classical example of domination, Pettit focuses on the relation of domination between master and slave. His theory thus comes to emphasise personal rather than institutionally mediated forms of power.

In Bourdieu's conception, slavery is the ultimate form of what he calls direct domination, where one dominates others by '"winning" them personally . . . creating a bond between persons'. While Bourdieu recognises this form of power, it is not, according to him, the central form of power in modern society. Instead, Bourdieu focuses on what he calls indirect domination – a form of power that 'no longer needs to be exerted in a direct, personal way . . .' but is mediated through 'a system of mechanisms' (Bourdieu 2010, 183, 190). Once this system is instituted, Bourdieu claims, the dominant no longer has to continuously and personally establish their domination; they 'have only to let the system they dominate take its own course' (Bourdieu 2010, 190). While in a pre-modern, pre-capitalist society, direct power is central, modern capitalist society is, according to Bourdieu, mostly reproduced through objective, institutionalised mechanisms – such as money. And while everyone is subordinated to the system, those with more power have more influence over it. Like Marx's concept of exploitation, Bourdieu's domination is both agent-driven and structural – placing itself somewhere between the intentional, personal power emphasised by Pettit and the agentless, aimless form of power at work in Jaeggi's theory.

135

Third, in comparison with other concepts of domination, such as Pettit's, Bourdieu's work is more commonly read in a Marxist rather than, for example, a republican tradition.[7] In drawing on Marx's concepts of capital and appropriation, Bourdieu maintains the social and material dimensions of Marx's theory, thus grounding it in social division and deprivation. In doing so, Bourdieu's concept of domination – described as 'mediated, lasting appropriation' – parallels yet, as we will see, enlarges Marx's concept of exploitation (Bourdieu 2010, 183).

Focusing on the concepts of appropriation and capital, I will show that when one expands the theory of exploitation – the capitalist's appropriation of the worker's labour – one gets to Bourdieu's concept of domination – what Bourdieu describes as the dominant's appropriation of 'the labour, services, goods, homage, and respect of others' (Bourdieu 2010, 190).[8] Domination is the appropriation not only of labour but of the full spectrum of human activities and their products – including, for example, care, services and education. We can thus define domination in the following way: *The subject is dominated when her appropriation is systematically impaired by the appropriation of more powerful subjects.*

What is appropriated in the relation and process of domination is the value of the subject's time and activity – the capacity to make constructive use of it. Bourdieu, following Marx, calls this value capital. In the following, I will show how Bourdieu's theory of domination expands the theory of exploitation by expanding the concept of capital.

The concept of capital is a central component of both Marx's and Bourdieu's theories. When one subject exploits or dominates another, she uses her capital to appropriate and accumulate more capital at the other's expense. You need capital to appropriate capital; and when you have less capital, you become vulnerable to exploitation and domination. Capital is thus, in both theories, understood as a form of social power – a power that, within a given social game, gives you the upper hand, enabling 'the appropriation of profits' (Bourdieu 2011, 84). Furthermore, capital lends you some power over the game itself: 'the power to impose the laws of functioning of the field most favourable to capital and its reproduction' (Bourdieu 2011, 84). With capital you can, to some extent, remake the rules of the game to your own favour. In these respects, capital, in Bourdieu's conception, has the same structure as in Marx's theory. However, for

Bourdieu, capital takes on many forms and shapes a wide range of social relations, not merely those of production.

There are, Bourdieu (1986) argues, three fundamental types of capital: economic, cultural and social capital. *Economic capital* is the form of capital that can clearly and directly be transferred into money. It mainly appears in objective, material forms, as goods. Economic capital constrains what objects the subject can appropriate, what she can afford. It can also take on institutionalised forms, for example as property rights.

*Cultural capital* can be objects – paintings, books and machines – or institutionalised statuses – titles, educational qualifications and professional legitimations. However, in its original form, cultural capital is embodied – as 'culture, cultivation, *Bildung*' (Bourdieu 2011, 83). Embodied capital does not materialise as a product or a title but as an integral part of a person: in her skills, schemes of perception, manners, tastes, gut feeling and moral intuition. Knowledge, manners, refined taste and artistic talent are all forms of cultural capital.

Embodied cultural capital is a central currency in many markets, including in cultural production, the matrimonial market and the social welfare market. With cultural capital you can acquire valuable goods, such as a partner, social welfare, cultural goods or social status (Bourdieu 2011, 84). For Bourdieu, the notion of cultural capital becomes particularly useful in his sociological studies of education. It allows him to explain how scholastic achievement varies between social classes and between class fractions. While children born into the intellectual class – the cultural class fraction of the dominant class – gain significant profit from education, children from the popular classes obtain less profit in the academic market. What the common-sense view would describe as a 'natural aptitude' or 'talent' for school work, often found among the children of 'intellectuals', stems, according to Bourdieu, from early training in the acquisition of cultural capital. Academic degrees are the central means by which embodied cultural capital is transformed into economic capital, guaranteeing, for example, a certain status and salary.

*Social capital* consists in social obligations, such as families, professional networks or political groups. A subject's social capital increases with her network – her standing within it, its number of participants and the participants' capital. While social capital cannot be reduced to cultural or economic capital, it derives its power from the aggregate cultural and economic capital of the members of one's group. Social capital allows the individual subject to borrow power from the other members of the group.[9] Like cultural capital, social capital can, occasionally, be converted into economic capital, by giving you a job or a good deal – or institutionalised capital, such as titles or nobility. However, social capital is mainly maintained through continuous activity. Social networks are constituted through rituals of engagement within the group, such as meetings, gifts and exchanges. Thus the 'measure of all equivalences is nothing other than labour time (in the widest sense)' (Bourdieu 2011, 89). Social capital 'presupposes a specific labour, i.e., an apparently gratuitous expenditure of time, attention, care, concern' (Bourdieu 2011, 89). Appropriating and maintaining social capital thus requires continuous work and care. While this becomes relatively easy for those who hold high cultural or economic capital – whose minimal attention is often gratefully received – it quickly becomes demanding for those with less capital.

Conversions between different forms of capital are, in Bourdieu's theory, crucial for maintaining a system of domination. Cultural and social capital enable capital – social power – to conceal itself. Even though the conversion of capital is costly and risky, it can be profitable when the transmission of economic capital, for example by inheritance, is obstructed by institutionalised measures, such as laws and taxes. '[T]he more the official transmission of capital is prevented or hindered, the more the effects of the clandestine circulation of capital in the form of cultural capital become determinant in the reproduction of the social structure' (Bourdieu 2011, 90). When economic domination is criticised, it can conceal itself by taking on clandestine forms – domination through social or cultural capital. And when you think that domination has been tamed, it might only have taken a new form. Conversions between different forms of capital make domination into a persistent social phenomenon that cannot easily be eradicated.

Although Bourdieu maintains that the different forms of capital cannot be reduced to one another, economic capital still maintains a particular status. Unless the subject can eventually transform her social and cultural capital into economic capital, she remains vulnerable to domination. She lacks the means of subsistence and thus real options. In this sense, domination resembles exploitation. Like the capitalist in Marx's theory, the dominant subject monopolises the means of subsistence, leaving the dominated without real options.

When applying Bourdieu's enlarged concept of capital to the concept of exploitation, it is thus transformed into the concept of domination. Dominant groups use economic, cultural and social capital to appropriate the activity of the dominated. As the dominated subject's time and activity loses its value, the activity of the dominant subject becomes more valuable. What is appropriated is not merely the productive activity of dominated people but also their cultural activities – art and education – and social activities – the care and solidarity invested in family, friends or political associations. Consequently, the conflict between capital and labour does not become the only possible breeding ground for conflict and class struggle in society.

While, in the theory of domination, the forms of power and lines of division in society are pluralised, they are no less central. The power at work in Bourdieu's theory functions in a similar way as in Marx's. Like Marx, Bourdieu claims that capital functions through competition and monopolisation:

> the relationship of appropriation between an agent and the resources objectively available ... is mediated by the relationship of (objective and/or subjective) competition between himself and the other possessors of capital competing for the same goods, in which scarcity – and through it social value – is generated. (Bourdieu 2011, 84)

A monopolised resource generates more capital – more effective power – for its owner. However, it also requires more capital to appropriate. '[T]he unequal distribution of capital', Bourdieu argues, 'is the source of the specific effects of capital, i.e., the appropriation of profits and the power to impose the laws of functioning most favourable to capital' (Bourdieu 2011, 84). The fewer the people that have capital, the more power they have.

Monopoly is, according to Bourdieu, crucial for maintaining the value not only of economic capital but also of social and cultural capital. It determines, for instance, the value of titles, talents, tastes or academic degrees. As an example, Bourdieu shows how when education was opened up to the popular classes in France, its value decreased. A more recent example of this phenomenon may be observed in Chile today, where higher education fees were recently removed from a significant part of the low-income population. As Bourdieu observes in *The Weight of the World* (Bourdieu et al. 1999),

139

the decreased value of education comes as a heavy disappointment to the parents and children from the popular classes who have invested in education, only to realise that the degrees have lost their value, bringing neither status nor a future career. Capital, as a social power, is conditioned on a division between those who have more and those who have less. It presupposes, on a theoretical level, a division that can serve as a breeding ground for actual social conflict.

For Bourdieu, the 'fundamental opposition' in society is thus not the division between capital and labour but that between the dominant and the dominated (Bourdieu 2013, 469). However, this division significantly diverges from Marx's conception of class antagonism in at least three respects.

First, in Bourdieu's theory, domination, and the social tensions that it can involve, is not organised according to a single, easily distinguishable line. While Bourdieu identifies some social groups with particularly high capital as the 'dominant classes', he also speaks of 'the dominant fraction of the dominant class' (Bourdieu 2006, 42). People can find themselves dominated to different degrees depending on who they interact with and how much capital they have. This can give rise to many different forms of antagonism, also within social classes.

Second, the subject's social position in a specific context depends not only on the volume of the capital she possesses but also on its composition – whether, for example, it is mainly economic or cultural. Thus, what Bourdieu sometimes describes as 'the dominant class' – including industrialists, private sector executives and college professors – is divided into several fractions, such as 'intellectuals' (possessing primarily cultural capital) and 'businessmen' (possessing mainly economic capital) (Bourdieu 2013, 470). The conflict with which domination is associated is not merely limited to the conflict between those with high and low capital but extends to that between competing class fractions possessing different forms of capital.

Third, in Bourdieu's theory, actual social conflict is related to, but not determined by, the social structure – the positioning of subjects depending on their volume and composition of capital. Structures can be understood in a variety of ways, and the social boundaries between collectives emerge through processes of social meaning-making.[10] For example, people with small volumes of capital do not necessarily identify with each other and see themselves as a collective. Furthermore, even when they do, there are no guarantees that they would mobilise politically. This depends, for example, on whether political organisations find frames and strategies that resonate with existing social groups (Benford and Snow 2000; Voss 1996).

Thus, while Bourdieu sometimes refers to the class division between the 'dominant class', 'the petty bourgeoisie' and the 'popular classes', such classes are not merely given by the social structure but are also based on empirical observations of the self-understanding of different professional groups (e.g. Bourdieu 2013, 114–16).[11] The question of the relation between social power structures, social collectives and political mobilisation is an important one that I will return to in Chapter 6. For now, it suffices to note that, while domination theoretically presupposes division which can serve as a breeding ground for social antagonism, the actual lines of conflict in society cannot be easily or completely predetermined.

### Domination as a dimension of alienation

By adding domination as a dimension of alienation, the concept of alienation is radicalised – able to capture unequal relations of power and antagonism. The question of antagonism is central. When rethinking alienation as a form of domination, we bring to the forefront a blockage to appropriation that has fallen out of focus in the recent alienation debate. Appropriation – experimental problem-solving – requires not only the *ability* to appropriate – a practical understanding of the world – but also real *possibilities*. The second type of appropriation is impaired by domination.

When dominated, the subject's appropriation – her constructive use of her time – is systematically inhibited by the appropriation of more powerful subjects. Appropriation – action and experimental problem-solving – requires that we can make constructive use of our time, that our activity can generate new abilities and possibilities. When the dominant subject appropriates and monopolises social resources, she blocks the dominated from appropriating it. This is a type of impairment to appropriation that only takes place in a society marked by systemic power inequalities. In such a society, appropriation – action and problem-solving – is not a neutral activity. It is fraught with antagonism: one person's appropriation can block another's. For many people, to be fully human – appropriating oneself and one's world – is to fight. For the dominated to overcome their alienation, they must struggle against the dominant.

Consequently, a concept of alienation linked to that of domination becomes conflictual and potentially radical.

Furthermore, although I have drawn on Marx's theories to radicalise the concept of alienation, the resulting concept is more open than Marx's in three respects. First, when alienation is linked to domination rather than exploitation, it is enlarged to cover a wider range of relations. Arguably, it thus avoids the pitfall of human essentialism. Alienation, in our conception, is not merely located within the process of economic production but also in education, art, childcare and political engagement. The theory presumes a subject who is not essentially a producer, but who can engage in a wide spectrum of activities.

At the same time, a possible objection remains. Although Bourdieu expands the conception of meaningful human activity, he still prioritises economic production and value. Ultimately, what separates the dominant from the dominated is their possession of the means of subsistence. In modern society, this mainly depends on economic capital. For social and cultural capital to be a source of power, it must, at some point, be convertible to economic capital. Productive activity thus remains particularly important to the subject.

Still, Bourdieu emphasises that social and cultural capital cannot be reduced to economic capital. Different forms of capital correspond to different logics; and conversions between them are often lengthy, costly and difficult to predict. Social, cultural and economic activities can all provide meaning and constructive value in different ways. While maintaining a particular emphasis on economic production and value, the economic reductionism of Marx's theory is largely avoided.

Second, the concept of alienation, linked to that of domination, avoids some of the deterministic tendencies of Marx's theory. Although alienation is an unequal and potentially antagonistic relation, the actual manifestation of this antagonism and the extent to which it is politically mobilised remains contingent.

Third, and lastly, I want to discuss the pitfall of idealising harmony, which seems, in this context, to be the most difficult to overcome. Avoiding domination, and, with this, the antagonism that it gives rise to, is both desirable and possible. Domination blocks us from appropriating the world and ourselves, and we should, therefore, strive to overcome it. Furthermore, since the problem of domination is social rather than existential, overcoming it should, at least in theory, be possible. It is both desirable and, theoretically, possible to eradicate domination and the form of antagonism to which it is related.

However, as opposed to Marx's exploitation, domination is, in practice, almost impossible to overcome. While domination, like exploitation – and the antagonism to which it is connected – can, in theory, be overcome, the process of doing so remains complex and unpredictable. The possibility of conversion between different forms of capital means that when domination in one form is resisted, it risks re-emerging in another. A final state of harmony free of domination thus seems, if not impossible, then highly implausible, and the path towards it remains unpredictable.

## IMPAIRED APPROPRIATION AS DISORIENTATION

Having included domination as a dimension of alienation, the concept of alienation as impaired appropriation has been made more genuinely radical. It becomes capable of capturing social antagonism and unequal relations of power. However, we seek a theory of alienation that involves not only impaired constructive use – domination – but also impaired orientation or practical understanding – what I have called disorientation.

One possible approach to this could be to assume that a dominated person will always be disoriented, and vice versa. However, this assumption does not hold. A subject with few opportunities may still find ways of orienting herself in the world. It is not impossible to find meaning in a job that you had no choice but to take, and where someone else reaps most of the benefits of your labour. When dominated, finding purpose and orienting yourself in the world can, for example, involve skilful quotidian acts of resistance. Only in its deepest form can we assume that domination would be so destructive that it would block the subject from experiencing herself as in charge of her own life. This may be the situation for those who are dominated to a point where they have been deprived of any social context that they can make their own, such as a place to live or a way of making a living. But if not in the process of domination, in what type of social processes is disorientation located? How can we socially ground the problem of disorientation – radicalising it into a form of social suffering – while maintaining its openness?

Recall from Chapter 3 that, although Jaeggi's theory of alienation takes important steps towards a theory of impaired orientation, it lacks social grounding. Her focus lies on the deeper structure of the subject's experience of the situation. She does not, on the other hand, specify the conditions for a functional orientation or the possible ways in which it could be blocked. For this reason, it becomes difficult to understand if and how disorientation can be described as a form of social rather than psychological suffering.

Beyond Jaeggi's work, the situation of disorientation has also been captured by contemporary cultural studies. In particular, the concept has grown influential through the work of Sara Ahmed (2006, 2010a, 2010b) who uses it, among other things, to capture queer desires and their disruptive potential. Ahmed describes disorientation as an experience of being out of place, of failing to want, move and behave – orienting oneself – in the way that is expected in a specific social milieu. Her work examines different cultural expressions of being out of place and of desiring the 'wrong' objects. It both draws on and breaks with Marx's theory of alienation, focusing, like Jaeggi, primarily on impaired practical understanding rather than the material aspects of Marx's theory.[12] She emphasises how the experience of disorientation can function as the 'necessary estrangement from the present' needed in order to develop a 'revolutionary consciousness' (Ahmed 2010b, 162). In focusing on the perspective of the marginalised rather than the privileged, and in connecting disorientation to marginalisation, Ahmed's work begins to socially ground the experience. However, Ahmed's study, like Jaeggi's, is focused on the structure of the subject's experience, rather than the relation between the subject and the social world. In order to complement this work and to further understand the relation of orientation and its conditions, I will once again turn to Bourdieu.

Pierre Bourdieu's concept of habitus is a fruitful tool for understanding how the subject relates to the social world and how this relation can be inhibited. Like Jaeggi, Bourdieu relies on a subject who interacts with the social world through continuous, experimental problem-solving. Bourdieu also observes that this experimental activity can be inhibited. He describes this process, which Jaeggi calls alienation, as one of 'disenchantment' or 'uprooting'. However, while Jaeggi primarily focuses on the experience of functional, as well as dysfunctional, problem-solving, Bourdieu focuses on the conditions for this activity. According to Bourdieu, the condition for the subject's capacity to solve problems and to orient herself in the world is her habitus.

The habitus is the subject's embodied dispositions – her sense of orientation – constituted in her continuous interaction with the world. It enables her to spontaneously and intuitively respond to new situations – to orient herself. If society is a game, in which the social order is the rules and the individual subjects are the players, the habitus is each player's sense of the game. The players – the individual subjects – have to obey the rules. However, 'the players' actual shots are actions that cannot be reduced to theoretical rules. They are improvisations', and the habitus is 'the capacity each player of a game has to improvise the next move, the next play, the next shot' (Calhoun 2003, 276). We develop our habitus, our sense of the social game, over time, by participating in social processes: 'As the word suggests, this is something we acquire through repetition, like a habit, and something we know in our bodies, not just in our minds' (Calhoun 2003, 276). The habitus is the habitual embodied disposition that allows us to orient ourselves in social processes from a given social position.

The habitus is the condition for, and the link between, subjects and the social world. For the subject to be able to act, she must be able to orient herself in a social process – she must have a functioning habitus. In Bourdieu's words, the habitus 'is what makes it possible to inhabit institutions, to appropriate them practically' (Bourdieu 1990, 57). The habitus is the condition for the subject's practical understanding – appropriation – of the world. Through this appropriation, both the subject herself, her habitus, and the social world are constituted. When we participate in and appropriate institutions, we 'keep them in activity, continuously pulling them from the state of dead letters, reviving the sense deposited in them, but at the same time imposing the revisions and transformations that reactivation entails' (Bourdieu 1990, 57). For social institutions to be sustained, subjects must actively claim – appropriate – them. Subjects and social processes are thus constitutive of each other. Through her active participation in the games of the social world, the subject develops a habitus that allows her to appropriate it. At the same time, the social game only exists as long as there are players who can understand it. The habitus enables subjects to appropriate the social world, spontaneously creating and recreating it. The condition for the subject's ability to orient herself is her habitus.

How, then, can the subject lose her sense of the game, her capacity to orient herself? The subject becomes disoriented when her

145

habitus – her embodied dispositions – no longer corresponds to her social world. She does not intuitively react to new events in a socially accepted way; or, conversely, the social world does not function in the way that the subject expects it to. Bourdieu empirically observes this crisis in the habitus for the first time in his studies of Algerian peasants in the remote mountain villages of Kabylia. In the wake of the war of national liberation and French military repression, changes that would normally take place over several centuries were rapidly imposed. In a process of what Bourdieu describes as a 'historical acceleration', the Kabyle people transitioned from a precapitalist to a modern economy. In the emerging capitalist society, however, their habitus no longer functioned. There was, according to Bourdieu, a 'mismatch between economic dispositions fashioned in a precapitalist economy and the economic cosmos imported and imposed, oftentimes in the most brutal way, by colonization' (Bourdieu 2000, 18). The social world of Kabylia, its practices and common forms of understanding, was disrupted. A significant part of the Kabyle peasant population became what Bourdieu called 'sub-proletarians' – peasants without land, farm workers, unemployed or temporal labourers. Furthermore, the 'mythico-ritual system' of gift-giving that had ordered and given meaning to Kabyle social life was replaced by a system of cost, profit and rational calculation (Bourdieu 2000). The Kabyle people found themselves 'uprooted', lost in a 'disenchanted' world that they could neither navigate nor understand (Bourdieu 1979).

From Bourdieu's theory of the habitus and its functioning, I will deduce three potentially disorienting social situations in which the habitus could become dysfunctional. These situations of disorientation, I will show, are also captured by Bourdieu in his early empirical studies of the Algerian sub-proletarians, as well as in his later studies of immigrants, peasants, factory workers, social workers and small business owners in modern France (see Bourdieu et al. 1999).

First, the subject can become disoriented in situations where her social world rapidly changes. When she finds herself in a completely changed social world or in a new social position, her habitus, which is slow to develop and slow to change, lags behind. The habitus is a 'durable, adjusted disposition', constituted in a continuous process that begins in early life (Bourdieu 1990, 57). By habitual repetition, we learn to orient ourselves in our social world from our social position. When the social world quickly changes, our sense of orientation might not catch up. Bourdieu describes how the Algerian sub-proletarians were '[t]orn from the social environment in which they lived their whole lives' and 'confronted with radically new problems'. Lacking the habitual disposition by which to orient themselves in their new world, they could, according to Bourdieu, 'only choose between indifference and superstition' (Bourdieu 1979, 69). As their social world was disrupted, the emerging sub-proletariat could not make sense of and find meaning in the real social world. Rapid social change left them disoriented.

Second, the subject's habitus can fall into crisis in social processes that make contradictory demands on their participants. It is difficult to develop a functioning habitus – a 'sense of the game' – when the game lacks a coherent set of rules. As the habitus develops in repetitive social interactions, contradictory impulses and experiences can be expected to impair its development.

Bourdieu also captures this type of crisis in the habitus in his studies of the uprooted Kabyle people. Bourdieu shows how the rational cost–benefit calculations demanded by their new social world fell into tensions with the old pre-capitalist economic order, which was still partly in place. The uprooted Kabyle people were thus, according to Bourdieu, stuck between conflictual standards resulting in an 'ambiguous reality' in which they could not orient themselves (Bourdieu 1979, 43). Even more significantly, the emerging group of sub-proletarians were blocked from developing a rational orientation. Stuck in a state of insecurity and unpredictability, the sub-proletarians were 'unable to work out a life plan' – leaving them 'totally barred from establishing a rational hierarchy of goals, the precondition for the calculation which is the basis of conduct defined as reasonable in terms of capitalist reason' (Bourdieu 1979, 68). Deprived of the objective preconditions for rational activity, they could not develop a habitual disposition of calculating cost and benefit. The new capitalist economy thus required new rational orientations while, at the same time, undermining the social conditions for such orientations to develop. Bourdieu's studies of the uprooted Kabyle people thus exemplify different ways in which contradictory social processes can disorient people, including by setting up contradictory or impossible social standards.

Third, and most importantly, the subject can become disoriented when the two aforementioned social processes are repeated and become habitual – when the disruptions in our habitus are repeated

147

so often they become normalised into a new habitus. We develop a habit of non-habit – accustoming and adjusting ourselves to a world without sense and meaning.

The habitus of those without a place in the world is a particular disposition that Bourdieu continuously returns to. Systematic disruption, he shows, corresponds to an embodied disposition in which emotional and temporal disequilibrium becomes a state of normality. In Bourdieu's words, 'the permanence of such a state of dependence sometimes brings on a profound demoralization ... Little by little a fatalistic resignation sets in; irresistibly, a parasitic existence becomes natural and then habitual' (Bourdieu 1979, 67). The new habitus is marked by an oscillation between resignation and dreams of a world beyond this. Bourdieu observes this in his interviews with the Algerian sub-proletarians: 'The discourse often proceeds in a jagged line, the leaps into a daydream being followed by relapses into a present that withers all fantasies' (Bourdieu 1979, 69). When the crisis in our habitus itself develops into a habitus, the subject has habitually detached from her real world and everyday life – oscillating between delusion and resignation. Disorientation becomes her mode of orientation.

From the concept of habitus as a condition for our orientation, we have thus derived three disorienting social processes – social disruption, contradiction and the systematic repetition of the former. In the last, and perhaps most extreme, case of disorientation, the social processes of disruption and contradiction become habitual and normalised. These forms of social disorientation can, as the example of the Algerian sub-proletarians reveals, be experienced by dominated groups. Furthermore, social disorientation can be assumed to be experienced by dominant social groups as well. Anyone could experience sudden social change, a sudden change of social status or contradictory social demands. And irrespective of one's social position, the habitus is, in Bourdieu's theory, slow to change. Even someone in an important professional position could, for example, become disoriented by a sudden shift in the professional ethic. However, although both dominated and dominant groups can be disoriented, people in dominated positions are particularly at risk of being caught in the most intense form of disorientation, when disruption turns into a new habitual state. When their lives are disturbed, dominant people may be able to make use of their money, networks or academic degrees to start anew. The highly placed professional, who no longer feels at home in her profession, may have more possibilities to shift to an entirely different workplace. The worker, however, who loses her job when the production plant is outsourced, might not have the same opportunities. When the lives of the dominated are disrupted, they are forced to grab any opportunities they can get – even those that are unstable and undesirable. From a dominated position, it can thus be particularly difficult to escape the state of disruption. Disruption is then likely to turn into a permanent state – obliging one to move from place to place, and between different temporary jobs. In these cases, disorientation turns into alienation.

### Disorientation as a dimension of alienation

In this section, I have drawn on Bourdieu to socially ground disorientation as a dimension of alienation. To be able to appropriate the world – making it your own through action and experimental problem-solving – you must be able to orient yourself in it. Bourdieu's theory of habitus elucidates how our way of navigating and making sense of the world, although it may seem subjective, is formed in our interaction with the social world. Our orientation in the world depends on our habitus – our embodied dispositions or orientations – which emerges over time through repetitive interactions. Disorientation occurs when the social world does not match our habitus. This may happen in disruptive or contradictory social processes as well as in social systems in which these processes are continuously repeated.

Disorientation, according to this understanding, is thus not merely psychological – a problem in the mind of the individual – or existential – an unavoidable part of the human condition. Rather, it is social. It is experienced in some forms of social processes and systems, but not in others. By providing a theory for how disorientation can be understood as a form of social suffering, the concept is radicalised. Disorientation, in our conception, is a social problem that requires political action and common solutions.

However, when socially grounding the concept of disorientation, and thus that of alienation, can it still remain open – avoiding common pitfalls? The concept of disorientation avoids essentialism. The subject is not predefined by a particular type of activity or way of life. She can find meaning in a wide variety of activities, as her way of orienting herself is constructed in her habitual interactions with the social world.

Furthermore, the theory of disorientation avoids the pitfall of idealising a final state of harmony. By reading Jaeggi with Bourdieu, the problem-solving activity of the subject becomes conditioned on her social world. This, however, does not change the underlying assumption of the subject as a problem-solver. The subject is marked by an activity by which she continuously encounters problems and seeks to resolve them – an activity that remains open-ended and never-ending. Given this conception of the subject, a stable state, free of inner and social conflict, is neither possible nor desirable.

Lastly, I want to discuss the pitfall of determinism, which, in this context, is the most difficult to avoid. When a theory is socially grounded, it could easily fall back on the assumption that the subject's actions can be determined by the social structure and her position in it. In Bourdieu's theory, however, important aspects of Marx's determinism are avoided. Although our purposes, values and gut reactions are constructed in our interactions with the social world, this process is contingent, complex and ongoing. At the same time, while there is room for contingency in Bourdieu's theory, the space for free human action – as emphasised, for example, by Hannah Arendt – is limited. The habitus both allows us to navigate the social world and binds us to it. The subject comes to embody and, therefore, often reproduce the social structure – including her own subordination. If I were to solely rely on Bourdieu's theory, I would be left with a theory of disorientation and alienation that leaves only a limited space open for human action.

For this reason, it is important to note that I am reading Bourdieu's theory of habitus alongside Jaeggi's theory of appropriation. My intention is not merely to replace Jaeggi's concept of appropriation – or what I have called orientation – with Bourdieu's concept of habitus. While the concept of habitus can be used to socially ground the concept of appropriation, the notion of appropriation can, in turn, be used to tease out the potential for action that lies dormant in the theory of habitus. The form of social freedom that Jaeggi emphasises – the freedom to make our world, ourselves and our own actions our own – is compatible with the idea of habitus. Although the concept of habitus can help us understand internalised domination, it also has another aspect. The habitus is what allows the subject to skilfully navigate the world. On the one hand, this ability enables the subject to do what is socially expected of her. But, on the other hand, it is also what allows her to do things in her own way. Jaeggi's concept of appropriation points towards the specific freedom that is realised in the activity of orientation. When we are able to skilfully orient ourselves in the world, we can make ourselves, our world and our actions our own. We remain fully ourselves – feeling our freedom and responsibility. Whether realising this freedom means resisting or reproducing existing social structures remains an open question.

Orientation is thus, in our conception, a multifaceted activity – enabling both social reproduction and resistance. This makes disorientation both an impairment to our capacity to act and experiment – to skilfully navigate our social world – as well as a potential for resistance – to break with a structure of domination that no longer makes sense. The possibility of disorientation, then, to some extent, opens up the concepts of habitus to make room not only for contingencies but also for radical breaks and the practice of freedom.

Let us take a closer look at what it means to be both dominated and disoriented – that is, in our conception, to be alienated. As discussed above, there are two sides to alienation. First, alienation is a situation of meaninglessness and powerlessness. When you are dominated and your only choice is that between different forms of subordination, disorientation becomes particularly difficult to overcome. Alienation is a situation in which our disorientation is deepened by domination and vice versa. Second, when making disorientation into an aspect of alienation, alienation becomes not only a blockage to but also a possibility for resistance. Losing your 'sense of the game' also means losing your sense of place. Disorientation may, as Ahmed (2010a) emphasises, motivate the dominated to challenge the structure of domination – to develop 'a revolutionary consciousness'. In order to challenge your place in society, you must be somewhat out of place. In Ahmed's words, 'revolutionary consciousness means feeling at odds with the world, or feeling that the world is odd' (Ahmed 2010b, 168). When we are disoriented, the world appears less natural and so might our own domination.

However, the experience of the world as odd also has a flipside. It can give you a critical distance, but it is also a burden: 'it can feel like a weight that both holds you down and keeps you apart', that makes you 'shift, drop your head, sweat, feel edgy and uncertain' (Ahmed 2010b, 168). As we have seen, when disorientation is experienced in combination with domination, it risks becoming a new embodied disposition: an expectation of thwarted expectations. To resist, both individually and collectively, requires not only a critical distance but also the capacity to find and orient oneself. When alienated, we lack both social opportunities – objects to constructively use – and practical understanding – the capacity that allows us to use those opportunities that we actually have. We cannot act and experiment. Alienation as domination and disorientation thus becomes both a problem and a possibility for political action and mobilisation.

## CONCLUSION

In this chapter, I have drawn on the work of Jaeggi, Marx and Bourdieu in order to radicalise the concept of alienation as impaired appropriation while, at the same time, maintaining its openness. In the resulting conceptualisation, the subject is alienated when she is dominated (when others systematically appropriate social power at her expense) and disoriented (when her practical understanding is socially impaired).

Each of the two dimensions of alienation – domination and disorientation – has been formulated in such a way that it should, as far as possible, avoid the pitfalls of determinism, human essentialism and idealising a final state of harmony. However, while the concept of domination that constitutes one of the dimensions of alienation is more open than Marx's concept of exploitation, it is not in itself fully open. In particular, it remains to be examined if the theory of alienation, when the concept of domination is combined with that of disorientation, avoids idealising harmony. In the next chapter, I will thus examine whether my attempt to reconstruct the concept of alienation in an open and radical way is successful, and how alienation, in our conception, can be distinguished from other, closely related concepts.

## NOTES

1. According to Marx, only communism implies the 'real appropriation of the human essence' (Marx 1975a, 296).
2. 'The sum total of these relations of production constitutes the economic structure of society, the real foundation, on which rises a legal and political superstructure and to which correspond definite forms of social consciousness' (Marx 1972d, 4).
3. The understanding of the relation between Marx's early and later

writings on alienation differ. Here, I follow Ollman's (1976) reading of *Capital* and the theory of surplus value as a refinement of theories already present in the *Economic and Philosophical Manuscripts of 1844* (Ollman 1976, 166). The theory of surplus value is read as a development of the theory of alienation (Ollman 1976, chap. 26). This approach differs somewhat from, for example, David Harvey's (2018) recent attempt to formulate a distinct concept of alienation based only on Marx's later writings, such as *Grundrisse* (Harvey 2018, 425).

4. 'Hence, the historical movement which changes the producers into wage workers, appears, on the one hand, as their emancipation from serfdom and from the fetters of the guilds, and this side alone exists for our bourgeois historians. But, on the other hand, these new freedmen became sellers of themselves only after they had been robbed of all their own means of production, and of all the guarantees of existence afforded by the old feudal arrangements' (Marx 1972a, 433).

5. Marx distinguishes between 'absolute surplus value' – stemming from the extension of the working day beyond the necessary labour time – and 'relative surplus value' – which stems from increased productivity due to technological and organisational innovation (for a short summary, see Harvey 2018, 26).

6. In his writings on exploitation, Nicholas Vrousalis (2013) conceptualises exploitation as a particular form of domination – domination for self-enrichment. Richard Bellamy (2007) argues instead that while domination, exploitation and oppression all signify unequal relations of power, domination does not necessarily involve the actual exercise of power, whereas exploitation and oppression do (Bellamy 2007, 151; see also Medearis 2015, 103; Pettit 1999, 78–9; Young 2011, 38).

7. Critics have pointed out both the potential of and remaining gaps in understanding Bourdieu's cultural theory as an expansion of Marx's theory of exploitation. See Beasley-Murray (2000, 111) for review, as well as a relevant discussion on how Bourdieu's theory can be developed into a theory of exploitation in which *time* would be conceived as the central source of value.

8. Bourdieu even occasionally refers to this as 'exploitation' (e.g. Bourdieu 2010, 192).

9. Bourdieu defines social capital as 'the aggregate of the actual or potential resources which are linked to possession of a durable network of more or less institutionalized relationships of mutual acquaintance and recognition – or in other words, to membership in a group – which provides each of its members with the backing of the collectively owned capital, a "credential" which entitles them to credit, in the various senses of the word' (Bourdieu 2011, 86).

10. See, for example, Michèle Lamont's (1992, 2009) comprehensive studies

on 'moral boundaries'. Drawing partly on the work of Bourdieu, she examines cultural divisions between as well as within the middle and working classes.

11. Bourdieu's theory of domination also goes beyond the discussion on capital, including other forms of symbolic domination, such as masculine domination (Bourdieu 2001). For this reason, the concept of class in Bourdieu's theory has been both praised for its complexity (Weininger 2002, 159) and criticised for being too inflated to lend itself to empirical research (Riley 2017, 113).

12. In so far as the theory is material, it is in the sense of new materialism – focusing on a materiality of the body (see Ahmed 2010a).

# CHAPTER FIVE

## *Alienation versus acedia*

Recall Jacob, Samira, Thomas and Emma from the Introduction. Caught in processes of precarisation, they all experience an inhibition in their relationship to the world in such a way that their relations to themselves become dysfunctional. The professional paths on which they had set out, as well as the social relations and forms of freedom associated with them, have gradually vanished. Thomas, stuck in unemployment, has lost the source of empowerment and relations of solidarity that a job, albeit a hard one, had offered. Samira, an educated journalist, can only get temporary jobs; the work she gets does not offer the professional integrity and freedom that had drawn her to the profession in the first place. Jacob lingers in uncertainty, stuck in an education that does not seem to be leading anywhere. His expectation, that education could lead to a new path in life, has been thwarted. And while Emma is still able to keep her job as a teacher, she sees her professional freedom continuously being undermined, leaving her unable to find herself in her work.

Having lost the object of identification from which they drew meaning, Jacob, Samira, Thomas and Emma are caught in precarious positions, lacking real options on how to manage their daily lives. To address these situations – in which the subject's relation to the object is disrupted and inhibited in such a way that her relation to herself becomes dysfunctional – we need a concept of alienation.

In the previous chapter, I reconstructed the concept of alienation in such a way that it should be able to address the meaninglessness and powerlessness experienced by dominated groups in societies marked not only by inequality but also by disorder and dislocation. Alienation is then conceptualised as an experience of domination – whereby others systematically appropriate social power at the subject's expense – and disoriented – whereby the subject's practical understanding is socially impaired. In other words, *the subject is alienated – her appropriation is impaired – when she is dominated and disoriented.*

In this chapter, I will examine this concept more closely. First, I study how the concept of alienation can be distinguished from other, similar concepts. Second, I examine whether it lives up to my criteria for an open and radical theory. Lastly, I return to Rahel Jaeggi's concept of alienation and argue that one of the distinct strengths of our reconstructed concept is its ability to distinguish between alienation and acedia – the painful uneasiness experienced by the dominant when they are disoriented.

## DEFINING AND DISTINGUISHING THE CONCEPT OF ALIENATION

The subject is alienated when she is dominated and disoriented. The concept of alienation and its dimensions are described and exemplified in Table 5.1.

Table 5.1 Disorientation, domination and alienation

| Disorientation | Domination | Alienation |
|---|---|---|
| The subject's practical sense-making is socially impaired. | Others appropriate social power at the subject's expense. | The subject's appropriation is impaired in the sense that she is both dominated and disorientated. |
| *Example:* A researcher does not feel at home in academia as it becomes increasingly dominated by a financial logic of productivity. She finds herself increasingly writing and publishing things she cannot commit to or care about. | *Example:* A man works at a car factory. Although the hours are long and his salary is low, he has little choice but to stay at the factory. | *Example:* When the production of the car factory is outsourced, the man loses his job, and he is unable to find a new one. Exhausted, he does not know what to do any more. |

The subject is alienated when she experiences a disorientation that is deepened by domination. Her dispositions and intuitions do not match the world in which she lives, making her unable to make sense of and find her way in the world. When she is alienated, this situation is aggravated by domination. The subject is stuck in a social position in which others appropriate social power at her expense. Her activity of appropriation – action and experimental problem-solving – is impaired. She lacks the opportunities to make constructive use of her time, and she cannot see the point in trying.

As suggested in the previous chapter, the situations of Jacob, Samira, Thomas and Emma can all be interpreted as examples of alienation understood as domination and disorientation. Thomas, having lost his job at the car factory when it got outsourced, is not merely exposed to the economic domination of others, he has also lost his world as he knew it: of long but regular work hours and union organising. Jacob finds that the business degree he is pursuing is not reputable enough to land him a job. Lacking cultural and social capital, he is vulnerable to domination in both the job market and the educational market. However, refusing to return to the social milieu in which he grew up, Jacob is stuck in an educational system in which he cannot orient himself. Samira – as an educated journalist – and Emma – a teacher whose professional status is gradually undermined – are on the verge of losing the cultural worlds in which they were once at home. Unable to make use of their cultural capital, they are left in situations where their options are severely limited. Lacking alternatives, Samira finds herself working for little or no salary, accepting jobs she finds unethical. Emma sees her work burden increase while her ability to control her own work diminishes. Both Samira's and Emma's professional autonomy is undermined to the extent that they are not only left disoriented – unable to navigate themselves and find meaning in their job – but also possibly dominated. Jacob, Samira, Thomas and Emma could all be considered both dominated and disoriented, and would thus, in our conception, be alienated.

The concept of alienation – defined as both domination and disorientation – thus captures contemporary experiences of precarisation. It addresses the meaninglessness and powerlessness experienced by dominated groups in societies marked not only by deepened inequality and dependence but also by increasing disorder and dislocation. When alienated, you are thrown back and forth by social

157

forces that you cannot predict or resist. The only form of resistance available to the alienated subject, whose sense of orientation is inhibited, is negation. As Pierre Bourdieu notices, '[r]evolutionary chiliasm and magical utopias are the only grasp on the future that offers itself' to this subject (Bourdieu 1979, 70). The possibility of resistance is an important question that we will return to in the next chapter. For now, it suffices to note that the alienated subject is not only dominated but also disoriented, and that this means that she cannot engage with the world as it is – neither actively sustaining it nor working for its transformation. Thus, the alienated subject can merely reject or resign herself to reality, not actively engage to challenge it. To understand the specificity of the concept of alienation, I will compare it with two similar situations – resilience and acedia – as well as its opposite – social ease.

The concept of alienation should be distinguished from its related concepts, as captured in Table 5.2.

First, alienation is related but cannot be reduced to resilience – the situation in which one is dominated but maintains the capacity to find and orient oneself in the world. To be resilient means to be able to withstand adversity, for example by adapting and developing. Notice that I am not referring to resilience primarily as the capacity to withstand a sudden crisis. Rather, what the resilient subject is able to withstand is her own subordination. Although she has few real options or opportunities, the resilient subject still discovers ways to

Table 5.2 Distinguishing alienation from acedia, resilience and ease

|  | Oriented | Disoriented |
|---|---|---|
| Dominant[a] | Ease | Acedia |
| Dominated | Resilience | Alienation |

[a] Recall that in a society organised by capital – which functions through scarcity – one subject's appropriation of capital always implies that someone else is blocked from appropriating it. For this reason, those who are not dominated are, to some degree, able to dominate others. I have, therefore, chosen to use the categories of 'dominated' and 'dominant', rather than, for example, 'dominated' and 'undominated' in the table. However, the categories of dominant and dominated are not a clear-cut dichotomy. Instead, people can be more or less dominant depending on social context. In many cases, the subject may, rather, find herself in between these two positions and would, thus, be difficult to place in the table. It can, for example, be difficult to decide whether someone suffers from alienation or acedia.

take command over her life and find meaning in the world. She is able to find herself in the social processes and positions she is in, including, for example, her work at the warehouse – finding creative ways of arranging products on the shelves – or her role as a mother – finding ways to put money aside for her children's college education.

Resilience means active engagement in the social world – in the sense of both reproducing and resisting it. The resilient subject might be successively playing her part in the social order – maintaining her dominated position and making it meaningful. However, resilience can also take the form of resistance. Such resistance can involve both individual quotidian acts, such as standing up for yourself and demanding respect when the manager treats you and other employees unfairly, and collective action, like joining a union and going on strike. Irrespective of which form resistance takes, you understand your conditions and are able to navigate through them.

However, it should be noted that although you need some grasp of a social system in order to resist it, it is not a sufficient condition for resistance. For this, you must, for instance, have acquired a critical distance from this system. To develop such a critical stance, resilience, can – but does not have to – be a blockage. If you are resilient enough to be able to navigate the social world from a dominated position, you might be less motivated to criticise it. On the other hand, if you actually do resist it, resilience means that you have sufficient practical understanding of the world to do so effectively.

Second, alienation should be distinguished from acedia, what Walter Benjamin describes as a 'heaviness at heart' (Benjamin 2009). Acedia can be understood as a sense of unease or negligence. In our definition, when a dominant subject is disoriented, she does not suffer from alienation but from acedia. The subject has the room to manoeuvre but has lost her flow. Every step is heavy. Although she has options, she cannot really see them. Her disposition, values and gut reactions no longer correspond to the social world in which she finds herself. What previously just happened by itself no longer makes sense to her – leaving her uncomfortable and uneasy.

Acedia, as a form of social disorientation, emerges in relation to social processes – including social change or a change in social position that sweeps you up in a process over which you feel out of control. This would be the case with the researcher who no longer feels at home in academia due to an ongoing logic of calculability and productivity. The academic finds that her work and, to a certain

159

extent, her life appear increasingly meaningless. Furthermore, as acedia is experienced from a dominant position, it might also involve participating in acts of domination that make you uneasy. For example, a woman from a working-class background gets offered a position as a manager within a type of business to which she has always been opposed. While accepting the job, she cannot feel at home in her dominant position. Acedia can be a moral uneasiness or a painful negligence of your own conscience.

Third, the concept of alienation can also be defined in relation to its opposite: social ease. When experiencing social ease, the actor is able to appropriate not only the world and her own activity but also the activity of others. She easily manoeuvres within social systems – as a manager, technician or artist. When she encounters problems or falls into conflict with others, she resolves them with ease – an ease that comes not only from having social power but also from knowing why and how she should be using it.

Our concept of alienation allows us to distinguish the alienated not only from those who experience social ease but also from those who are resilient and who experience acedia. In practice, however, it is important to notice that we cannot expect there to be a ready-made social group collective that corresponds to the category of the alienated. This is both a potential strength and a challenge with the concept of alienation. It can give some guidance to, but not determine, the limits of the political struggle against the problem of alienation. I will return to this issue in the last chapter, when I examine how the radical democratic strategy for political mobilisation should be reformulated in response to the problem of alienation. For now, however, we can merely note that a real political movement against alienation cannot mobilise according to any given social category, but would have to be shaped in an open and complex way, where participants from a multiplicity of social milieus actively listen to each other's claims.

## RADICAL AND OPEN?

The aim has been to formulate a concept of alienation that is both radical – retaining a dimension of social suffering, power and antagonism – and open – avoiding the pitfalls of human essentialism, determinism and the ideal of a final state of harmony. Does the concept of alienation as domination and disorientation live up to these criteria?

By drawing on conceptual resources from Marx and Bourdieu, the concept of alienation as impaired appropriation has been radicalised in three senses. First, the concept of alienation has been linked to that of domination. Domination, and thus alienation, is located in systemic unequal relations of power, where one social group – the dominant – systematically appropriates the time and activity of another group – the dominated. Second, this means that alienation involves a form of power that is partly agent-driven and that benefits one agent at the expense of another. The concept of domination thus draws attention to social division and antagonism, making it suitable to be mobilised for political struggle. Third, alienation in its other dimension – what I have called disorientation – has been developed into a form of social suffering – taking place in relation to certain social systems and processes. I have established that our capacity to orient ourselves in the world depends on what Bourdieu calls our habitus, which in turn depends on social processes. When the subject is caught in contradictory or disruptive social processes and systems, her habitus can fall into crisis – leaving her disoriented.

The concept of alienation thus captures a form of suffering that is social rather than subjective and interprets this suffering in a context of social power and antagonism. Alienation means that some people benefit from others' disadvantage. Overcoming suffering thus involves a struggle against those in power. But while it is radical, is the concept also open?

Radicalising the concept comes, as we have seen, with the risk of lapsing into human essentialism, or the assumption that the subject can be predefined by a particular type of activity or way of life; determinism, the assumption that the subject's actions are determined by the social structure and her position in it; and idealising a final state of harmony, the assumption that a stable state free of inner and social conflict is possible and desirable.

Recall, first, how Jaeggi avoids the pitfall of *human essentialism* by broadening and abstracting the conception of human activity. Appropriation can take place in many ways, not merely, as in Marx's theory, through labour. Human essentialism is thus avoided. However, in my attempt to radicalise the theory of alienation, I have brought back elements of Marx's concept. Have I, with this, also lapsed into essentialism?

By drawing on Bourdieu's theory of domination, I have sought to enlarge Marx's concept of alienation and its related concept of exploitation. In Bourdieu's theory, many different activities, not merely labour, are valuable to human beings. There are no essentialist restrictions on what the subject can do and find meaning in. Bourdieu emphasises at least three types of activity that people value: cultural activity – such as reading and creating art; social activity – such as taking care of a family member or joining a political organisation; and economic activity – wage labour. Each of these activities corresponds to a form of value or capital – cultural, social and economic – that cannot be reduced to another. When one social group dominate another, they monopolise a particular form of capital, thus blocking the other's appropriation of it. As such, appropriation and domination can take place in many spheres of life. As the sphere of human activity, and its impairment, is enlarged, human essentialism is avoided.

And yet, a potential problem remains. Although cultural capital and social capital function separately from economic capital, and although the possession of one does not guarantee the possession of another, transaction is possible. And even though Bourdieu emphasises the monopolisation of any type of capital as a form of domination, economic capital remains his priority. Both social and cultural capital ultimately depend on their relation to economic capital. If transaction becomes impossible, they lose their function as capital.

Here, we see an important trace of Marx's concept of exploitation in Bourdieu's theory. The underlying power relation seems, in my analysis, to be the monopolisation of the means of subsistence, which, in modern society, depends mainly on economic capital. Without economic capital, we become vulnerable to domination, truly lacking alternatives if we are to sustain ourselves. By emphasising economic capital and activity, we risk falling back into the assumption of the human subject as essentially a producer.

However, in emphasising the distinct functioning of each type of capital, Bourdieu avoids this essentialism. Cultural, social and economic activity remain separate and valued for different reasons and, often, by different people. Although the different forms of capital to which they correspond – cultural, social and economic – can be transformed into one another, this process is far from straightforward. Transformation is costly, slow and hard to predict. For example, the accumulation of cultural capital may take years, and the result might still not be successful, or at least not equally so as it would be for someone who had cultural capital to begin with. Although

162

linked, each form of capital belongs to separate social processes. In emphasising the underlying relation of exploitation – that of monopoly over the means of subsistence – while significantly broadening it and emphasising the irreducibility of different forms of activity, the theory of domination enlarges the concept of exploitation while maintaining its key power relation: the monopolisation of value and, ultimately, over the means of subsistence.

Having seen that, in most relevant respects, the concept of alienation avoids the pitfall of human essentialism, let us instead turn to that of *determinism*. Recall that Jaeggi avoids it by relying on a conception of the subject marked by appropriation – an activity that is experimental and open-ended. My aim has been to socially ground the concept of appropriation, in particular in the dimension of orientation, while maintaining its experimental character. For this, I turned to Bourdieu's concept of habitus. The habitus – the subject's embodied disposition – allows the subject to understand and navigate the world. It is constituted throughout the subject's life in repetitive social interactions. The idea of habitus thus provides a theory for how our ability to orient ourselves depends on, and can be impaired through, social processes. At the same time, the theory of habitus is compatible with the conception of the subject as experimental and open-ended. The habitus does not, like a rule, determine how we act. As we saw in Chapter 4, habitus can be described as the subject's 'sense of the game'. The best player is rarely the predictable one, who rigidly follows a set of strict guidelines; it is someone who invents new and surprising manoeuvres. The more skilfully the subject is able to navigate, the more freely she can move. The habitus is what allows us to solve problems and respond to new challenges in an open-ended and experimental way. While the concept of habitus can be used to socially ground the concept of alienation, it also maintains an element of spontaneity and contingency.

However, while it allows for contingency, the theory of habitus does not, at least initially, seem to leave much space for human freedom. The subject's habitus develops in her early interactions with her social world. Already as a child, she begins to learn how the world is ordered and what her place is in it. Learning how to capably navigate the world also means learning to reproduce the world as it is – including one's own social position. When drawing on the theory of habitus, we come to rely on a subject who has deeply internalised the

163

social structure and her position in it. The subject is not determined by the social structure, but her freedom within it is restricted.

At the same time, in reading the theory of habitus alongside Jaeggi's theory of alienation, one can tease out the potential for human freedom that lies dormant in Bourdieu's theory in two ways. First, the idea that the subject's orientation can be impaired – that she can become disoriented – can, to some extent, open up the theory. Disorientation should be understood as an impairment of our capacity to act and experiment, as well as a potential for resistance. It means that we can fail to reproduce the social structure and its relations of power. The possibility of disorientation, largely corresponding to what Bourdieu calls *déracinement* or 'uprooting', is not emphasised by Bourdieu but becomes important in the theory of alienation.

At the same time, our conception of disorientation differs from that of contemporary cultural theory, in that it emphasises to a greater extent the empowering potential of orientation and the disempowering aspect of disorientation and alienation. As we have seen, when disorientation is experienced in combination with domination, it risks becoming a new embodied disposition – an expectation of disrupted expectations. To resist, individually as well as collectively, requires not only a critical distance but also the capacity to find and orient oneself. When alienated, we lack both objects to constructively use and the practical understanding that allows us to do so. We cannot act and experiment. Alienation as domination and disorientation thus becomes both a problem and a possibility for political action and mobilisation.

Second, by drawing on Jaeggi's theory we tease out the capacity for authenticity and individuality that marks a subject constituted by a habitus. Reading Bourdieu with Jaeggi sheds light on an important, but rarely emphasised, potential of Bourdieu's subject to appropriate herself and her world. The habitus can easily be read merely as a form of internalised domination – making Bourdieu's subject capable only of social reproduction. Jaeggi, however, shows us that there is another side to skilful orientation: the ability to make ourselves and our actions our own. The idea of appropriation as orientation opens up a space for the individual subject. It emphasises the potential of the subject to act in authentic and unexpected ways – a potential that remains even as we assume that the capacity for orientation depends on a functioning habitus.

Jaeggi's concept of appropriation shows us that being able to orient oneself in the world does not merely involve internalised power. On the contrary, our self-imposed limitations are often even stricter when we are insecure and cannot fully make sense of the social situation that we are in. Jaeggi illustrates this with her example of the 'ambitious junior editor, who has his hair cut, buys himself a suit that fits just a little too well, and begins to imitate his boss's mannerisms' (Jaeggi 2014, 69). The junior editor is unable to orient and find himself in his milieu and his role. He rigidly follows his boss's manners. When we are disoriented, we might try so hard that we lose ourselves and our ability to resist. Conversely, imagine, for example, a worker who has worked for many years at the car factory and is engaged within a union. She knows exactly how her world functions and her place within it – but also how to mobilise resistance.

Even if we cannot rely fully on the potential for disorientation to maintain the openness of the subject, we can do so by emphasising the subject's potential to, even when her options are severely delimited, do things her own way: to be herself. This potential is maintained precisely in the situation where the subject is able to orient herself. Orientation does not only mean internalised domination; and disorientation does not necessarily mean emancipation. This realisation is central to our concept of alienation and distinguishes it both from common readings of the theory of habitus and from the concept of disorientation in contemporary cultural theory.

The last, and perhaps most important, pitfall that we have sought to avoid is *the ideal of a final state of harmony*: the assumption that a stable state free of inner and social conflict is possible and desirable. This, as we have seen, is an assumption strongly associated with the theory of alienation – and, in particular, in its most radical conceptions. It suggests that when we have overcome our alienation and the social antagonism to which it is linked, we are in harmony with ourselves, each other and our social world at large. The risk is that in associating alienation with domination and antagonism, we also assume that once alienation is overcome, so is conflict. Politics becomes superfluous.

Domination, as I have conceptualised it, is a social problem, which should, at least in theory, be possible to overcome. However, this does not mean that all types of conflict are eradicable. Instead, I will argue, we must distinguish between two forms of conflict. When we suppress one, we spur the other.

165

Conflict of the first type is theoretically ineradicable; it is intrinsic to the process of appropriation constitutive of the subject. The subject constitutes herself and the world through problem-solving – an activity that, by definition, cannot take place without problems. In the activity of appropriation, the subject encounters something that is foreign to her and makes it her own. In this process, both she and the initially foreign object change. The process presupposes both an adversarial dimension – a distinction between an 'I' and an 'other' – and some form of resolution.

Such a resolution, however, does not imply harmony. In Jaeggi's words, 'The openness of the process of appropriation and its experimental character imply that overcoming alienation need not be described as a "coming to oneself" or as reconciliation but can be conceived of instead as an open-ended and never-ending process' (Jaeggi 2014, 153). The subject's problem-solving is an ongoing activity without any final resolution. And since appropriation is an ongoing activity without any end point, overcoming alienation – impaired appropriation – does not imply harmony. On the contrary, it involves conflict and difference. To assume a subject constituted through appropriation – an activity of experimental problem-solving – means assuming that, at least some form of, conflict is ineradicable.

The second form of conflict is social, stemming from our alienation and, in particular, the risk of antagonism inherent in its dimension of domination. In the process of domination, the dominant use their power to appropriate the activity of the dominated to accumulate more social power. In societies ordered by capital and domination, the subject's activity of appropriation turns into a competition that can, at any time, erupt into antagonism. This conflict has social roots and can therefore, at least in theory, be eradicated.

However, an end to alienation and the conflict it breeds is practically unlikely. Alienating social processes are marked by two interlinked dimensions – domination and disorientation. Domination is highly conflictual and, by its very dynamic, almost impossible to finally overcome. It is a dynamic that resembles that of exploitation, where a small imbalance in power eventually increases. According to Bourdieu, this mainly takes place in modern society through its institutions, such as the labour market or education. And, when we seek to reform one of these institutions, power may conceal itself by moving into another. As we have seen, power can take on many forms; it can be economic, cultural or social. For instance, when we make reforms to delimit the power of economic capital – say, by tax reforms – capital can be converted to more subtle forms, such as cultural capital.[1] The modern dynamic of domination – where small differences grow exponentially, and where power can conceal itself – means that power inequalities will continuously reappear. Domination is thus hard to eradicate, and so is the antagonism that it breeds. In combination with disorientation – which impairs our ability to accurately make sense of problems and resolve them – this becomes even harder.

Alienation is a form of domination that is particularly difficult to overcome. When the subject is alienated – when her domination is deepened by disorientation – she cannot accurately make sense of the world and accurately respond to problems – including the problem of domination. To be able to accurately respond to problems is crucial for overcoming them. For example, according to Rahel Jaeggi and Nancy Fraser, the struggle against capitalism has continuously failed to identify and attack the root of the problem, and, for this reason, capitalism has continuously been able to preserve itself by transforming into a new mode (Fraser and Jaeggi 2018, 13–15). While alienation and the social antagonism that it involves is thus, in theory, possible to overcome, the attempts to do so are, in practice, unlikely to succeed completely.

In capturing two forms of conflict, where only one can be quenched at a time, the concept of alienation escapes the pitfall of idealising harmony. The subject is herself constituted by her engagement with difference and conflict. And as this activity is impaired – when the subject is alienated – conflict risks emerging in another, more antagonistic, form. Erasing all forms of conflict is thus neither possible nor desirable.

Thus, finding a concept of alienation that is both radical and open does not come without challenges. However, in reconstructing alienation as domination and disorientation, the concept is not only radicalised but also made more open. Before concluding this chapter, I will return to Jaeggi's theory and examine how our reconstructed concept of alienation differs from hers.

## ALIENATION VERSUS ACEDIA

Having radicalised the concept of alienation as impaired appropriation, it is now possible to compare it with Rahel Jaeggi's theory. Our concept of alienation both retains central elements of Jaeggi's theory – in particular the idea of alienation as impaired appropriation – and rethinks it – locating it in unequal power relations. I will show that when alienation is reconstructed as a form of domination, it comes to include other subjects and situations than Jaeggi's theory. The theory comes to address a broader spectrum of marginalised people, including people like Jacob, Samira, Thomas and Emma from the Introduction. A central distinction that I introduce is that between those who are alienated – dominated and disoriented – and those who suffer from acedia – disorientation experienced from a dominant position.

## Jaeggi's alienation as acedia

Jaeggi's examples of alienated subjects include, among others, a researcher who has become indifferent to his work, and a previously bohemian man who – without knowing how he got there – is living a conventional suburban family life. The fact that neither of the men appears to belong to any of the most marginalised groups in society is perhaps not just a coincidence. Recall that, in Jaeggi's theory, the alienated subject 'experiences a process that she can in principle influence (or should be able to influence) as beyond her influence – or that something that can in fact be decided on appears to her as if it could not be'. According to Jaeggi, the alienation of the bohemian man can be 'traced back to a lack of awareness of the possibilities of action that are open to him' (Jaeggi 2014, 57). Jaeggi's concept of alienation concerns people with options but without awareness of them – thus making the indifferent researcher and the previously bohemian man, who, presumably, both have many possibilities available to them, typical examples of alienation. According to Jaeggi, the presence of possibilities distinguishes alienation from 'straightforward coercion or manipulation' (Jaeggi 2014, 51). Not having options means, in her terms, being 'coerced' or 'manipulated' – not alienated. What I have called alienation, Jaeggi describes as coercion.

Jaeggi's concept of alienation thus differs from our reconstructed concept. In a society structured by relations of domination – where some systematically appropriate and monopolise social power at the expense of others – the theory of alienation becomes a theory mainly for those who remain relatively powerful, capable of dominating others. It addresses itself to those with many possibilities rather than those who lack significant options. Recall how domination, like exploitation, is sustained by a lack of options. In Jaeggi's theory, Marx's worker, who has to sell her labour to the capitalist in order to sustain herself, would not be alienated. The worker has no real choice: she can only choose which capitalist to work for. The typical example of an alienated subject, in Jaeggi's conception, would thus not be Marx's worker but a subject with sufficient capital to keep her options open. From our perspective, this means turning the terms on their head. Alienation is, in our theory, a concept for the dominated – not the relatively powerful.

Jaeggi successfully distinguishes her concept of alienation from what she calls coercion or manipulation. At the same time, however, the concept loses its capacity to capture the experience of the subject who lacks real options – including the experience of subjects who, in a society ordered by capital and relations of domination, would be dominated. While one of my central aims in reconstructing the concept of alienation was to capture experiences of relative subordination, Jaeggi, to a greater extent, leaves this work to other concepts.

Table 5.3 illustrates how Jaeggi's concept of alienation distinguishes itself from other concepts with respect to the subject's domination and disorientation. If we compare this with Table 5.2, outlining our reconstructed concept of alienation, we can see that many of the situations that I would categorise as alienation would, for Jaeggi, be considered manipulation or coercion. Conversely, many of the situations that Jaeggi would consider to be alienation would, in our conception, fall under the category of acedia.

Consider, for example, Jaeggi's description of the bohemian man who has a child and soon finds himself living a conventional suburban family life. For Jaeggi, the suburban family man is a typical case of alienation, whereas, in our conception, he is just as likely to suffer from acedia. The man – uprooted from the cultural bohemian milieu in which he felt at home – is likely to be disoriented. His bohemian,

Table 5.3 Distinguishing Jaeggi's concept of alienation from coercion and social freedom

|  | Oriented | Disoriented |
| --- | --- | --- |
| Dominant | Social freedom | Alienation |
| Dominated | Coercion | Coercion |

cultural disposition does not match his new, conventional suburban milieu. However, while he is suffering from disorientation, he is not necessarily dominated. He was not, for example, economically obliged to move to a suburb; it just felt like the right thing to do once he had a child. What for Jaeggi is a typical case of alienation could, in my conception, be a situation of acedia.

## Why distinguish alienation from acedia?

Our concept of alienation, in which alienation is a form of domination, does not include everyone. It might even, as we have seen, exclude some of the cases that in Jaeggi's conception would have been typical of alienation. This might initially seem problematic. Recall from Chapter 1 that the left in the post-war period turned from a focus on exploitation to focusing on alienation because the concept of alienation was considered more inclusive. When the concept of alienation is linked to domination – a similar concept to that of exploitation – it can no longer appeal to everyone. Why, then, do we distinguish alienation from acedia?

Recall from Chapter 4 that the general reason for adding a dimension of domination to the concept of alienation was to radicalise the theory. In relation to this overarching aim, there are at least three particular reasons why a concept of alienation linked to domination and distinguished acedia is more suitable as a left concept of alienation.

First, a concept of alienation distinguished from that of acedia addresses itself specifically and directly to marginalised groups. While a theory of alienation that does not take domination into account is general enough to capture the experiences of many people, it will explicitly – like Jaeggi in her attempt to distinguish alienation from coercion – or subtly – by failing to capture the specificity of the situation of the marginalised – exclude important cases of marginalisation. This is not suitable for a radical left theory, which should function as a tool for marginalised groups.

Second, a concept of alienation linked to that of domination is more apt for addressing the form of alienation – of dysfunctional relations to the world and to oneself – that is most likely to trigger the social struggle that the left seeks. Although the concept of alienation has traditionally often included the dominant, it is in relation to the dominated that the concept becomes particularly forceful and potentially mobilising. For example, in a comprehensive study of Walmart workers in the US, sociologists Adam Reich and Peter Bearman (2018) found that although resistance and unionisation were almost impossible under contemporary working conditions at warehouses, some workers were still mobilised. What inspired the workers' engagement were what they perceived as unfair differences and abuse of power, manifesting as acts of disrespect and micro-aggressions. When alienation is linked to the concept of domination, it can capture this abuse of power. Our concept of alienation, by being linked to that of domination, thus maintains the particular strength of the concept of alienation: its capacity to address situations that not only hinders but also inspires resistance.

Third, and for this reason, a concept of alienation that fails to make sense of domination risks becoming reconciliatory rather than mobilising. This would make it more suitable as a concept for the left – aiming not only at unifying people but also at mobilising them. It is when linked to a concept of exploitation or domination that the concept of alienation really becomes one of struggle.

At the same time, as we have seen, our concept of alienation, in being distinguished from that of acedia, is radicalised without losing important aspects of its openness. When we base our concept of domination, and thus that of alienation, on Bourdieu's theory it becomes less restrictive than Marx's theories of exploitation and alienation. 'The dominated' is a more inclusive and flexible category than that of 'the worker'. Our concept of alienation is thus oppositional while remaining complex and relatively inclusionary.

## CONCLUSION

My aim has been to reconstruct a concept of alienation that is genuinely radical – retaining a dimension of social suffering, power and antagonism – yet open – avoiding the pitfalls of human essentialism, determinism and the ideal of harmony. In the resulting concept, *the subject is alienated – her appropriation is impaired – when she is dominated and disoriented*. This concept of alienation allows us to distinguish alienation – a form of domination deepened by disorientation – from acedia – the unease experienced by the dominant when they become disoriented. With this, the concept of alienation is radicalised – capturing social suffering as well as unequal power relations and social antagonism.

171

The question of conflict and antagonism is central. As a more conflictual concept of alienation – where alienation partly stems from the domination of one group over another – it maintains the potential not only to capture the disempowering effects of the social suffering that alienation involves but also to mobilise political struggle. The theory of alienation shows how some forms of conflict – those triggered by domination – could, at least theoretically, be overcome. At the same time, it opens up a space for continuous, ineradicable conflict – the form of conflict involved in the free, unalienated activity of the problem-solving subject. The distinction between these two forms of conflict is key for maintaining both the openness and the radicalism of the concept of alienation and thus, as we will see, for integrating the concept into the theory of radical democracy.

## Notes

1. In Bourdieu's words, 'the more the official transmission of capital is prevented or hindered, the more the effects of the clandestine circulation of capital in the form of cultural capital become determinant in the reproduction of the social structure' (Bourdieu 2011, 90).

# PART III

# Against alienation:
# Redirecting radical democracy

# CHAPTER SIX

# *Reformulating agonistic democracy and its subject*

The aim of Chantal Mouffe's radical democracy – both as a normative theory of agonistic democracy and as a political strategy – is the open and radical mobilisation of people experiencing marginalisation. Consequently, this requires a subject who is both open and radical. When experiencing marginalisation, the subject should be ready to listen, but also to fight. While these demands may initially seem contradictory, they are not. The reason for this, I showed in Chapter 2, is that Mouffe's theory comes to fall back on three underlying assumptions about the subject: the subject as flexible, strong and conflict-seeking. The subject, thus conceived, is both committed enough to be radical and sufficiently disconnected to be open.

At the same time, I pointed out that this is precisely where agonistic democracy risks becoming socially weightless – unable to address social suffering experienced by marginalised groups in society. The open and radical subject – who can act even when deeply disconnected – cannot be alienated. Radical democracy is left unable to theoretically accommodate and politically address marginalisation in the form of alienation. The first part of the study thus left us with a challenge: to find a subject who can, at least theoretically, be both open and radical, but who is also capable of experiencing alienation. Is there a subject that can accommodate alienation – and can it still be open and radical?

In this chapter, I seek to reformulate the subject of agonistic democracy to include alienation without undermining or creating a tension between the openness and radicalism of the theory. More specifically, I examine, first, how the subject can be reformulated to include alienation. Second, I study whether it is possible to integrate this conception of the subject into agonistic democracy without creating a conflict between its aims, those aims being an open and radical political practice. Third, I reformulate the theoretical approach that underpins both the agonistic model of democracy and the radical democratic strategy in order to adjust it to the new conception of the subject. I discuss whether the theory, thus conceived, still remains open and radical – if it remains radical democratic.

## REFORMULATING THE SUBJECT

### The problem with the agonistic democratic subject

Recall from the first part of the book that Mouffe's agonistic democracy corresponds to an individual subject who is both open – capable of responding to new claims and to form plural associations with people of diverse opinions – and radical – able to passionately commit to a political association that seeks to challenge and transform existing power relations. However, while these demands first appeared to fall into tension – requiring a subject who is both passionately committed and able to, at any time, let go of her commitments – they do not. Mouffe's theory, I argued, relies on an underlying conception of the subject as what I called an agonist. The agonist can be described as flexible, capable choosing her own object of identification; strong, relying on nothing but herself in willing and acting; and conflict-seeking, spurred into action by conflict itself. The subject thus conceived reacts to disruptions and inhibitions in her social relations in a particular way. She is capable of acting even when she is deeply disconnected and her social relations are inhibited. This enables her to be, at the same time, radical and open – committed and disconnected.

With this conception of the subject, however, agonistic democracy fails to include people like Jacob, Samira, Thomas and Emma, as described in the Introduction. It cannot include marginalised people today, people who, in Richard Sennett's words, lack the 'particular strength of character' that contemporary precarious society demands: 'that of someone who has the confidence to dwell in disorder, someone who flourishes in the midst of dislocation' (Sennett 1998, 62). Like the 'flexible subject' that the current social order demands, the agonist – flexible, strong and conflict-seeking – is perfectly suited to straddle today's conditions of precarity and disconnection. Agonistic democratic theory is thus left unable to conceive of the challenges in mobilising marginalised people today in an open and radical way.

176

How can we reformulate the subject of agonistic democracy to include alienation? In other words, if we incorporate our theory of alienation – domination and disorientation – into agonistic democracy, how should we then characterise the subject? In order to answer this, I examine whether the agonist's characteristics – her flexibility, strength and propensity to seek conflict – are compatible with our theory of alienation, and, if not, how they should be reconsidered. The subject of agonistic democracy is thus reformulated to correspond to the subject assumed in our theory of alienation.

## Social, not flexible

In Chapter 2, I showed that the subject on which Mouffe's theory relies – the agonist – is flexible. She can identify with any object that comes into view, and any of these identities will, in the most relevant respects, fit her equally well. Can the flexible subject experience alienation, conceived as domination and disorientation?

Even a flexible subject can experience domination – the situation whereby others systematically appropriate social power at her expense. Flexibility has to do with the process of identification. And although the experience of domination can affect the subject's capacity to form affective relations, it does not determine it. It could, for instance, be difficult to identify as an academic if you do not have enough social or cultural capital to get a qualified job. Even so, the fact that you are dominated does not necessarily mean that you cannot maintain the identities from which you draw meaning. It is not impossible to find purpose in a job that you had no choice but to take, and in which someone else reaps most of the benefits of your labour. When dominated, finding purpose and orienting yourself in the world can, for example, involve skilful everyday acts of resistance, joining a union, or finding ways of making seemingly menial tasks more stimulating. The assumption that the subject is flexible does not, therefore, block agonistic democracy from accommodating a theory of domination.

Disorientation, on the other hand, cannot, by definition, be experienced by the flexible subject. While the flexible subject can form affective relations with any objects, it is precisely this ability to find meaning in the world that is inhibited when we are disoriented. For agonistic democracy to be able to provide a theory of alienation, we must, for that reason, reformulate its conception of the subject. If not flexible, how should we characterise the subject?

To find a suitable conception of the subject, I will instead turn to our theory of alienation, as outlined in Chapters 4 and 5, and examine the subject to which it corresponds. This subject, I showed, relies on what Pierre Bourdieu calls habitus: a certain 'durable, adjusted disposition'. The habitus 'is what makes it possible to inhabit institutions, to appropriate them practically' (Bourdieu 1990, 57). The habitus allows us to orient ourselves in our social world and from our social position. Only when her habitus fully functions can the subject realise and orient herself in the world. The habitus, in turn, is constituted in the subject's habitual interactions with the world, and thus depends on certain social relations. Rather than flexible – able to identify with any object that comes into view – the subject can be described as *social*: she depends on social relations to navigate and find meaning in the world.

Drawing on this concept of habitus, we can assume that the subject is social in two respects. First, her particular ways of orienting herself – her tastes, skills, moral impulses and objects of identification – are social. They are shaped over time in the subject's interactions with the social world. The subject is thus social in the sense that her specific orientations – her particular habitus – are formed in relation to and depend upon social processes.

Second, and even more importantly, the subject is social in the sense that her very *ability* to orient herself is social; it depends upon, and can be inhibited by, social processes. As we saw in Chapter 4, the subject's orientations – her habitus – can become dysfunctional. This can happen in disruptive and contradictory social processes, and, in particular, in situations of repeated, systemic disruptions. In these situations, the habitus, which is slow to develop and slow to change, falls into crisis. The subject's orientations no longer correspond to her social world – leaving her disoriented. For the social subject, not only her particular orientations but also her general capacity to orient herself is social.

When we incorporate the theory of alienation – domination and disorientation – and the conception of the subject on which it relies into agonistic democracy, we come up with a subject who is social rather than flexible. She does not have an innate ability to orient herself in the world. Instead, her practical understanding is social; it can be socially inhibited.

178

### Dependent, not strong

The subject – the agonist – that Mouffe's agonistic democracy relies on is not only flexible but also strong. She relies only on her own strength in deciding and acting. For the agonist, who does not depend on social objects to act, deprivation is not disempowering – it is the starting point of radical action (Laclau 2004, 286). This constitutes the 'radical optimism' of agonistic democracy (Laclau 1990, 35): the subject can, as Mouffe claims, 'always intervene in the relations of power in order to transform them' (Mouffe 2013, 132). Even when deprived, the subject can act to change things. But can the strong subject, on whom Mouffe's radically optimistic theory relies, be alienated?

The agonist's innate strength does not necessarily preclude disorientation. Even a subject who relies only on herself in willing and acting may fail to see the alternatives that are actually available to her. However, while she can become disoriented, the agonist is too strong to be dominated. She does not depend on social resources from which she can be deprived.

In Chapter 4, it was explained that the relation of domination is based on deprivation. When dominated, the subject lacks the capital that she needs to appropriate the world and herself. She is left exposed to the domination of more powerful agents who systematically appropriate more social power at her expense. The characteristic of the subject that leaves her vulnerable to domination is thus her dependency. She depends on social resources that she can constructively use.

The theory of alienation thus relies on a specific type of subject: a subject who is dependent. This means that when social objects are monopolised by others, she is left vulnerable to domination, such as in the form of alienation. Consequently, for agonistic democracy to be able to provide a theory of alienation, it should reconsider its subject. The subject on whom such a theory relies is not strong; she is dependent.

### Problem-solving, not conflict-seeking

For agonistic democracy to be able to include a theory of alienation, it should reformulate its conception of the subject: she is social rather than flexible, dependent rather than strong. Can the subject, thus conceived, still be conflict-seeking?

In Chapter 2, I showed that it is the subject's natural propensity to seek out conflict that allows her to be flexible and strong. She does not need specific social connections to be passionately engaged, because she is spurred by conflict itself. She can be mobilised by rhetorical distinctions between 'we' and 'they', irrespective of the distinct meaning of these categories. Furthermore, the subject's conflict-seeking can also, at least to some extent, explain why the subject does not depend on social objects to act. She does not need objects to act, because her actions are not mainly those of constructive use, but rather of negation. Even a social movement, in Mouffe's conception, is formed mainly around negation. It involves construction only in so far as it requires the construction of an opponent, such as the elite or the oligarchs.

When the subject is assumed to be social rather than flexible, and dependent rather than strong, the assumption that the subject can be spurred into action by conflict itself no longer holds. What spurs the social subject is not an abstract division between 'we' and 'they' but her particular moral intuitions. While the flexible subject can identify with, and distinguish herself from, any object, the social subject cannot. For her, identification – and antagonism – is social. Her moral intuitions, including the way she distinguishes herself from others, develop over time in relation to her social milieu and position. The social subject is spurred not by conflict itself but by particular social conflicts. Whether a specific antagonistic rhetoric will appeal to the social and dependent subject will be contingent on her social relations and experiences, and, in particular, on her experiences of domination.

Having reformulated the subject as social, we can thus no longer assume that she is naturally conflict-seeking. How, then, should we describe her? Is she, in fact, naturally harmonious? The subject assumed in our theory of alienation is neither conflict-seeking nor harmonious; she is problem-solving. Recall from Chapters 4 and 5 that the subject assumed in the theory of alienation is marked by her activity of appropriation, an activity by which she makes use of and orients herself in the world. In appropriating the world, she encounters otherness and makes it her own – changing both the other and herself. She continuously runs into, and resolves, problems. Conflict is constitutive of the subject. This characteristic is shared with the agonist. As opposed to the agonist, however, she is not essentially spurred by conflict itself. She does not seek problems but seeks to resolve them. When integrating our theory of alienation into agonistic democratic theory, it comes to rely on a subject characterised by her problem-solving rather than her conflict-seeking.

A subject driven by conflict is not the same as a subject driven by the desire to resolve conflict. Recall from Chapter 2 that for division to mobilise the conflict-seeking agonist's passions, it must tap into the deeper antagonism that, in Mouffe's theory, constitutes the subject. Conflict cannot be 'a mere difference of position' but should be 'envisaged in terms of a frontier, indicating the existence of an antagonism between respective position and the impossibility of a "centre position"' (Mouffe 2019, 84–5). Antagonism is, in Mouffe's ontology, not 'mere difference' but radical negation – a type of conflict that cannot be resolved. Being spurred by a type of conflict to which there is no resolution, the agonist does not and cannot seek to resolve conflict. The problem-solving subject, however, is constituted by a different type of conflict. In this type of conflictual situation, the subject can experiment with different types of solutions, and some of her solutions will be more accurate than others. If and how a particular conflict can be resolved cannot be predetermined, but neither can the possibility of a resolution be precluded.

We can therefore conclude that in order to integrate the theory of alienation into agonistic democracy, the subject can no longer be assumed to be flexible, strong and conflict-seeking. Instead, agonistic democracy should rely on a conception of the subject as social, dependent and problem-solving. Having reformulated the subject to accommodate alienation, it is time to examine what implications this has for agonistic democracy at large.

## From antagonism to alienation

As we saw in Chapter 2, Mouffe's radical democracy can be divided into three parts: a normative theory of democracy, what she calls agonistic democracy; a political strategy, sometimes called left populism; and a set of theoretical assumptions underpinning both. Reformulating the subject of agonistic democracy has implications for radical democracy in all its forms. In the rest of this chapter, I will discuss the implications of my reformulation of the subject on the normative theory of agonistic democracy and the theoretical approach that underpins it. Can we integrate the reformulated conception of the subject into agonistic democratic theory without creating a theoretical conflict between its two aims – openness and radicalism?

Before reformulating agonistic democracy, let us first recall the aims of Mouffe's agonistic democracy and what she perceives as the main challenge in achieving them.

### Taming antagonism: the challenge of Mouffe's agonistic democracy

Recall from Chapter 2 that the overarching normative aims of Mouffe's agonistic democracy are openness and radicalism. It seeks political association that is open, in the sense that it is capable of responding to a multiplicity of demands and new claims, but that, at the same time, can challenge existing power relations. For this, it should be agonistic rather than antagonistic, in the sense that it is able to see adversaries as legitimate opponents rather than enemies to be destroyed (Mouffe 2019, 91). An agonistic association avoids 'non-negotiable moral values or essentialist forms of identification' (Mouffe 2019, 93). At the same time, the struggle should be radical. The aim of agonistic democracy is, in Mouffe's words, 'a profound transformation of the existing power relations and the establishment of a new hegemony' (Mouffe 2005a, 52).

We have also seen that in Mouffe's agonistic democracy, antagonism is a central challenge. In Mouffe's words, 'one of the main challenges for pluralist liberal-democratic politics consists in trying to defuse the potential antagonism that exists in human relations so as to make human co-existence possible' (Mouffe 2019, 91). According to Mouffe, we reach the normative aims of agonistic democracy by channelling and taming antagonism. We do so by maintaining institutions that can channel conflict – in particular, liberal democratic institutions like elections – and, even more importantly, by making use of the liberal democratic institutions that we have. Mouffe's main point is that democratic political parties and movements must remain conflictual enough to channel antagonism. We need, Mouffe argues, real divisions in democratic politics: divisions between 'the left' and 'the right' or between 'the people' and 'the oligarchs'. Only then can we tame 'antagonism'[1] – 'the struggle between enemies' – into 'agonism' – 'the struggle between adversaries' (Mouffe 2019, 91). In order to maintain the radicalism and openness that an agonistic democracy aims for, the main challenge becomes to channel antagonism through the democratic institutions.

## The new challenge for agonistic democracy: overcoming alienation

In my reformulation of agonistic democracy, I seek to keep the aims of an open and radical political practice. I will show that when reformulating the subject of agonistic democracy, these aims can fall into conflict – but not necessarily. For a reformulated agonistic democracy, avoiding the tension between openness and radicalism becomes a practical rather than theoretical challenge.

I will seek to show this by re-examining the two central moments of Mouffe's agonistic democracy: the moment of disconnection and the moment of connection. As described in Chapter 2, the subject in Mouffe's theory is assumed to be constituted in the oscillation between connection and disconnection. This constitutive movement of the subject is what allows her to be both open and radical. The flexible, strong and conflict-seeking subject – the agonist – is assumed to react to disconnection in a radical way, by forming a new strong connection. Dislocation becomes the starting point of radical action (Laclau 2004, 286). At the same time, the agonist who is strongly committed to a hegemonic project still remains open – always ready to let go and reconsider her attachments. However, having reformulated the subject of radical democracy, the subject's reaction to the experience of connection and disconnection must be rethought. The question is whether the subject can still remain both radical and open, or if these aims fall into tension.

Let us first examine the experience of disconnection, where the relation of identification is severed. I will then turn to the experience of strong connection. For the social, dependent and problem-solving subject, the moment of disconnection is not necessarily emancipatory, enabling open and radical engagement. Recall, for example, Jacob from the Introduction, who cannot engage in the education he is pursuing. Having discovered that it does not lead anywhere, Jacob finds no reason to involve himself in it. But neither does he see any reason to leave. The education and the traineeships can, at least temporarily, hold off what seems like an inescapable future of unemployment or low-income jobs. Jacob thus stays, lingering in uncertainty, disconnected from his social context.

Jacob does not respond to disconnection in the way that Mouffe's agonist would, challenging and replacing his object of identification. He does not, for example, come together with others like him to challenge the education system from which he seems to be subtly

183

excluded. Instead, he disengages; he sees no other possibility than remaining in the system and playing his part. Jacob's reaction makes sense when we assume a subject who is social. The social subject's capacity to act and experiment is constituted in her relations with the world. The subject that has become alienated from the world – connected to it merely through a relation of relationlessness – is not radically engaged, but indifferent.

Is disconnection from our identities always disempowering? Do we not need some distance from our commitments within the established order in order to radically break with it? In Jaeggi's words, 'To the extent that indifference includes the experience that a world of established meanings can suddenly become meaningless . . . it is also an emancipatory, even a "dereifying" experience.' Detachment can both be a sign of alienation and a condition for escaping it; it is 'not only an experience of powerlessness but also of power' (Jaeggi 2014, 150).

But if detachment, as Jaeggi claims, can be emancipatory, how can it also turn into an experience of meaninglessness and powerlessness? Are we not, in fact, free when we become indifferent to the social world and are no longer trapped by its conventions? Drawing on Hegel, Jaeggi argues that the detached person is free only in the abstract. She lacks positive freedom – the freedom to do something.[2] Indifference is a defensive stance that we take on in order to minimise hurt and loss. Detached from worldly objects, after all, worldly events can no longer harm us. On the other hand, our lack of attachments means that we no longer have any real aims to pursue. We cannot practise our freedom to will and act. Disconnection turns into powerlessness when it blocks us from making affective ties to and orienting ourselves in the world.

The concept of alienation reveals that, although disconnection can be empowering, it has a flipside: apathy. The subject can only respond to the experience of disconnection as agonistic democrats expect – with radical engagement – when she is not deeply disoriented. This type of paralysing disorientation is made worse in systems of continuous repeated disruption from which – often because of domination – the subject cannot escape. In these cases, the subject might internalise disconnection as a new embodied disposition. Disconnection becomes a new normality rather than a trigger for action. The social, dependent and problem-solving subject is thus in a better position to respond to disrupted connections in a radical way if she is not alienated.

184

This being said, we should not dismiss the radical potential of disruption and disconnection. Critical distance is crucial for challenging domination, especially when it is deeply internalised. Yet such distance only has a radical potential if we are sufficiently related to the world to make sense of and orient ourselves in it. Only when we can appropriate the world are we able to truly engage with, and actively work to, change it – both by small daily acts of resistance and by coming together with others. There are many possible forms of disruption that could enable critical distance without being deeply disorienting. For instance, we could develop critical distance by sharing our views with others, through art, theatre, movies or critical education. Here, disruption might trigger resistance rather than disorientation. As long as it is not alienating, disconnection can encourage radical engagement.

Let us turn, instead, to the moment of connection, when a strong relation of identification is established or sustained. A strong affective relation can spur us into action, including radical action. But is connection always good – breeding agonism? This, we will see, is not the case when the subject is alienated and cannot respond to new claims in an open-ended way.

One might think that the subject cannot be alienated while also being strongly committed. However, there are at least two practical ways in which commitment can be alienating – both of which become problematic from an agonistic democratic perspective. First, as Jaeggi shows, the subject might strongly identify with her social roles but remain unable to appropriate them. In this scenario, the subject has adopted a social role that she remains strongly committed to, but that she cannot fully make her own (Jaeggi 2014, 92). Imagine, for instance, someone in Jacob's position, moving between different traineeships at different companies. In order to be hired, he might try to do everything exactly right: to follow the rules and be like everyone else. In these types of situations, the subject becomes the role but loses himself. He cannot find himself in the role and make it his own. The relation of identification becomes alienating.

Alienated, rigid role-playing is likely to reproduce the current order rather than enable resistance. When the dominated are also disoriented, they are trapped in the roles to which they are assigned, unable to make their own path. At the same time, not all role-taking blocks radical action. On the contrary, social roles can be crucial in inspiring political mobilisation. For example, teachers can mobilise

185

as teachers in order to challenge their working conditions. Their professional roles enable them to come together and be recognised. An activist can also identify as an activist, enabling her to remain committed. However, when alienated, even these potentially radical roles remain rigid. They block us from being open to new claims and a plurality of perspectives. The activist may, for example, rigidly follow certain principles while excluding potential allies or failing to grasp the real consequences of her political strategies. From an agonistic democratic perspective, rigid rule-following becomes problematic. It risks turning into dangerous antagonism, by which the boundary between 'we' and 'they' becomes too fixed to allow for a plurality of claims. Strong commitments to social roles can thus become alienating. This, in, turn, becomes problematic from an agonistic democratic perspective, since it blocks the subject's capacity to remain open.

Second, the alienated subject can form strong commitments – but to imaginary, rather than real, objects. Recall Bourdieu's description of the uprooted peasants in Algeria. While some of them resigned themselves to their conditions, others escaped into a dream world – a complete negation of this world. In Bourdieu's words, for those lacking a grasp of the present, '[r]evolutionary chiliasm and magical utopias are the only grasp on the future that offers itself' (Bourdieu 1979, 70). When alienated, the subject cannot appropriate the world; she cannot form affective attachments by practically engaging with it, but only by transcending it in her imagination, attaching herself to its complete negation. As her attachments are formed in her imagination rather than in her practical engagement, they cannot accommodate real problems and experiences.

Jaeggi's and Bourdieu's observations suggest that, while alienated relations of identification may be radical – spurring us into action that challenges the current order – they are not open. In negating her current conditions while failing to make sense of them, the subject falls into the antagonistic forms of relation that agonistic democrats seek to avoid. Agonistic democrats fear that, when we are antagonistic, we fail to take into account the real consequences of our actions and the suffering that we may cause. Instead, we justify violence by references to rigid rules or transcendental ideals. Mouffe argues that, in an agonistic democracy, we must seek to avoid 'non-negotiable moral values or essentialist forms of identification' (Mouffe 2019, 93). However, when the alienated subject encounters a problem, she cannot experiment and try different solutions. She remains rigid and trapped. She fails to appropriate her actions, and thus, to take responsibility for them. Our commitments become alienating, as well as problematic from an agonistic democratic perspective, when the object we have committed to is imaginary rather than real.

The two examples show that, although strong connections and commitments can inspire radical action, they have a flipside: antagonism. When we rigidly follow predetermined patterns, we fail to accommodate complexity and plurality as well as to respond to new claims. Alienated relations structurally resemble the antagonistic relations that agonistic democrats fear: a type of relations that, according to them, enable exclusion and violence.

The condition for the subject to be able to form strong connections while remaining open is thus that she is able to appropriate her roles, world and actions – that she can overcome her alienation. Relations of appropriation enable the subject to form strong but open relations of identification – and to do so not merely with the 'empty symbol' of a leader or a slogan, like Mouffe suggests, but also with its actual positive contents. The reformulated subject of agonistic democracy does not mainly commit herself to slogans but to real people, communities and particular political programmes. Overcoming alienation – appropriating the world and herself – enables the subject to be both radical and open. The challenge in an agonistic democracy – seeking to maintain agonism while avoiding antagonism and apathy – thus becomes to overcome alienation.

Table 6.1 illustrates how alienation relates to the agonism – open and radical engagement – that agonistic democracy seeks, as well as to the problems that it seeks to avoid, that is, antagonism and apathy. When we reformulate the agonistic democratic subject and integrate a theory of alienation, we can see that open and radical engagement, agonism, remains theoretically possible. However, the practical conditions for such engagement can be enforced or undermined depending on the subject's possibilities to appropriate the social processes in

Table 6.1 Alienation, agonism, apathy and antagonism

|  | Alienation | Resilience |
|---|---|---|
| **Disconnection** | Apathy | Agonism |
| **Connection** | Antagonism | Agonism |

which she is involved, to make them her own. The main challenge for an agonistic democracy striving for open and radical engagement of marginalised people becomes to overcome alienation.

Agonistic democracy can no longer only focus on channelling conflict in order to tame antagonism. There are at least two central reasons for this. First, a lack of democratic channels for antagonism can no longer be considered the sole central reason for the outbreak of antagonism. Agonistic democracy must thus take a wider range of social relations and processes into account than merely the liberal democratic political institutions. The central question is whether people are able to appropriate the different social and political practices in which they are involved.

Second, having reformulated the subject, antagonism is not the only problem that agonistic democracy must seek to avoid. It must also concern itself with the problem of disengagement and apathy. It can no longer rely on the subject's essential qualities to maintain engagement. When the subject is alienated, her attachments are either so strong that she cannot remain open or so detached that she cannot radically engage. Overcoming alienation thus becomes crucial for agonistic democrats – not only in order to tame antagonism but also to avoid apathy.

When the subject is reconsidered, the oscillation between connection and disconnection no longer constitutes the subject. Neither is it a condition for her to remain both open and radical. An important movement is instead that which occurs between the alienated and resilient subject. When the subject goes from being alienated – dominated and disoriented – to being resilient – dominated but oriented – she becomes able to practically engage with and make sense of the world. She can engage agonistically – in a radical and open way to challenge her marginalisation.

This, however, does not mean that overcoming alienation guarantees radical engagement. Radical engagement depends on a number of factors, including organisation, resources, education, time and so on. For dominated groups, with fewer resources to exert power individually, the political organisation and its structure can be particularly important. I will discuss this further in the next chapter. Conversely, alienation can be an important factor for mobilisation. But while alienation can be a trigger for resistance, it can also become a corruptive force – turning openness into apathy and radicalism into antagonism. When, on the other hand, we remain resilient – dominated yet

188

oriented – disruption can become a critical distance that allows us to engage in radical action. Commitment can be both radical and open.

At the same time, the difficulty in overcoming alienation partly explains why antagonism can be difficult to avoid and why a radical democratic movement must struggle against alienation – not only in the social world at large but also within the movement itself. As opposed to Mouffe and Laclau's theory, however, this is conceived as a strategic problem for the radical democratic movement rather than a theoretical dilemma in the model of agonistic democracy. For this reason, agonistic democracy can loosen some of the demands on the subject to be intrinsically flexible, strong and conflict-seeking, while still not worsening the possible tension between its aims of openness and radicalism. For the subject to be radical and open, she is no longer assumed to be both connected and disconnected, or both marginalised and strong. The problem of simultaneously maintaining openness and radicalism becomes a social and political problem, not a theoretical one: it becomes a problem of alienation.

In our reformulated model of agonistic democracy, antagonism is important, but not as central as in Mouffe's theory. Taming and channelling antagonism is no longer the main challenge. The main challenge for agonistic democracy, I have argued, is alienation. Still, antagonism remains important. Recall that alienation, in itself, is an antagonistic relation, retaining a dimension of power and antagonism. The problem of alienation thus remains closely related to that of antagonism. Furthermore, antagonism also remains a part of the solution to the problem of alienation. The struggle for democracy and for overcoming alienation is, by definition, highly conflictual, involving a struggle of the dominated against the dominant.

## Is the theory still agonistic?

The previous section showed that it is possible to integrate the theory of alienation into agonistic democracy, while also retaining its normative emphasis on open and radical engagement, and without creating a theoretical tension between these aims. Let us thus turn to the deeper theoretical assumptions on which agonistic democracy relies, most notably its ontological assumption that politics and society are marked by antagonism. Having reformulated the subject as problem-solving rather than conflict-seeking, we can no longer assume that antagonism is ineradicable. What happens when you integrate the theory of alienation and its corresponding conception of the subject into the deeper assumptions of the theory? Is it still agonistic?

If we define agonistic democracy by its aims of theoretical openness and radicalism, it should be. In Chapter 5, I showed that our reconstructed theory of alienation is both open and radical. It avoids assumptions of human essentialism, determinism as well as the ideal of a final state of harmony. At the same time, it retains a dimension of social power, suffering and antagonism. The theory thus maintains an open space for contingency, spontaneity and pluralism but also a radical emphasis on the need for social struggle and transformation. It should therefore be possible to integrate our concept of alienation into agonistic democracy without undermining the theory's openness and radicalism.

However, while the openness and radicalism that marks Mouffe's theoretical approach is maintained, our reformulation of the subject implies a significant shift in the theory's ontological assumptions. Ontological discussions are central to agonistic democracy, and in Mouffe's theory, the most important assumption is that of 'the political' – ineradicable antagonism. There is, according to Mouffe, an ineradicable 'adversarial dimension of society' involving a confrontation between 'we' and 'they' (Mouffe 2005a, 5). For Mouffe, this antagonism cannot be eradicated, only tamed. The assumption of the political is key to her theoretical approach. It is this assumption that allows the theory to retain the radical, antagonistic dimension of traditional socialism without assuming that such antagonism can be overcome and result in a final state of harmony. In my reconstruction of the theory, however, the assumption of the political in the sense of ineradicable antagonism is not fully maintained. The subject, in my conception, is not unavoidably antagonistic. She seeks not conflict but its resolution. Have I thus abandoned the most central thesis of Mouffe's theory – that antagonism is ineradicable and central to politics – and adopted its most problematic ideal – the ideal of a final resolution? If so, how, as I have claimed, can the theory still remain open and radical?

Having reconsidered the underlying conception of the subject in agonistic democracy, I have reformulated but not completely rejected Mouffe's central thesis. In my conception, conflict is ineradicable, but antagonism is not – or at least not in theory. At the same time, antagonism is emphasised as an important and recurrent risk. In this way, I avoid assuming that a final state of harmony can be reached while

190

at the same time maintaining Mouffe's emphasis on the risk of antagonism. This is how the theory can remain both open and radical.

## TOWARDS A MULTI-SCALAR AGONISM

The resulting theory of agonistic democracy, what I call multi-scalar agonism, both resists and retains elements of Mouffe's model. It remains agonistic in the sense that it regards conflict as ineradicable and central to democracy. However, it differs from Mouffe's agonistic pluralism in that the agon is not singular – stemming exclusively from the ontological condition of the political – but multi-scalar. Conflict cannot be traced back to a single point of origin. It cannot be reduced to a specific social pathology, such as the capitalist system, nor can all conflict be traced back to the ineradicable antagonism between 'we' and 'they', what Mouffe calls 'the political'. Instead, the model of multi-scalar agonism emphasises how conflict can emerge at several different scales, and that none of these scales takes precedence.

While the scales of conflict can be imagined in different ways, I will here take my point of departure in, and seek to problematise, Mouffe's division between the social and the political. As agonistic democracy is made multi-scalar, it can no longer exclusively focus on taming antagonism by channelling 'the political', constitutive conflict, through the political institutions. Instead, it becomes a form of democracy which also continuously interrogates its social conditions of existence, in order to maintain them. Resistance to alienation is conceived as both a condition for and a part of the agonistic democratic struggle.

Thus, in our model of multi-scalar agonism, two types of conflict are central. While related, they involve different forms of power, at different scales, which cannot be reduced to one another. Conflict of the first type is ontological, intrinsic to the process of appropriation in which the subject and her social world is constituted. This process presupposes a division between an 'I' and an 'other' that can become conflictual. When appropriating the world, the subject encounters something that is foreign to her and makes it her own. The process thus presupposes an adversarial dimension – a distinction between an 'I' and an 'other' – that can be more or less conflictual.

In this sense, it resembles what Mouffe calls antagonism. However, there is one important difference. Mouffe's antagonism stems from what she describes as a 'radical negativity' (Mouffe 2019, 87). The

'I' and the 'other' are, in Mouffe's ontology, opposed to each other in such a way that a resolution is impossible. The activity of appropriation, on the other hand, presupposes not only some form of conflict but also a resolution. Unlike Mouffe's hegemony, this resolution is not a mere manifestation of power. But neither is it an end point. As we have seen, the resolution inherent in the process of appropriation is not harmonious. Each resolution implies new problems and new conflicts. The model of multi-scalar agonism thus presupposes a form of ongoing conflict-resolution that differs from Mouffe's antagonism in that it involves not only continuous conflicts but also continuous resolutions that are more than mere manifestations of power.

Even more importantly, the model of multi-scalar antagonism differs from Mouffe's agonistic democracy in that it also emphasises a second type of conflict, located not at the ontological scale but at the social. As we have seen, the process of appropriation that marks the subject can be inhibited by another form of conflict: alienation.

Alienation is a type of conflict that is social in the sense that it is contingent and can appear in some societies but not in others, and in comparison with the first type of conflict, more prone to manifest itself as dangerous antagonism, where opponents regard each other as enemies to be destroyed. Recall that alienation – a form of domination deepened by disorientation – involves a division between the dominant and the dominated. And, as I argued above, domination, when combined with disorientation, easily turns rigid and antagonistic. While disoriented, we might possibly be radical – committed to a counter-hegemonic struggle, but not open. Disorientation distorts our understanding of the situation that we are in, leaving us unable to fully grasp the consequences of our actions. Alienation, if politicised, might thus breed what Mouffe sometimes calls 'dangerous antagonism' or simply 'antagonism' – the struggle between enemies seeking to eradicate each other. A conflict that turns antagonistic is dangerous, potentially violent, and unlikely to be resolved.

Through this second type of conflict, we bring back the properly antagonistic dimension of the theory. However, since this antagonism has social roots, it is – at least in theory – possible to overcome. Yet, while it is theoretically possible, an end point to alienation and the conflict that it breeds is practically unlikely. Alienation as a particular form of domination is difficult to fight successfully. As we saw in Chapter 5, the dynamics of domination makes it particularly hard to overcome. It continuously transforms and reinforces itself.

In combination with disorientation – which impairs our ability to accurately get to the root of problems and resolve them – it becomes even more difficult.

The model of multi-scalar agonism thus equally emphasises conflict at the social and ontological scales – as well as the difficulty in separating the two. Taking these two forms of division together, the possibility of conflict is always present: either predominately as appropriation or as alienation.

When alienated, the subject's agonistic problem-solving is blocked, and conflict becomes more antagonistic. When, on the other hand, the subject begins to overcome her alienation, agonism is enabled and some of the antagonism that alienation involves is tamed. What Mouffe calls 'the political' – ineradicable antagonism – is therefore, in our conception, not only ontological but also social. Or, rather, the radical democratic distinction between the social and the political is, if not completely dissolved, significantly muddled. With this, the theory remains both open, in the sense that it avoids idealising harmony, and radical, in the sense that it maintains a dimension of antagonism.

The model of multi-scalar agonism thus opens up a space for conflict that is both social, in the sense that it involves a struggle for social freedom, and political, in the sense that it is ineradicable. While a theory of multi-scalar agonism opens up for the (unlikely) possibility of overcoming the form of antagonism that stems from alienation, this does not imply a decreased emphasis on conflict in democratic politics. On the contrary, the aim is to make agonistic democracy more genuinely radical, able to address forms of power and antagonism that it previously ignored. When we integrate a dimension of social alienation into agonistic democracy, the theory becomes better equipped to understand and mobilise contemporary experiences of social suffering into a struggle for social transformation.

Having reconceived the subject, the main challenge for an agonistic democracy is no longer merely to tame ineradicable antagonism but to overcome alienation. Only when alienation is overcome can the subject remain truly open and radical. If the aims of openness and radicalism fall into conflict, this conflict is not a theoretical tension but a social and political problem – a problem of alienation. Such a problem can be handled through political strategy and struggle.

Even if alienation may never actually be permanently eradicated, it can, through continuous struggle, be significantly decreased.

The struggle against alienation – as opposed to Mouffe's counter-hegemonic struggle – is difficult, but not hopeless. It is, at least in theory, something that could be won. The double nature of alienation – inspiring and corrupting, mobilising and demobilising – is central to my understanding of the link between alienation and agonistic democracy. It also becomes central to radical democracy as a political strategy. A political movement struggling against alienation must, at the same time, struggle against the corrupting effects of alienation on the movement itself. In the next chapter, I will examine how radical democracy, given my reformulation of the subject, should reconsider its political strategy.

## NOTES

1. Mouffe uses the word 'antagonism' to denote both the form of conflict – 'we/they distinction' – that in her theoretical assumptions is ineradicable – as well as its more dangerous expression – 'the struggle between enemies' (e.g. Mouffe 2019, 90–1).
2. 'Becoming a person for Hegel means "putting one's will into something," and that also means giving oneself specific properties by willing something in the world. In such a relation to the world, the person first realizes herself as a person, and in that her freedom first becomes concrete' (Jaeggi 2014, 148).

# Chapter Seven

# Redirecting the radical democratic strategy

Radical democracy is not only a theoretical approach and a normative model of democracy but also a political strategy. Before concluding this study on radical democratic theory, I will turn to this third aspect of radical democracy: radical democracy as strategy. What does our reformulated conception of the subject allow us to understand, now, that we could not previously? Which issues become relevant to a radical democratic movement seeking to maintain an open and radical struggle against marginalisation in a context of alienation?

Having reformulated the subject of radical democracy – as social, dependent and problem-solving, rather than flexible, strong and conflict-seeking – we are left with a theory of radical democracy better equipped to address alienation. And while the radical democratic ideals of openness and radicalism do not theoretically fall into tension, maintaining both becomes a social and political problem, which I define as the problem of alienation. In this chapter, I will show that the reformulated conception of the radical democratic subject makes the theory more politically relevant – apt for addressing problem of alienation, as well as the complex strategic challenges that it gives rise to.

To do so, I will, first, examine the central challenge to the radical democratic movement under conditions of alienation. I show that a radical democracy that seeks to mobilise radically and openly against alienation does so in a situation wherein, precisely because of this alienation, the type of mobilisation that radical democrats strive for is undermined. I go on to discuss some of the strategic challenges that our reformulated conception of the subject reveals with respect to three central questions of political mobilisation: who should the social movement include? How should it organise? And what should it demand?

## THE STRUGGLE WITH AND AGAINST ALIENATION

Chantal Mouffe and Ernesto Laclau's radical democracy is not merely theoretical but also practical. Their thorough ontological investigations have implications for the strategic dimension of radical democracy. In their seminal work *Hegemony and Socialist Strategy: Towards a Radical Democratic Politics* ([1985] 2001), Laclau and Mouffe develop a theory of hegemony and the political – ineradicable antagonism – which ultimately results in a new socialist strategy they term 'radical democracy' or 'left populism'. With the turn from the social to the political, the mobilising strategy of the left changes. The main line of conflict in society and in politics is no longer a given social division, such as the division between capital and labour. For radical democrats, antagonism is not social but ontological – it arises not from particular social practices and the struggle for more social freedom but from an ineradicable part of any society. Division, Laclau and Mouffe argue, springs from the ontological condition of the political, and its shape is determined in the political debate. In order to mobilise people, the key question is not 'who suffers?' or 'how should social suffering be alleviated?' Instead, mobilisation depends on discourse and, in particular, on language.

Mouffe and Laclau thus argue that a successful social movement should adopt a 'populist strategy', consisting of a particular type of discourse. The populist discourse consists of a symbol around which people can gather, such as a leader or the slogan of 'the people', and an adversary towards whom they can direct their antagonism – their example is 'the oligarchs' (Mouffe 2019, 79). To mobilise people, the political movement must be built around a rhetorical formulation of a 'we' and a 'they'. However, the actual content of these categories does not matter. To mobilise the flexible, strong and conflict-seeking subject, any adversary will suffice. The subject is not spurred into action by a specific social antagonism but by antagonism itself.

In response to the problem of alienation today, I have reformulated the underlying assumptions of radical democracy, focusing, in particular, on its conception of the individual subject. In my assumptions, the subject is not flexible, strong and conflict-seeking, but social, dependent and problem-solving. The subject, thus conceived, is spurred not by conflict itself but by her aspiration to overcome it. To engage in this problem-solving activity, she depends on her social relations. When the subject is alienated – when her social rela-

196

tions turn into relations of relationlessness – her problem-solving activity is impaired. She is disoriented and dominated – unable to practically understand and find meaning in her world, while others systematically appropriate social power at her expense. In this situation, I have argued, conflict is more likely to turn into dangerous antagonism. Although conflict is ontological – a part of the subject's problem-solving activity – dangerous antagonism is not. Conflict is more likely to turn into antagonism when our problem-solving capacity is impaired – that is, when we are alienated.

In integrating a theory of alienation into radical democracy, we have revealed a new strategic challenge for the radical democratic movement. Radical democracy today must mobilise openly and radically against alienation in a situation wherein, specifically because of alienation, this type of mobilisation is undermined. Alienation, being impaired appropriation, corrupts the very relation that the radical democratic association seeks – the relation of appropriation. Relations of appropriation enable us to maintain the commitment and resources we need to engage in radical action while simultaneously remaining open to new impulses and ideas. Alienation, on the other hand, distorts radicalism into antagonism and openness into apathy. Radical democracy thus finds itself in a paradoxical situation: the alienation it seeks to overcome tends to block precisely the engagement that is needed for this struggle. However, the paradox of alienation is not the end of radical democracy but its starting point.

A radical democracy that takes the problem of alienation seriously must seek to organise radically and openly in a context wherein such engagement is consistently eroded. It must struggle with and against alienation – engaging in the activity of appropriation while simultaneously seeking to overcome the forces that block this appropriation. The activity of appropriation and the struggle to overcome the blockages to this activity go hand in hand.

Having reconsidered the radical democratic subject and association, we can now begin to make sense of the challenges that the problem of alienation poses: how to appropriate the world while, at the same time, overcoming the aforementioned blockages. In being able to address this problem, the radical democratic movement can also address a range of related tactical challenges that it previously ignored. I will at this point try to delineate some of these challenges, focusing on three questions that are central to any social movement: who to include, how to organise and what to demand.

## WHO TO INCLUDE?

The question of inclusion is central to any social movement. How can we, having redirected radical democracy towards the problem of alienation and reconsidered its conception of the subject, reconsider its response to this question? Which challenges and potential strategies for the radical democratic movement seeking to mobilise alienated groups are we now able to see?

Before answering these questions, let us first return to Mouffe and Laclau's left populist strategy, and why the radical democratic movement cannot, by using this strategy, fully include alienated groups. For Mouffe and Laclau, anyone can be mobilised into the left populist struggle as long as the populist leader appeals to their natural antagonism. Furthermore, there are no specific people or groups in society who are alienated. Instead, the closest Mouffe and Laclau come to a concept of alienation are the notions of 'antagonism' and 'lack' – the experience of a gap within the current hegemony. This lack can be experienced by anyone and, consequently, anyone can be mobilised into a counter-hegemonic struggle – including the struggle against alienation.

Anyone can be mobilised, and in order to mobilise people, no positive recognition of particular social positions, divisions and values is needed. The movement is constituted around various negative experiences of lack, and an 'empty' symbol, often a leader or a slogan, around which people can gather. The leader names an equally empty symbolic enemy. He constructs a division between 'we' and 'they' that activates 'the political' – the ineradicable antagonism inherent in any social formation. In this way, people's ontologically given passions and antagonism are channelled. Mouffe and Laclau's theory and strategy thus provide no means to identify or positively recognise alienated people.

When we reformulate the subject of radical democracy as social, dependent and problem-solving, we can better make sense of the tactical challenges involved in including alienated people – in identifying alienated groups and lending them recognition. Having reconsidered the subject of radical democracy, the problem of political inclusion and mobilisation becomes broader than that of empty symbols and antagonistic language. When the subject is no longer assumed to be flexible, strong and conflict-seeking, the question of political mobilisation can no longer be decoupled from real social processes, positions and patterns of meaning-making. Not everyone can be alienated – and not all antagonistic discourses will be mobilising. By including and recognising alienated groups, a central task becomes to identify who is alienated – dominated and disoriented – and to find a political rhetoric that resonates with their own narratives, experiences and demands.

## Identifying the alienated

Who is alienated today? As we saw in Chapter 5, not everyone suffers from alienation. We are alienated when we are simultaneously dominated and disoriented. The alienated subject finds herself in a social system and position where she lacks the capital – social, cultural or economic – to make constructive use of her own time, and where her social world is continuously disrupted in such a way that it leaves her unable to engage and manoeuvre. The theory of alienation allows us to distinguish the situation of alienation from other experiences, such as those of ease, resilience and, in particular, acedia – the unease experienced by the dominant when they are disoriented.

In practice, however, there are no ready-made social groups today that correspond to the category of the alienated. Already in the Introduction, we saw that an important manifestation of alienation today is precarity – a state of dependency and disruption linked to the labour market dynamics that an extensive scholarship describes as the new state of normality for many people (e.g. Berlant 2011, 192; Bourdieu 1998). However, we cannot say that all of the workers, everyone lacking stable employment or everyone within certain occupational categories is alienated. This is both a potential strength and challenge to do with the theory of alienation. It can, furthermore, give some guidance to, but not predetermine, the limits of the political struggle against alienation. My purpose, here, is not to empirically determine who is alienated today, but rather to highlight some of the ambiguities in identifying the alienated – when not only traditionally exploited groups, such as low-skilled routine workers, but also seemingly privileged groups, such as professionals and semi-professionals, can experience both disorientation and domination.

Precarious social processes and systems are often characterised by dependency and systematic disruptions – or, in our terminology, by domination and disorientation. 'What's peculiar about uncertainty today', Richard Sennett states, 'is that it exists without any looming historical disaster; instead it is woven into the everyday practices of a vigorous capitalism. Instability is meant to be normal' (Sennett 1998, 31). This disruptive precarity becomes alienating when its disorientation is deepened by domination. The literature on precarisation suggests that precarity can be experienced in several different ways. Those who experience precarisation but remain in a dominant position may not find themselves alienated. In fact, they might even flourish in a precarious social system – making use of the general insecurity to advance their own power. More likely, however, they might find themselves suffering from acedia – the painful unease experienced by the dominant when they are disoriented. But if not everyone is alienated – disoriented *and* dominated – in which milieus can we expect the experience of alienation to be the most prevalent?

First, drawing on Bourdieu's studies on domination as well as the broader literature on precarity, precarious popular milieus – those coming from a family or a personal history of low-skilled labour – may be particularly exposed to alienation. Lacking the economic, cultural and social capital to manage the insecurity 'woven into our everyday lives', they may not meet the demands of the precarious regime. In fact, according to Sennett, these demands 'become more self-destructive among those who work lower down in the flexible regime' (Sennett 1998, 63). Recall, for example, Jacob from the Introduction, caught in a social process of precarisation blocking him from succeeding not only in the labour market but also in the educational market. Coming from what seems like a popular social milieu, he enters the educational programme without the cultural capital and social networks needed to succeed and to get a job. Without being able to appropriate cultural, economic and social capital, he lingers within an education system in which he is not at home, and one which he cannot navigate. Thomas, too, is stuck is in a similar situation. When he loses his job at a car factory, his life situation turns highly precarious. The world as he knew it is lost, and he lacks the capital – such as perhaps the educational degrees or social networks – needed to set out a new path for himself. Jacob and Thomas are caught in precarious situations, being both dominated and disoriented.

Second, alienating precarity today might be experienced not only in popular social milieus but also within deprofessionalised intellectual ones. While accumulated and institutionalised cultural capital combined with social capital might help one 'flourish in the midst of dislocation' – for example, moving between different consultancy jobs or academic projects – bearers of cultural capital can also be left vulnerable to domination – with devalued degrees and expertise, as well as a loss of status, professional autonomy and employment security.

To elaborate on this particular situation, we know that a person is dominated in situations when her appropriation is systematically impaired by the appropriation of more powerful actors. Instead of her increasing her social, cultural or economic capital through her work, someone else is appropriating the value of her activity. The more efforts she makes, the less she has. The literature on precarisation and deprofessionalisation suggests that domination is experienced not only among unskilled workers but also among groups commonly considered as semi-professionals or even professionals. Through processes of precarisation and deprofessionalisation, previous professionals risk losing the specific forms of capital that distinguished them as professionals, including the possession of scarce but valuable knowledge and the control over organisational assets. Having lost these resources, the former professional would find herself in a position wherein she is left vulnerable to the domination of other agents, such as clients or managers.

Samira and Emma from the Introduction are good examples of this. Samira – an educated journalist – and Emma – a teacher seeing her professional freedom undermined – have lost the cultural worlds in which they were at home. Unable to make use of their cultural capital to take control over their own work, they find their options to be severely delimited. Lacking options, Samira finds herself working for little to no salary, and accepts jobs that she finds unscrupulous. Emma sees her work burden increase – with a growing amount of administration and diagnostic tests – but the extra time she spends on this does not seem meaningful to her. Both Samira's and Emma's autonomy and professional freedom are undercut to the extent that they are not only left disoriented – unable to navigate themselves and find meaning in their job – but they are also, possibly, dominated.

As we saw in the Introduction, many professionals today may suffer from these types of losses. As her knowledge is no longer considered scarce or valuable, the professional's cultural capital is undermined. Unsurprisingly, literature on deprofessionalisation has observed a general decline in the value of professional knowledge. A number of processes have been found to drive this development, including declining public trust in professionals, automatisation of knowledge-work tasks (Collins 2013), general education, greater availability of information and the need for continuous re-education due to technological advancement (Kalleberg 2009; Smith 2010). At the same time, scholars have demonstrated how professionals lose control over organisational assets, professional self-governing is undermined, and freelance work grows increasingly common (Kalleberg 2011; Srnicek 2017). The implication is, then, that many professionals and semi-professionals today could be experiencing domination.

However, the literature on deprofessionalisation also suggests that the very process of deprofessionalisation does not affect everyone equally – not even within the same profession. Let us briefly return to the examples of teachers and journalists. While teachers today increasingly experience domination, this varies significantly between teachers in different positions and types of schools. A teaching aid, high school substitute teacher, or a part-time university lecturer is more likely to be exposed to domination than professors or tenured associate professors. The level of domination can also vary between different types of schools, such as between private and state schools. A teacher or associate professor might be less likely to experience domination at a self-governing university or a private school run as a teacher cooperative (Filson 1988, 316).

Similarly, while, in the last decade, the profession of journalism has been severely affected by the decline in public trust (Carlson 2017) and the digitalisation of news production – processes that scholars claim have disrupted tens of thousands of individual careers in Europe and the US (Alexander 2015, 12) – these processes do not necessarily affect all individual journalists equally. Without real possibilities of stable employment, some risk finding themselves in positions of domination, wherein they are forced to work cheaply, or even for free, and to accept jobs that lower rather than increase their cultural and social standing. At the same time, journalists with large social capital and sufficient security may do relatively well in a situation of freelance work. Some might perhaps even experience an increased professional freedom. As journalism is deprofessionalised, journalism schools have come to emphasise the importance of journalistic entrepreneurship (Besbris and Petre 2020). Social capital – including social networks and Twitter followers – may be decisive in how an individual journalist experiences the shift towards digitalisation and freelancing, as opposed to full-time employment (see Revers 2017 on digital media in journalism). Accordingly, the experience of deprofessionalisation can, but does not have to, be one of disorientation and domination. Whether someone within a deprofessionalised profession also experiences domination may depend on a number of factors, such as her position and her workplace, as well as her individual volume of cultural, economic and social capital.

As we have seen, 'the alienated' do not correspond to a preexisting social category. The experience of alienation is likely to be prevalent in both popular and intellectual milieus, such as among precarised routine workers and the deprofessionalised professionals. At the same time, far from everyone in these contexts is alienated – and in particular not among professionals and semi-professionals. While the concept of alienation can serve as a guide for the radical democratic struggle, it cannot be used to predetermine and delimit it. It does not point to a single, clearly demarcated social or professional group – such as the workers, the precariat or the professionals – as the subject of social change. The degree of alienation people experience can vary significantly between individuals and between contexts, even within the same broader social and professional milieus.

A political movement against alienation thus faces several challenges. First, in order to identify who is actually experiencing alienation, it has to be shaped in an open and complex way, whereby participants actively listen and respond to the claims of others. If the aim is to include the alienated, participants must be ready to listen to people from a wide variety of social milieus. Second, a movement against alienation faces the challenge of uniting these different people – including people from both popular milieus and precarised, but less marginalised, milieus. Its social complexity can become both a problem and a pathway for the movement against alienation.

### Recognising the alienated

Having identified some of the people that the radical democratic movement concerned with alienation could include – the precarised within primarily popular and intellectual milieus – it is time to examine how to recognise them. What should they be recognised for? First, elaborating on Mouffe and Laclau's strategy, the left populist struggle can recognise the negative experiences of alienated groups. However, I will argue, this strategy also comes with risks. Given the disconnection and disempowerment that the alienated experience, calling for action without rebuilding connection risks turning into what Lauren Berlant (2011) describes as a 'cruel optimism' – becoming yet another burden on top of existing individual responsibilities. Instead, a possible way forward could be to recognise alienation as a collective experience of disengagement and, in this way, rebuild a real relation between alienated people that may energise the struggle.

Recall that in Mouffe's left populist strategy, people's negative experiences of deprivation vary, but can, if they are named, be mobilised around the same symbol, such as a movement's leader or main slogan. However, when the subject is reformulated as social and dependent, we can no longer assume that people's negative experiences are always particular and dispersed. Experiences, including that of alienation, are shared and social. Alienation – that is, impaired relations of appropriation – is experienced within certain social systems and not in others. Although blocking our relations, alienation can, at the same time, serve as a uniting force across social milieus. For this to happen, it does not suffice, as Mouffe claims, for the leader to name people's various grievances and call for action. On the contrary, this strategy risks having a demoralising effect: disregarding rather than recognising people's suffering and thereby aggravating their alienation. The inability to engage, and to be heard, is an integral part of the condition of alienation from which they suffer.

For the experience of alienation, of an inhibited relation, to be transformed into political engagement, the movement must seek to build new mobilising relations. One way to do so would be to recognise people's collective experience of alienation. Seeing how the experience of alienation is shared with others could serve as a relief from the insecurity and powerlessness that is also an intrinsic part of the experience.[1] However, to be able to challenge alienation, it may not suffice for the radical democratic movement to address alienation in words only. It may, as we will see, also require strategic representation, action and behaviour.

When we reformulate the subject of radical democracy and integrate a theory of alienation, the radical democratic movement is not, as in Mouffe's left populist strategy, limited to mobilising around negation and negative experiences. There is another form of recognition that the radical democratic movement can offer alienated groups: positive recognition. While the experience of 'lack' that Mouffe emphasises can be experienced by anyone, alienation is a particular social experience; it is a specific form of social suffering experienced in specific social milieus and situations. In order to fight alienation, the radical democratic movement must extend its mobilising strategy *beyond* lack, negativity and the language of 'we' and 'they'. Radical democracy needs strategies for positive recognition of existing social discourses and forms of understanding within certain social milieus.

A radical democratic movement could seek to recognise positive aspects of alienated social milieus by adopting their cultural narratives, language and/or behaviour.[2] There are at least two central elements of alienated social milieus that the radical democratic movement could seek to create a correspondence or resonance with.

First, the radical democratic movement can seek to adopt and communicate the positive values and cultural narratives that already exist in those social milieus in which alienation is prevalent. For this, the movement would have to describe political problems and solutions in a way that makes sense and seems viable and reasonable within these milieus. The challenge, here, would be to seek to identify problems and solutions that could be shared between diverse contexts – stretching between both precarious popular milieus and intellectuals. Alienation, or some version of this, could possibly serve as a common formulation of a particular problem. Its effectiveness as a mobilising narrative would, however, have to be examined empirically.

Second, an equally important form of resonance, when it comes to including and mobilising alienated people, is what I will call embodied resonance. Drawing on Bourdieu's concept of habitus, we can describe this form of resonance as embodying the habitus of alienated people. Embodied resonance is achieved not merely by discursively capturing the values, narratives and experiences of the social milieus where alienation is prevalent, but by embodying their style.

Embodied resonance in public means lending public recognition to alienated, marginalised people. This is a central reason why embodied resonance could be particularly effective in recognising and mobilising alienated groups. As we saw in Chapter 4, one of the dimensions of alienation is disorientation. Drawing on Bourdieu, I argued that disorientation means that the subject's habitus – her embodied dispositions – no longer functions. The social world to which the subject and her habitus corresponded has been lost. When these embodied ways of being are displayed in public by a movement or its leaders, it can thus be particularly forceful. It could aid people to reconnect with the social world – in this case, the movement – and even themselves, by finding a space where their habitus functions.

Whether embodied resonance would actually be effective for mobilising alienated people is an empirical question that would have to be tested. This idea is, however, supported by strands of the contemporary literature on populism, in particular the work of Pierre Ostiguy (2017, 2009). In Ostiguy's conception, the leader is not, as Mouffe and Laclau assume, an 'empty' symbol capable of representing anything. Instead, the populist leader embodies a certain sociocultural position. The important thing, Ostiguy argues, is the 'ways of relating to people' that 'go beyond "discourses" as words', and that 'include issues of accent, levels of language, body language, gestures, and ways of dressing. And as a way of relating to people, they also encompass the way of making decisions, in politics' (Ostiguy 2017, 77). The populist leader is able to mobilise people from certain sociocultural milieus, not merely by presenting a certain political position – such as a left or right position – but through her embodied dispositions, similar to what I have called habitus. The leader forms a relation to a particular sociocultural milieu through her way of being. Such embodied dispositions are, according to Ostiguy, slow to develop and slow to change. 'These different traits', Ostiguy claims, 'may be in fact more difficult to credibly change than left–right positioning' (Ostiguy 2017, 77). Embodied resonance may explain why people sometimes support leaders who express values and opinions that differ from their own. It is thus, Ostiguy shows, particularly fruitful in explaining the success of populist movements. Embodied resonance could, for example, partly explain how right populist leaders can attract support from traditionally left-leaning groups.

What role, then, could embodied resonance play in the radical democratic struggle against alienation? The work of Ostiguy and Bourdieu can give us some indication on how to answer this question. According to Ostiguy, the populist movement emerges through 'a particular form of political relationship between political leader and the social basis, one established and articulated through "low" appeals which resonate and receive positive reception within particular sectors of society for social-cultural historical reasons' (Ostiguy 2017, 73; see also Ostiguy 1999, 2009). The relationship is established through what Ostiguy describes as a 'flaunting of the "low"'. Ostiguy's notions of 'the low' and 'the high', in their sociocultural dimension, roughly correspond to Bourdieu's notions of high and low embodied cultural capital. While on the side of 'the high', 'people publicly present themselves as well behaved, proper, composed, and perhaps even bookish', people on 'the low' 'frequently use a language that includes slang or folksy expressions and metaphors, are more demonstrative in their bodily or facial expressions as well as in their demeanour, and display more raw, culturally popular tastes' (Ostiguy 2017, 78). The political leader can thus achieve resonance with his target groups by embodying and displaying a similar level of cultural capital.

This strategy also has an antagonistic dimension. In a populist movement, Ostiguy argues, the populist leader not only embodies 'the low'; he demonstrably and antagonistically 'flaunts' it. We see such flaunting in 'the utterly incorrect Berlusconi, the speeches of Jean-Marie Le Pen, the biting insults of Hugo Chávez, or the mischievous escapades of Carlos Menem' (Ostiguy 2017, 76). By refusing to be 'proper' or 'politically correct' or to show 'good taste', the populists challenge the rules of the game and the established power (Ostiguy 2017, 92). At the same time, the political challenge of 'the low' is, according to Ostiguy, met by a political defence of 'the high'. Politicians on the side of 'the high' respond by, in a similarly assertive and antagonistic way, 'flaunting the high'. By 'relishing . . . their transgressions', populist leaders politicise the high–low dimension (Ostiguy 2017, 92). This antagonistic representation, or 'flaunting', can thus become an effective means for mobilising people, resulting in what Linus Westheuser (2020) describes as a 'symbolic class struggle'. And if, as Bourdieu claims, symbolic, embodied capital is a concealed class division, political mobilisation along this divide can be described as a concealed class struggle. In being concealed, it can be mobilised for very different political agendas.

Drawing on Bourdieu's theory of capital, I will argue that mobilisation by embodied resonance poses problems, but it also offers new possibilities for a radical democratic struggle against alienation. A problem for the radical democratic movement is that the strategy of symbolic resonance seems – following Ostiguy's observations – to be most effectively used by right populists. Ostiguy's theory of populism, combined with Bourdieu's theory of capital, would, for example, explain some of the relative success of right populist leaders within some traditionally left, white working-class milieus. The habitus of the financial fraction of the dominant class and the dominated classes are similar in the sense that both tend to have low cultural capital. Some of these may also share what Ostiguy describes as 'nativist' characteristics, marked by a 'culturally localist ("from here") way' – which can function as a provocation towards their common opponent, the cosmopolitan, intellectual class (Ostiguy 2017, 80). The right populist leader's flaunting of low cultural capital and nativism may thus resonate both with the 'businessmen' – the financial fraction of the dominant class – as well as within some precarious popular and countryside milieus. Embodied resonance can thus be utilised by right populists to unite the financial fractions of the dominant class with – in particular – white and countryside popular milieus. It reinforces the conflict between those with high and low cultural capital as well as those with nativist rather than cosmopolitan ways. The right populists' use of embodied resonance thus risks blocking the radical democratic struggle against alienation, seeking to unite precarised groups with different amounts of cultural capital.

At the same time, embodied resonance can be used not only by right populists but also by labour movements and left-wing leaders. There are at least two reasons why it could be an effective strategy in the struggle against alienation.

First, under conditions of alienation, embodied resonance can work as a 'moral battery', inspiring engagement. In an emerging literature on social movements and emotions, James Jasper (2010) argues, for example, that while the shame and self-blame often connected to the experience of subordination can block political engagement, countering such emotions with their opposite – with pride and a sense of power – can be a forceful 'moral battery', inspiring engagement and action (Jasper 2010). Moreover, the commitment to collective action can be further strengthened by pride in one's group and its 'moral worth' (Jasper 2011; Tilly and Wood 2020).

Such 'moral batteries' could be particularly powerful in mobilising alienated groups. In being both dominated and disoriented, those who are alienated suffer not only from subordination but also from disorientation: a loss of social place and purpose. When social dispositions resonating with their own are proudly 'flaunted' by a political leader, it can function as a moral battery, turning the shame of domination and the displacement of disorientation into pride and belonging. By establishing bonds of embodied resonance, a political movement and its leader can open up a space for those who are out of place.

Second, the antagonism involved in the 'flaunting' of margin-alised social dispositions can inspire passions among dominated groups, at least as effectively as the discursive antagonism described by Mouffe and Laclau. A symbolic flaunting can, like language in Mouffe and Laclau's theory, challenge dominant groups and serve as a vindication for the daily micro-aggressions that the dominated suffer. Ostiguy shows how, by 'flaunting the low', the populist leader disrupts and challenges the rules of the political and social game. To this challenge, politicians on the side of 'the high' respond in a similarly assertive and antagonistic way by 'flaunting the high' – or, in Michelle Obama's words, 'When they go low, we go high.' What emerges is a political conflict that partly follows the sociocultural lines of high and low cultural capital. The potential antagonism that domination – as a dimension of alienation – may inspire can thus be challenged not only discursively but also through the strategy of symbolic division and resonance.

Symbolic resonance could thus be a potentially useful strategy for radical democratic mobilisation against alienation. At the same time, it has several drawbacks, in particular the differences in habitus between precarised groups. Precarised, alienated people can be found in many different social milieus and vary in both their cultural capital and nativist dispositions. Some of the most intense processes of precarisation have taken place in relatively white, nativist milieus in the countryside as well as in racialised milieus in both the countryside and the city suburbs. To complicate things further, precarisation has also affected academic social milieus, such as the deprofession-alised professionals. While well-mannered and polished politicians might serve as a provocation to deeply precarious people with low cultural capital, representatives with a more relaxed and personal manner might be perceived as rude and aggressive to deprofession-alised academics. This poses a challenge for a movement seeking to mobilise alienated groups.

Having reformulated the subject, we can broaden our perception of the strategies and challenges facing a radical democratic move-ment. When we assume a radical democratic subject who is social, dependent and problem-solving, we can see that a radical democratic strategy can include more than language. A main challenge for a broad radical democratic movement struggling with and against alienation is to find resonance within a variety of precarised social milieus that differ in many respects, notably in their level of cultural capital. This also reveals new tactical challenges for the radical democratic movement. In order to engage people who are alienated – disengaged from their own situation – negative discursive resonance may not suffice. In these cases, positive recognition and resonance may be particularly important, not only in respect to values, narratives and experiences, but also when it comes to embodied dispositions. At the same time, it is precisely in these aspects that alienated people, with different levels of cultural capital, differ. This emerges as a central challenge facing the radical democratic movement concerned with alienation.

## HOW TO ORGANISE?

In the wake of the Occupy Wall Street movement – for which the internal organisation of the movement itself was one of its central aims – the organisation of democracy movements has been widely discussed by both democracy theorists and practitioners. In Mouffe's left populist strategy, however, the movement's internal relations are of little importance. Participants in the movement do not need to relate directly to each other. Instead, their relationships are mediated by a symbol, often a leader. Having reformulated the subject of radical democracy and integrated a theory of alienation, the question of internal organisation becomes relevant. Which new challenges and tactical considerations, when it comes to the internal organisation of the movement, now come into view?

Before answering this question, let us briefly recall Mouffe's left populist strategy and the internal movement organisation that it proposes. In the left populist approach, activists' diverse claims and experiences are mediated by the leader or the slogan. Each person has their own relation to this symbol, and no direct relations between participants are needed. The flexible, strong and conflict-seeking subject does not depend on her relations to others in order to engage. Rather, she is spurred by conflict itself, or, more specifically, by the division between 'we' and 'they'. The relations between people within the movement therefore consist of little more than the common symbol that unites them, as well as the equally symbolic adversary to which they are all opposed. People merely have to be able to get along under the same symbolic roof – 'equality', 'the people' or 'the 99 per cent' – and remain opposed to the same opponent – 'the elite', 'the oligarchs' or 'the 1 per cent'. While the antagonistic construction inspires radical engagement – triggering the subject's natural tendency to seek conflict – the lack of closer relations between participants enables openness, by leaving space for a multiplicity of social groups with different aims and experiences. The symbolic division between 'we' and 'they' is assumed to be sufficient to maintain an engagement that is both open and radical.

Having reformulated the subject of radical democracy, we can no longer assume that this type of loose social relations, mediated by 'empty symbols', would be sufficient to mobilise people. A subject who is social, dependent and problem-solving, rather than flexible, strong and conflict-seeking, is not moved by mere symbols or symbolic conflicts. Open and radical engagement requires real, functioning social relations – relations of appropriation. For this, a commitment to an 'empty symbol', such as a slogan, does not suffice. Recall from Chapter 6 that, while such a commitment may be strong, it is not necessarily open. Rather, this might turn into an alienated relation wherein the subject forms affective attachments not by practically engaging with the world, but by transcending it in her imagination, attaching herself to its complete negation. For the precarious subject, who lacks a grasp of the presence, '[r]evolutionary chiliasm and magical utopias are', in Bourdieu's words, 'the only grasp on the future that offers itself' (Bourdieu 1979, 70). The alienated subject cannot practically engage with the real world through action and problem-solving. Instead, her commitments are merely formed in her imagination. For this reason, it is unlikely that they will accurately respond to the real problems that she faces. Without functioning relations, the social subject's capacity to respond to the experiences and claims of others is inhibited. For the subject to be able to engage politically in an open and radical way, the political movement should thus be built by functioning practical relations – relations of appropriation – rather than around empty symbols.

When reformulating the subject of radical democracy, we are thus able to shed light on the importance of internal organisation for a properly radical democratic strategy. This also means that we are better equipped to make sense of some of the key challenges that the radical democratic movement faces.

211

*Domination and disorientation in the political association*

Domination and disorientation, the two dimensions of alienation, are forms of relations that might manifest themselves not only in society at large but also within the radical democratic movement. And both pose specific challenges for a movement that seeks to remain open and radical. While disorientation blocks us from accurately addressing and making sense of problems, domination distorts the movement's internal power dynamic. In a movement against alienation that includes people with various levels of capital, there is a risk that people with more social and cultural capital may appropriate the organisational resources while blocking those with less from making the movement their own. To seek to organise in a way that breeds neither disorientation nor domination becomes a central organisational challenge for a radical democratic movement against alienation.

Whether alienation – domination and disorientation – is a problem within social movements today, however, is an empirical question. Although this has not been directly examined, social movement studies have identified a number of problems within contemporary movements that could be interpreted as indications of alienation. Research has, for example, found that burnout – 'the end result of a process in which idealistic and highly committed people lose their spirit' (Pines 1994, 381) – is not only a work-related problem, it is also a problem within social movements and parties. Activists' emotional investment in the activity, even social movement scholars argue, renders them particularly vulnerable (Kovan and Dirkx 2003; Maslach and Gomes 2006; Plyler 2006). This may be an indication that alienation is a risk in social movement organisations. Furthermore, although political engagement is commonly observed to be empowering, this is not always the case. When political processes are experienced as dominating, or as 'procedurally unjust', they risk having the opposite effect, resulting in political apathy (Helander 2016). Irrespective of these empirical findings, however, we can, at least theoretically, assume that people can be dominated and disoriented in political processes – systematically undermined in processes that they are unable to navigate. This risk is something that a radical democratic movement that takes alienation seriously must take into account.

## Possible solutions

As we have seen, internal alienation within the movement is a possible problem faced by the radical democratic movement. As such, it needs tactics for counteracting internal processes of alienation in both of its dimensions: domination and disorientation; however, the risk is that the attempt to avoid one could breed the other. If we take this risk into account, what are the organisational tactics that a movement against alienation can adopt? While fully answering this question lies beyond the scope of this study, I want to briefly discuss some of the benefits and problems with three organisational tactics that have grown popular among contemporary democratic movements: prefiguration, exclusion and peer-education.

A common tactic in radical and democratic movements is *prefiguration* – the attempt of a political association to cultivate within its own organisation the same 'social relations, decision-making, culture, and human experience' that it seeks to achieve in society at large (Boggs 1977). The idea of prefiguration can be illustrated by the Indignados' slogan '¡Democracia Real YA!' (real democracy NOW!), which is directed both towards the political system and towards the internal organisation (Calvo 2013; Flesher Fominaya 2017). The Occupy Wall Street movement and the Alter-globalisation movement are commonly understood as prefigurative (Maeckelbergh 2011). In the Occupy movement, the prefigurative strategy included an emphasis on direct and deliberative democratic ethos and procedures. At this point, these strategies have been thoroughly examined, and they have in several cases been found to be successful in fulfilling their internal democratic ideals (Flesher Fominaya 2017; Maeckelbergh 2012). For example, the Global Justice Movement has been found to organise along lines with (deliberative) democratic ideals (C. Haug 2010; Della Porta and Rucht 2015) and to foster democratic attitudes (Della Porta 2005, 2009). The democratic prefigurative strategy has thus proven its potential as a radical democratic strategy, seemingly inspiring engagement and openness.

What are the possibilities and problems of prefiguration when it comes to the problem of alienation? Prefiguration commonly involves open discussions, which may serve as a way to build relations of appropriation – enabling participants to make the movement their own. At the same time, there are two possible risks with this strategy from an alienation perspective. First, associations characterised by openness, discussion and non-hierarchical structures can also enable groups with more cultural and social capital to dominate those with less – resulting in further alienation. Studies indicate that openness and a non-hierarchical structure pave the way for informal elite dominance (Freeman [1972] 2013; Staggenborg 2013; Bondesson 2017).

Second, the prefigurative political culture with its priority of ethics and democratic procedures may disorient rather than resonate with some alienated social groups. As we have seen, Ostiguy shows, for example, that the preferred type of leadership may vary depending on the participants' sociocultural background – and in particular, in Bourdieu's terms, on their cultural capital. Ostiguy's division into 'the high' and 'the low' has a politico-cultural dimension that cannot be fully separated from the sociocultural one. The dimension 'is about forms of political leadership and preferred (or advocated) modes of decision-making in the polity' (Ostiguy 2017, 81). While 'the high' involves 'formal, impersonal, legalistic, institutionally mediated models of authority' where 'niceties' are valued, 'the low' involves 'very personalistic, strong (often male) leadership' (Ostiguy 2017, 81). On the side of the low we hear that '"Doubt is the boast of intellectuals," "Better than to talk is to do"'. It 'entails a preference for decisive action often at the expense of some "formalities"' (Ostiguy 2017, 82). This suggests that the prefigurative organisation and leadership – centred on deliberation and discussion – might not always appeal to those with low cultural capital, preferring a style of effective goal-oriented action. There is, thus, a risk that the attempt to avoid domination by means of prefiguration could result in disorientation and further alienation among some alienated groups.

Conversely, grass-roots organisations might inspire passionate mobilisation and relations of appropriation among dominated groups, without having any explicit prefigurative ambitions. An example of this is the French Gilets jaunes (yellow vests) movement. The movement originated with protesting against an increase in fuel taxes, wearing the yellow vests that, under a 2008 French law, all motor vehicles are required to carry. It combined aims for a strengthened democracy with claims for social and fiscal justice. However, while it was concerned with democracy, the aim was not necessarily to manifest democratic deliberation in the movement itself. Rather, protesters demonstrated, and blocked roads and fuel depots – actions that sometimes developed into major riots and violent clashes with the police. The movement came to inspire passionate mobilisation, not least among the rural working class, such as motorists from rural areas who had long commutes and were heavily affected by increased fuel taxes. It remained clearly horizontal and owned by its grass roots, with a rejection of any emerging leadership figure (Chamorel 2019).

In contrast, the 2016 movement Nuit debout (rise up at night), which occupied the Place de la République in Paris after protests against labour reforms, inscribed itself in the prefigurative model. Assemblies were organised in the square every night for three months, with sub-assemblies or discussion groups specialising in certain themes and struggles; and its main mode of action was the refusal to designate any kind of leadership and instead to protect at all costs the movement's impersonality and horizontal structure. If the movement spread to other cities for a few days, it remained – in the image of Occupy – a Parisian phenomenon, with a certain sociological homogeneity (young educated urbanites). And if Jacques Rancière argued with much hope that the May 68 movement started with the same social group but succeeded in converging with the working class, this never really happened to Nuit debout (Confavreux 2016).

While the prefigurative tactic is thus potentially promising, it also comes with the risks of cultivating informal elite dominance and of further disorienting participants. How widespread these two problems are in prefigurative movements, and how they can be avoided, remains to be examined. There are, however, some empirical indications that, when wrongly adopted, the prefigurative strategy could reinforce rather than counteract both domination and disorientation.

Let us take a look at the example of Occupy Sandy, which arguably struggled particularly with both of the aforementioned problems. In the wake of Hurricane Sandy in 2012, activists from the Occupy Wall Street movement travelled to the socially vulnerable area Rockaway, Queens. Their aim was to help the locals rebuild the area after the hurricane, while at the same time politically empowering them. The activists initiated a support project in which anyone could engage and whose aims were open for deliberation and reformulation. In her study of the movement, Sara Bondesson (2017) found that in the initial phase of acute relief work, the project was successful. Ten thousand volunteers distributed food and water, provided medical aid and helped with the reconstruction. However, when the work moved from the most pressing practical issues to political organising and lobbying, the collaboration between locals and the Occupy activists faltered and conflict ensued. Bondesson concludes that the local Occupy Sandy hub had failed to live up to its democratic organisational ideals (which she describes as openness, flexibility and horizontality) and became dominated by the Occupy activists from outside the area. For example, the locals never truly gained control over the budget, and although the organisation was said to be flat, informal leadership structures had developed with mainly outsider activists in central positions. This outside dominance was met with resistance from the locals and the local organisations.

Beyond the problem of elite dominance emphasised by Bondesson, her interviews also suggest that there was a more fundamental discord between Occupy activists and locals. I interpret this as an indication that the local participants questioned elements of the prefigurative ethic and form of decision-making. For some of the local activists, the Occupy movement's ideals and functioning did not make sense. They questioned why the goals of the movement should continuously be discussed, saying, 'We know what the problems are' (Bondesson 2017, 141). One of the local activists expressed discontent with the idea of becoming empowered and being taught about democratic organising. In interviews, residents explained that it seemed to them like the Occupy activists had come directly from school and were over-eager to implement their ideals, even when it meant overruling the local understanding already in place. The Occupy activists' attempts to teach them how to do things democratically were experienced by local activists as patronising (Bondesson 2017, 162). Other local activists criticised the movement's ideal of shared leadership. Some suggested that the Occupy activists, coming from the outside, should not have an equal say. The influence of outside activists, they claimed, resulted in unnecessary conflict and fragmentation (Bondesson 2017, 149). On a deeper level, it can thus be questioned whether the prefigurative tactic – marked by long discussions where everyone has a say – resonated with some of the most precarious people in the movement.

Experiences of the prefigurative tactic suggest that it can potentially be successful, but also that it risks both cultivating informal elite dominance and failing to resonate with precarious groups. A radical democratic movement adopting this tactic should thus do so with an awareness of these problems.

Can the possible risks associated with the prefigurative strategy be counteracted? Let us turn to another popular organisational tactic among contemporary democratic movements that more directly targets the problem of domination within the movement: *exclusion*. By excluding people who are in a position to dominate others in the movement, such as men or white people, for example, domination is prevented. A broader movement can also practise tactical exclusions in some, but not all, of its activities (e.g. Dovi 2009; Medearis 2015, 144).

In a movement mobilising alienated groups, occasional tactical exclusion could be used to counteract the risk that those in the movement with more cultural and social capital would dominate those with less. Participants with more social and cultural capital might, for example, more easily be able to dominate the conversation, to shape the agenda of the association, to be selected for important positions and to gain recognition for their work. Conversely, those with less capital might put in a lot of work without gaining recognition or being selected for important positions. Tactical exclusions could be used here to create branches of the movement solely controlled by groups that otherwise would risk domination.

However, while tactical exclusions may be efficient in preventing domination, they could also be experienced as disorienting, failing to resonate with the moral intuitions and self-perception of some of the participants. For example, some have understood the tactical exclusions of white people as a racist separation according to race. Tactical exclusions may in particular be disorienting for those who are excluded, unsettling their understanding of themselves as oppressed, feminist, antiracist or the champion of the oppressed. This disorientation might be particularly painful for those who are alienated in society at large – experiencing continuous disrespect and disorientation. The risk that tactics for countering domination could, in turn, breed disorientation is one of the practical dilemmas that a movement against alienation should take into consideration.

Beyond organisational tactics that directly target internal domination, there are also tactics that could be used to target disorientation. As we have seen, disorientation means impaired meaning- and sense-making. It blocks people's ability to accurately make sense of the problems that they encounter. To counteract disorientation, the movement against alienation could turn to the various strategies that have been formulated for building radical consciousness through education, and, in particular, through peer-education, where dominated people come together to learn from each other.

217

The idea of radical education can be traced back to the work of Paulo Freire. In *Pedagogy of the Oppressed* (1996) he argues that oppressed groups can develop a revolutionary consciousness through a pedagogy based on love. This idea has influenced contemporary radical practice and theory (e.g. Sandoval 2000). There are several examples, both classical and contemporary, of movements built around the idea of radical and critical education – including the system of study-circles used in the Swedish labour movement, the autonomous French university Centre universitaire de Vincennes created to enable critical consciousness, and Université debout, arranged by the French movement Nuit debout. Studies of the Swedish labour movement have shown, for example, that workers' education organised through non-hierarchical study-circles was particularly important in developing a common identity and establishing a sense of belonging, while at the same time taming tendencies towards antagonism (Jansson 2012, 2016). At the same time, we have also seen how, as in the case of Université debout, radical education does not always reach the marginalised groups that it seeks to target. These mixed results suggest that education, if organised in the right way and with the right ethos, may be a means through which relations of appropriation can be established within the movement, while at the same time overcoming some of the blockages to alienation.

In sum, having reformulated the subject of radical democracy, we can shed light on organisational challenges and tactics that were previously overlooked. In particular, it opens up for tactics aimed at shaping the relations within the movement, such as prefiguration, tactical exclusion and peer-education. At the same time, the concept of alienation also sheds new light on the possible risks associated with some of these strategies. A general challenge in organising against alienation is that strategies aimed at one of its dimensions – such as domination – can aggravate the other – such as disorientation – and vice versa. Struggling with alienation within the movement means seeking solutions that contest domination without disrupting the world of the participants in a disorienting way. At the same time, a successful strategy against alienation cannot merely cling to old sociocultural ideals, narratives and ways of doing things when these, in fact, sustain domination. Although it takes time, our disposition and orientations – what Bourdieu calls habitus – can change. Tactics aimed at cultivating new orientations – such as prefiguration and peer-education – can become both disorienting and successful. To

218

avoid aggravating alienation, the radical democratic movement may find fruitful ways of combining different tactics. Beyond the organisational tactics discussed here, there are, of course, many more. When we integrate a theory of alienation into radical democracy we open up for a variety of new ways of organising. Like the struggle against alienation, the struggle with alienation within the movement is likely to be a reoccurring one – requiring continuous action and experimentation.

## WHAT TO DEMAND?

The questions of what issues to focus on and what concrete demands to make are central strategic concerns for any social movement. The concrete demands that the movement makes can affect the support for and success of the movement, as well as the future prospects for radical struggle. However, in Mouffe's populist strategy, the substantial aims of the movement are of little strategic importance. Instead, Mouffe emphasises the strategic importance of discursive construction of a 'we' and a 'they'. Having reformulated the subject, radical democracy can begin to take seriously the question of what to demand.

Recall that for Mouffe and Laclau, the actual social outcomes of the movement are not of strategic importance. Instead, the focus lies on the discourse, and the goal is to gather many different claims of deprivation under the same symbolic roof. These claims do not have to add up into a coherent political programme. Instead, the priorities of the left populist movement have often come to be decided by the leader.[3] Assuming instead a social subject, whose political engagement, like all her engagements, is shaped in social processes, the political aims and outcomes of the movement become central. Political engagement does not take place in a vacuum but in a social context that can be either alienating or empowering. The political outcome of the movement can affect this context and thus the possibilities for future political mobilisation.

When we reformulate the radical democratic assumptions of the subject, the question of political demands once again emerges as a potentially significant strategic concern. The theory of alienation reveals that pushing for strategic social changes that counter alienation in the present may also enable future democratic mobilisation. This opens up, for instance, for the type of strategies that broadly

219

could be described as reformism. Reformism has been practised by the Swedish social democratic party, for example. By implementing welfare policies supposed to benefit everyone, the goal was not only to advance the party's social aims but also to ensure broad popular support for the welfare state in general as well as for further social democratic rule.

For the radical democratic movement, the reformist strategy would involve identifying and strategically pushing for changes that could counter alienation and enable radical and open resistance.[4] For this, the movement would have to identify policies that could strengthen the struggle against domination and diminish processes of disorienting precarisation. What, more specifically, this would involve depends on the specific social context in which the movement engages, as well as its participants and their experiences. Policies for reducing precarity could, for example, aim at strengthening social security or union rights. A general challenge in this regard lies in finding reforms that are relevant for different alienated groups, whose views, as we have seen, might both align and differ. Incorporating a theory of alienation into radical democracy thus opens up for a range of new strategic considerations when it comes to making demands.

## NOTES

1. Recent social movement literature has found support for this type of strategy, sometimes described as 'emotional resonance'. Here emotional resonance is found to be particularly mobilising among vulnerable groups. For example, according to Schrock, Holden, and Reid, it can function as 'relief from shame, fear, powerlessness, alienation, and inauthenticity' (Schrock et al. 2004, 61).
2. This strategy of social movements is often described in the social movement literature as 'frame resonance'. For review, see, for example, Benford and Snow 2000.
3. Errejón, secretary for policy and strategy and campaigning of Podemos, emphasises, for example, that the party and the leader 'represent and in doing so it constructs' (Errejón and Mouffe 2016, 113). Although Podemos has relied heavy on centralised organising as an electoral strategy, leaders have indicated a plan towards opening up to grass-roots organising (Agustín and Briziarelli 2018, 11–12).
4. Or, in times of regress, it could also mean defending existing measures, against reforms that would aggravate alienation.

CONCLUSION

# Antagonism and alienation in the process of precarisation and beyond

I started this book by telling you the stories of four people lingering indefinitely in uncertainty. Jacob is caught in an education that seems to be leading nowhere, and Thomas, in long-term unemployment. Samira moves between jobs that she cannot commit to, while Emma sees her professional freedom gradually eroded, leaving her unable to find herself in her work. While Samira and Emma have the cultural capital that a professional degree can lend, neither Jacob, Samira, Thomas nor Emma can remain in the world in which they felt at home. They are left unable to take command over their own lives and to project themselves into the future. Their relations to their work – and, by extension, to their social world – are inhibited in such a way that their relationships to themselves become dysfunctional.

In this book I have argued that the problem of alienation challenges some of the central assumptions of radical democratic theory, and most notably the assumptions about the subject. In order to include the alienated, the subject is reformulated. The reconceived subject is characterised by her activity of appropriation, an activity of problem-solving that involves division and conflict but not the radical negativity that Mouffe calls antagonism. In rethinking the subject in this way, alienation – a social problem – rather than antagonism – an ineradicable part of any society – becomes the central challenge to democracy.

The resulting theory both resists and retains elements of Mouffe's model. It remains agonistic in the sense that it regards conflict as ineradicable and central to democracy. However, it differs from Mouffe's agonistic pluralism in that the agon is not singular – stemming exclusively from the ontological condition of the political – but multiscalar. It can no longer exclusively focus on taming antagonism by channelling 'the political', constitutive conflict, through the political

221

institutions. Instead, it becomes a form of democracy which also continuously interrogates its social conditions of existence, in order to maintain them. Resistance to alienation is conceived as both a condition for and a part of the agonistic democratic struggle.

Although this study is theoretical, it is also of practical significance. I turned to radical democracy in order to address the problem of alienation, which is a social and political problem. Having broadened the radical democratic conception of the subject, we can also broaden our conception of radical democracy as a practice, and as political strategy. Before ending this book, I would like to, first, reiterate some insights from the last chapter, asking what light our reformulated theory of radical democracy can shed on the present problem of alienation and the possibilities of democratic mobilisation against it. What can one do with this new model of radical democracy and its subject that one could not do before? Second, the book ends with a discussion on the possible forms of alienation that, in our focus on precarity, have been obscured. I suggest that in seeking to understand these problems, researchers could use insights from the analysis and conceptual framework developed in this book.

## LESSONS FOR THE RADICAL DEMOCRATIC STRUGGLE

Having reformulated the subject of radical democracy, a potential radical democratic strategy opens up: the possibility of uniting people like Jacob, Samira, Thomas and Emma – precarious youth, routine workers, professionals and semi-professionals – in a common struggle against alienation. At the same time, we are also in a better place to grasp the challenges that such a struggle would involve. Today, people from many different social milieus are precarised, and some of them are also alienated. The effort to unite these people risks turning into alienation in and of itself, reproducing existing forms of domination and producing new forms of disorientation. The struggle against alienation, then, requires a complex set of strategies. Having reformulated the subject of radical democracy, we can take at least three previously concealed challenges and opportunities into account.

First, Mouffe's populist movement – wherein participants are recognised merely for their negative experiences, and their relationship to each other only consists of a common, symbolic adversary – might no longer suffice. Calling for alienated people to act without constructing any new, empowering relations of appropriation risks turning into what Lauren Berlant (2011) calls 'cruel optimism' – adding pressure to individuals who are already overburdened.

Second, the strategies against alienation can produce multiple and contradictory effects. Tactics that protect some people from being dominated – such as a prefiguration or tactical exclusions – may leave others disoriented. While, for example, a prefigurative, deliberative leadership style that democracy movements like Occupy Wall Street have adopted may almost always seem sensible to some groups, in particular intellectuals, it risks alienating others. Not everyone feels at ease with long discussions in which everything is put into question, and particularly not in situations of urgency and deprivation. Having reconsidered the subject of radical democracy, the types of challenges that movements face today can be comprehended and addressed. Meeting them becomes a part of the radical democratic strategy.

Third, the radical democratic strategies can be broadened, beyond merely the construction of antagonistic relations. For instance, a strategy can be to construct new, positive relations. This may be particularly relevant for movements mobilising alienated people who experience meaninglessness and powerlessness. In that situation, people can be strengthened by movements that offer new and meaningful relations – a new world to orient oneself in – and a leadership based on resonance, such as leaders who embody their social dispositions. A radical democracy relying on a social subject can recognise existing social divisions and systems of meaning. These divisions manifest themselves not only in language but also in the subject herself – in her body and her deep-seated moral intuitions. Our embodied social dispositions can make us dislike someone for their bad taste – or for their overly correct one. The rise of right populism testifies precisely to this – to how the mere manners of politicians can determine who we vote for and who we despise, irrespective of whether they are left-wing or right-wing. When class divisions are concealed as cultural divisions – as good or bad manners – a right populist leader can become the champion of the workers. Having reconstructed the radical democratic conception of the subject, this is something that the radical democratic left can no longer ignore.

## ALIENATION BEYOND THE PROCESS OF PRECARISATION

Our reformulation of radical democracy has allowed us to shed light on some of the central challenges that the problem of alienation poses to contemporary democracies. However, in the focus on labour market precarisation, other important problems of alienation today have been left largely unaddressed. At the very beginning of the book, I argued that the most important manifestation of alienation today is precarity. Precarity, I showed, is not only, as previous researchers have argued, the new state of normality for an increasing amount of people, but also an experience that, in its deep structure, corresponds to that of alienation. However, precarity coexists, overlaps and interacts with other forms of intensified insecurity. In concluding this book, I would like to open the discussion to three important forms of insecurity today that have fallen beyond the scope of this book: climate alienation, pandemic isolation and asylum-seekers' waiting. While these issues deserve to be considered in their own right, with attention paid to the specific forms of suffering and possibilities of resistance that each involves, I would like to point to some of the ways in which such an engagement could make use of the analysis and conceptual framework developed in this book.

First, drastic climate changes and the inability of our societies to sufficiently respond to them have resulted in an increased burden on individuals to bear the responsibility for a crisis that can only be resolved collectively. This, in turn, is connected to experiences of intensified existential uncertainty as well as of denial and what is sometimes described as 'climate alienation'.

In our terminology, where alienation is generally understood as impaired appropriation, this can be observed particularly on the level of the collective. The climate crisis has proven to be a problem that is particularly difficult for our societies to accurately and sufficiently respond to. Despite intense debates and efforts, carbon dioxide emissions continue to increase each year and global temperatures keep rising. This inability of a society to sufficiently reform itself in response to a crisis is characteristic of what Rahel Jaeggi describes as an alienated form of life. Here, it is not so much an individual subject's problem-solving that is inhibited, but the problem-solving or 'learning' capacity of an entire group (Jaeggi 2018, 48).

However, while the climate crisis could be described as a form of collective alienation, it is not necessarily always experienced as such. The relation between collective and individual alienation is far from straightforward, and the climate crisis is a good example of this. In order to be able to grasp the climate crisis from an alienation perspective, we would need further studies into the individual experience of collective alienation. While most of us are affected by climate change, we are so in different ways and to widely different degrees. I will suggest that the conceptual framework developed in this book can help us to recognise and make sense of our different responses to climate change.

According to the United Nations High Commissioner for Refugees (UNHCR), an annual average of 21.5 million people have, since 2008, been forced to move due to weather-related events, such as floods, storms, wildfires and extreme temperatures. In these acute cases, the experience of the climate crisis may be one of alienation in the more specific sense that has been defined here: leaving people not only in situations of disorientation, but also in situations of domination. Simply put, while some people, companies and nations have built their wealth on an economic process highly reliant on fossil fuel, the same process is an important cause behind the extreme weather that has rendered millions of people homeless.

However, for others, the experience of the climate crisis lacks the type of urgency and immediacy that disrupts one's life and compels one to react. People read about melting glaciers, see the smoke from wildfires, experience increasingly intense weather and worry about the future of their children. In these situations, people may experience the hopelessness and powerlessness of alienation, but also the painful negligence that I have called acedia. In the latter case, the subject finds herself using her power to contribute to the climate crisis, and does so largely against her own will. Those experiencing acedia today could be managers, shareholders, lobbyist or politicians who, in different ways, act to promote the intense production and distribution of carbon dioxide; or just citizens who have their pension funds invested in fossil fuel. When experiencing acedia, the subject has power, such as economic or social capital, but fails to take responsibility for how she uses it.

As we saw in Chapter 7, the mobilisation against acedia and alienation involves particular challenges. The debate on the climate crisis is often highly technical – sometimes unavoidably so – and risks provoking new forms of domination and disorientation, especially outside of academic social milieus. Furthermore, as democratic societies

225

struggle to respond to the crisis and diminish their carbon dioxide emissions, individual consumers are left to shoulder the burden of a crisis that can only be resolved collectively. Such a context of frustration and powerlessness risks further strengthening the appeal of false information and conspiracy theories.

However, although difficult, broad mobilisation against climate alienation is not impossible. In recent years, new radical actors have emerged on the local, national and global arena. Youth-led movements such as Fridays for Future have mobilised broadly by calling attention to the urgency of the climate crisis for an entire young generation. Parents in suburbs mobilising for a safer local environment for their children have shown how the struggle for environmental justice – for clean air and the preservation of green areas where children can play – can be linked to other urgent local struggles against gang violence, police violence and racial profiling (Ouassak 2020). These movements demonstrate that even around an issue that can seem distant and highly theoretical, people can find ways to organise that have an immediate importance to and impact on their own community.

Another type of environmental movement aims at actively appropriating parts of the economic system that are experienced as being beyond democratic control. People have gathered to shape new forms of production through cooperative gardening, food stores and, in its more militant form, by occupying land and physically blocking development projects (what in France is called a *zone à défendre*, or ZAD for short). Another initiative aimed at appropriating elements of the economic system is local currencies and community currencies. The latter is surprising from an alienation perspective, as the aim is to democratically 'appropriate' money, what Karl Marx describes as the most powerful object in the capitalist system and the ultimate manifestation of man's alienation (Marx 1975a, 323). Local and community currencies – a form of associative money run voluntarily by a group of people gathered around a shared project – can be distinguished from contemporary ordinary forms of money in that they can only be used to buy specific products in certain places (Blanc 2018, 51–2). In this way, they are intended to promote local and sustainable production. At the same time, the aim is democratic. Under the slogan 'for a local and democratic appropriation of money', the influential Mouvement Sol in France seeks to 'construct an economic citizenship and a monetary democracy' (Mouvement Sol 2022). By

offering a complementary currency, governed through citizen participation and deliberation, local currencies are intended to extend the
scope of democratic decision-making into the sphere of the economy,
allowing citizens to take command over, and appropriate, social
practices that fall beyond the reach of the traditional democratic
institutions (Mouvement Sol 2021, 10). Given their aim at challenging climate alienation by appropriating the social, initiatives such as
local currencies are particularly promising in countering the alienation from the radical democratic perspective developed here. This
calls for further studies evaluating whether these initiatives actually
live up to their democratic potential.

A second form of intensified insecurity today relates to the Covid-
19 pandemic and the confinement policies enacted by governments.
Strategies of social distancing have left many people in new forms of
intensified insecurity and isolation, unprecedented in today's democratic societies. As a disruption of people's social relations, the
experience of pandemic isolation may structurally resemble that of
alienation. This, however, will depend on whether social isolation is
followed by a deeper inhibition, a disruption in the subject's relationship to herself. While several studies have observed that people have
experienced 'apathy' and profound 'loneliness' during confinement
– particularly within the older population (Dahlberg 2021; Groarke
et al. 2020; Hwang et al. 2020) – a more in-depth analysis of these
phenomena would be required in order to determine whether such
loneliness also involves processes of de-subjectification.

Furthermore, because the very cause of this insecurity is social
isolation, any attempt at countering it through collective mobilisation becomes particularly difficult. From our perspective, focused on
alienation as a democratic problem, a central question is whether the
experiences of pandemic isolation are suitable to analyse through a
political framework – centred on conflict and domination – or if it
would be more suitable to examine as a subjective, psychological
problem, that is, loneliness as an individual state. Recent years have
seen the rise of new forms of protest and antagonism, manifesting
themselves as heterogeneous mobilisations against vaccine passes
and government restrictions. However, social distancing measures
are likely to hit hardest against the same people who, at the same
time, they would most benefit. This involves the people particularly
exposed to the pandemic, such as those with physically demanding jobs, those who live in crowded accommodation or those who

already suffer from poor health. An in-depth analysis of each particular measure would be required in order to determine whether it actually involves domination, that is, whether it systematically allows some people to appropriate social power at others' expense. Needless to say, the pandemic has given rise to a collective distress that, due to its deeply isolating nature, has been very difficult to accurately address. Examining it through the alienation framework developed here could be a step towards a better understanding of what the phenomenon of pandemic isolation did to democratic societies and how it affected our possibilities for radical democratic resistance.

Finally, while this book has emphasised the alienating structure of imposed speed and movement, we should not forget its flipside: waiting. When they are waiting, people are stuck – often in both time and space. Time is not moving fast enough; it is 'endured rather than traversed' (Kohli and Kaukko 2018, 490). Just like speed, waiting can render the subject deeply insecure. It is a type of 'liminal experience', a 'transitory and transformative space which lies in between life stages, statuses and material contexts' (Sutton et al. 2011). Its outcome is often unknown. And when this is the case, it can become deeply painful, in particular for those who are already in a vulnerable position.

On the one hand, waiting as a 'transformative space' is an experience that we all share: it is an inherent aspect of growing up and moving through life. On the other hand, waiting can also be a politically imposed, structural experience that entails specific forms of power. Martin Luther King, Jr. captured the relation between power and waiting in a letter from prison:

> For years now . . . I have heard the word 'Wait!' It rings in the ears of every Negro with piercing familiarity. This 'Wait' has almost always meant 'Never.' The poor will always be with us; the poor will always wait. Their time is not money. (Martin Luther King, Jr., qtd in Sutton et al. 2011, 31)

While everyone waits, those with less power – the poor, the marginalised and the disadvantaged – wait longer. Until recently, the forms of power that waiting entails have remained largely untheorised. However, recent literature has revealed how some marginalised groups, and in particular asylum-seekers, are exposed to a specific form of waiting sometimes described as 'prolonged' waiting (e.g.

Andersson 2014; Bendixsen and Eriksen 2018; Griffiths et al. 2013; Rotter 2016). As we will see, the experience of prolonged waiting bears a structural resemblance to that of alienation.

Scholars show that while 'situational, instrumental waiting' is a normal part of life, the 'prolonged open-ended waiting' of migrants, and in particular asylum-seekers, caught in situations of ambiguity and dependence, can be deeply disempowering. The places where refugees wait are often located at a geographical distance from the rest of society; they become 'static holding places where everything, time and people, stay still' (Kohli and Kaukko 2018, 491). Their inhabitants are left in a place of '"no place" and as being "no one"' (Kohli and Kaukko 2018, 492). Refugees' experiences of waiting vary, but are also similar in at least one important aspect. Time in the spaces where refugees wait is continuously depicted as being 'long and empty', a type of 'limbo' (Brun 2015). In limbo you are neither fully present, nor do you have anywhere else to go (Mountz 2011, 382). Instead, you are stuck in the 'waiting room for real life' (Kohli and Kaukko 2018, 496). Refugees waiting for asylum have fled their homes, but without really arriving anywhere: 'located within . . . dislocation', they lack social ties and habits that can bind them to time and life (Kohli and Kaukko 2018, 496).

In its deep structure, the experience of prolonged waiting thus seems to resemble that of alienation: the waiting subject's relation to the social world is impaired in such a way that it risks inhibiting her relationship to herself – leaving her unable to find meaning in her activity and to make constructive use of her time. The social disruption of migration, then, when prolonged through the asylum process, is linked to a deeper problem: the disruption of the subject's relationship to herself. This is sometimes described as a form of 'de-subjectification' (Vitus 2010, 41). Held in a state of passivity, asylum-seekers who wait risk losing the sense of being in command of their own lives (Brun 2015; Kohli and Kaukko 2018).

As the experience of prolonged waiting in its deep structure resembles that of alienation, it could potentially be further analysed through the prism of the conceptual framework developed in this book. This framework is suitable if one wants to examine prolonged waiting as a social and political, rather than mainly psychological, problem – as a problem that can and should be resisted through democratic struggle. It may also provide some ways of understanding how such a struggle can emerge.

As I have demonstrated in this book, resistance to alienation requires the formation of new, unalienated relations among alienated subjects. Although difficult, creating such relations is not impossible. In a study of unaccompanied asylum-seeking girls in Finland, Kohli and Kaukko (2018) observed how, despite being stuck in conditions over which they had little or no influence, and in spite of their explicit lack of motivation to 'change something so temporary', the girls kept making collective efforts to reconstruct their lives and to take charge of their time. Even when lacking a shared language, the girls managed to communicate with one another and organise shared activities: showing each other music from their countries and finding Finnish artists that they all liked. Together, the girls found different roles and functions in their shared life and started to fill the time with routines – creating and recreating a rhythm suitable for everyone (Kohli and Kaukko 2018, 500). In this way, the girls managed to create social bonds and habits that built resilience in the midst of the 'permanent impermanence' of prolonged waiting. The transformation of alienation into resilience is difficult, but not impossible, and, as I have demonstrated, it is a key to democratic engagement.

In opening up the discussion on alienation beyond the process of precarisation, we see how the experience of alienation is also a particular experience of time: of time going too fast, slipping out of our grasp, or of time going too slowly, fixing us in a limbo that is neither 'here' nor 'there'. It all depends on whether we can appropriate our time and, in this way, our lives – making the time that we have our own. This, I have shown, is not merely a problem that each of us has to deal with on our own; it is often also a problem of systematic social disorientation and domination. From the radical democratic outlook developed in this book, alienation is a social, political and, ultimately, a democratic problem. Collective action, providing its participants with an experience of collective problem-solving and embodied resonance with each other, becomes crucial – not only for alienated people themselves but also for sustaining democratic life.

# Bibliography

Agustín, Óscar García, and Marco Briziarelli, eds. 2018. *Podemos and the New Political Cycle*. Cham: Palgrave Macmillan.

Ahmed, Sara. 2006. *Queer Phenomenology: Orientations, Objects, Others*. Durham, NC: Duke University Press.

———. 2010a. 'Orientations Matter'. In *New Materialisms: Ontology, Agency, and Politics*, eds. Diana Coole and Samantha Frost, 234–58. Durham, NC: Duke University Press.

———. 2010b. *The Promise of Happiness*. Durham, NC: Duke University Press.

Alexander, Jeffrey C. 2015. 'The Crisis of Journalism Reconsidered: Cultural Power'. *Fudan Journal of the Humanities and Social Sciences* 8(1): 9–31.

Althusser, Louis. 2005. *For Marx*. London; New York: Verso.

Andersson, Ruben. 2014. 'Time and the Migrant Other: European Border Controls and the Temporal Economics of Illegality'. *American Anthropologist* 116(4): 795–809.

Arendt, Hannah. 1998. *The Human Condition*. Chicago: University of Chicago Press.

Balibar, Étienne. 2007. *The Philosophy of Marx*. London; New York: Verso.

Bauman, Zygmunt. 2000. *Liquid Modernity*. Cambridge; Malden, MA: Polity Press.

Beasley-Murray, Jon. 2000. 'Value and Capital in Bourdieu and Marx'. In *Pierre Bourdieu: Fieldwork in Culture*, eds. Nicholas Brown and Imre Szeman, 100–19. Lanham, MD: Rowman & Littlefield.

Bellamy, Richard. 2007. *Political Constitutionalism: A Republican Defence of the Constitutionality of Democracy*. Cambridge: Cambridge University Press.

Bendixsen, Synnøve, and Thomas Hylland Eriksen. 2018. 'Time and the Other: Waiting and Hope among Irregular Migrants'. In *Ethnographies of Waiting: Doubt, Hope and Uncertainty*, eds. Manpreet K. Janeja and Andreas Bandak, 87–112. London: Bloomsbury Academic.

Benford, Robert D., and David A. Snow. 2000. 'Framing Processes and

Social Movements: An Overview and Assessment'. *Annual Review of Sociology* 26(1): 611–39.

Benjamin, Walter. 2009. *On the Concept of History*. New York: Classic Books America.

Berlant, Lauren Gail. 2011. *Cruel Optimism*. Durham, NC: Duke University Press.

Bernstein, Richard J. 1999. *Praxis and Action: Contemporary Philosophies of Human Activity*, new edition. Philadelphia: University of Pennsylvania Press.

Besbris, Max, and Caitlin Petre. 2020. 'Professionalizing Contingency: How Journalism Schools Adapt to Deprofessionalization'. *Social Forces* 98(4): 1524–47.

Bialakowsky, Alejandro. 2019. 'Alienations, Cleavages, Reclassifications'. *Constellations* 27(2): 285–99.

Blanc, Jérôme. 2018. 'Making Sense of the Plurality of Money: A Polanyian Attempt'. In *Monetary Plurality in Local, Regional and Global Economies*, ed. Georgina M. Gómez, 48–66. London; New York: Routledge.

Boggs, Carl. 1977. 'Marxism, Prefigurative Communism, and the Problem of Workers' Control'. *Radical America* 11(6): 99–122.

Bondesson, Sara. 2017. *Vulnerability and Power: Social Justice Organizing in Rockaway, New York City, after Hurricane Sandy*. Uppsala: Department of Government, Uppsala University.

Bourdieu, Pierre. 1979. *Algeria 1960: The Disenchantment of the World*. New York: Cambridge University Press.

———. 1986. 'The Forms of Capital'. In *Handbook of Theory and Research for the Sociology of Education*, ed. John G. Richardson, 241–58. Westport, CT: Greenwood.

———. 1990. *The Logic of Practice*. Stanford: Stanford University Press.

———. 1998. *Contre-feux: propos pour servir à la résistance contre l'invasion néo-libérale*. Paris: Éditions Liber.

———. 2000. 'Making the Economic Habitus: Algerian Workers Revisited'. *Ethnography* 1(1): 17–41.

———. 2001. *Masculine Domination*. Stanford: Stanford University Press.

———. 2006. *The Rules of Art: Genesis and Structure of the Literary Field*. Stanford: Stanford University Press.

———. 2010. *Outline of a Theory of Practice*. Cambridge: Cambridge University Press.

———. 2011. 'The Forms of Capital (1986)'. In *Cultural Theory: An Anthology*, eds. Imre Szeman and Timothy Kaposy, 81–93. Chichester: Wiley-Blackwell.

———. 2013. *Distinction: A Social Critique of the Judgement of Taste*. Hoboken, NJ: Routledge.

Bourdieu, Pierre, Alain Accardo, Gabrielle Balazs, Stéphane Beaud, François Bonvin, Emmanuel Bourdieu, Philippe Bourgois, et al. 1999. *The Weight of the World: Social Suffering in Contemporary Society.* Stanford: Stanford University Press.

Brante, Thomas. 2005. 'Om begreppet och företeelsen profession'. *Tidskrift för Praxisnära forskning* 1.

Brun, Cathrine. 2015. 'Active Waiting and Changing Hopes: Toward a Time Perspective on Protracted Displacement'. *Social Analysis* 59(1): 19–37.

Butler, Judith. 2006. *Precarious Life: The Powers of Mourning and Violence.* London; New York: Verso.

Calhoun, Craig. 2003. 'Pierre Bourdieu'. In *The Blackwell Companion to Major Contemporary Social Theorists*, ed. George Ritzer, 274–309. Malden, MA: Blackwell.

Calvo, Kerman. 2013. 'Fighting for a Voice: The Spanish 15-M/Indignados Movement'. In *Understanding European Movements: New Social Movements, Global Justice Struggles, Anti-Austerity Protest*, eds. Cristina Flesher Fominaya and Laurence Cox, 236–53. London: Routledge.

Carlson, Matt. 2017. *Journalistic Authority: Legitimating News in the Digital Era.* New York: Columbia University Press.

Chamorel, Patrick. 2019. 'Macron versus the Yellow Vests'. *Journal of Democracy* 30(4): 48–62.

Collins, Randall. 2013. 'The End of Middle Class Work: No More Escapes'. In Immanuel Wallerstein, Randall Collins, Michael Mann, Georgi Derluguian, and Craig Calhoun, *Does Capitalism Have a Future?*, 27–88. Oxford: Oxford University Press.

Confavreux, Joseph. 2016, April 30. 'Jacques Rancière: "La transformation d'une jeunesse en deuil en jeunesse en lutte"'. *Mediapart.* https://www .mediapart.fr/journal/culture-idees/300416/jacques-ranciere-la-transfor mation-d-une-jeunesse-en-deuil-en-jeunesse-en-lutte.

Connolly, William E. 1995. *The Ethos of Pluralization.* Minneapolis: University of Minnesota Press.

———. 2002. *Identity, Difference: Democratic Negotiations of Political Paradox*, expanded edition. Minneapolis: University of Minnesota Press.

———. 2004. 'The Ethos of Democratization'. In *Laclau: A Critical Reader*, eds. Simon Critchley and Oliver Marchart, 167–81. London: Routledge.

Critchley, Simon. 2004. 'Is There a Normative Deficit in the Theory of Hegemony?' In *Laclau: A Critical Reader*, eds. Simon Critchley and Oliver Marchart, 123–32. London: Routledge.

———. 2014. *The Ethics of Deconstruction: Derrida and Levinas.* Edinburgh: Edinburgh University Press.

Dahlberg, Lena. 2021. 'Loneliness during the COVID-19 Pandemic'. *Aging & Mental Health* 25(7): 1161–4.

Dean, Jodi. 2016. *Crowds and Party*. London; New York: Verso.

Della Porta, Donatella. 2005. 'Deliberation in Movement: Why and How to Study Deliberative Democracy and Social Movements'. *Acta Politica* 40(3): 336–50.

———. 2009. *Democracy in Social Movements*. New York: Palgrave Macmillan.

Della Porta, Donatella, Sakari Hänninen, Martti Siisiäinen, and Tiina Silvasti, eds. 2015. *The New Social Division: Making and Unmaking Precariousness*. New York: Palgrave Macmillan.

Della Porta, Donatella, and Dieter Rucht. 2015. 'Power and Democracy: Concluding Remarks'. In *Meeting Democracy: Power and Deliberation in Global Justice Movements*, eds. Donatella Della Porta and Dieter Rucht, 214–35. Cambridge: Cambridge University Press.

Dominelli, Lena, and Ankie Hoogvelt. 1996. 'Globalization and the Technocratization of Social Work'. *Critical Social Policy* 16(47): 45–62.

Dovi, Suzanne. 2009. 'In Praise of Exclusion'. *The Journal of Politics* 71(3): 1172–86.

Errejón, Íñigo, and Chantal Mouffe. 2016. *Podemos: In the Name of the People*. London: Lawrence & Wishart.

Ferrini, Cinzia. 2009. 'The Challenge of Reason: From Certainty to Truth'. In *The Blackwell Guide to Hegel's Phenomenology of Spirit*, ed. Kenneth R. Westphal, 72–91. Malden, MA: Wiley-Blackwell.

Filson, Glen. 1988. 'Ontario Teachers' Deprofessionalization and Proletarianization'. *Comparative Education Review* 32(3): 298–317.

Flesher Fominaya, Cristina. 2017. 'European Anti-Austerity and Pro-Democracy Protests in the Wake of the Global Financial Crisis'. *Social Movement Studies* 16(1): 1–20.

Foucault, Michel. 1997. 'The Ethics of the Concern for Self as a Practice of Freedom'. *Ethics: Subjectivity and Truth* 1: 281–301.

Fraser, Nancy, and Rahel Jaeggi. 2018. *Capitalism: A Conversation in Critical Theory*. New York: John Wiley & Sons.

Freeman, Jo. [1972] 2013. 'The Tyranny of Structurelessness'. *WSQ: Women's Studies Quarterly* 41: 231–46.

Freire, Paulo. 1996. *Pedagogy of the Oppressed*, new rev. edition. London: Penguin Books.

Fromm, Erich, and Karl Marx. 2017. *Marx's Concept of Man*. London: Bloomsbury Academic.

Glynos, Jason. 2003. 'Radical Democratic Ethos, or, What Is an Authentic Political Act?' *Contemporary Political Theory* 2(2): 187–208.

Gramsci, Antonio. 1971. *Selections from the Prison Notebooks*, ed. and trans. Quintin Hoare and Geoffrey Nowell Smith. London: Lawrence & Wishart.

Griffiths, Melanie, Ali Rogers, and Bridget Anderson. 2013. 'Migration,

Time and Temporalities: Review and Prospect'. *COMPAS Research Resources Paper* 3.

Groarke, Jenny M., Emma Berry, Lisa Graham-Wisener, Phoebe E. McKenna-Plumley, Emily McGlinchey, and Cherie Armour. 2020. 'Loneliness in the UK during the COVID-19 Pandemic: Cross-Sectional Results from the COVID-19 Psychological Wellbeing Study'. *PloS One* 15(9): e0239698.

Haber, Stéphane. 2007. *L'aliénation: vie sociale et expérience de la dépossession*. Paris: Presses universitaires de France.

———. 2013. *Penser le néocapitalisme: vie, capital et aliénation*. Paris: Prairies ordinaires.

Hall, Stuart. 1988. *The Hard Road to Renewal: Thatcherism and the Crisis of the Left*. London; New York: Verso.

Hardimon, Michael O. 1994. *Hegel's Social Philosophy: The Project of Reconciliation*. Cambridge: Cambridge University Press.

Harvey, David. 2018. *Marx, Capital and the Madness of Economic Reason*. New York: Oxford University Press.

Haug, Christoph. 2010. 'Discursive Decision-Making in Meetings of the Global Justice Movement: Cultures and Practices'. PhD diss. Free University of Berlin.

Haug, Marie R. 1972. 'Deprofessionalization: An Alternate Hypothesis for the Future'. *The Sociological Review* 20: 195–211.

———. 1975. 'The Deprofessionalization of Everyone?' *Sociological Focus* 8(3): 197–213.

Healy, Karen, and Gabrielle Meagher. 2004. 'The Reprofessionalization of Social Work: Collaborative Approaches for Achieving Professional Recognition'. *British Journal of Social Work* 34(2): 243–60.

Hegel, Georg Wilhelm Friedrich. 2005. *Hegel's Preface to the Phenomenology of Spirit*. trans. and running commentary Yirmiyahu Yovel. Princeton, NJ: Princeton University Press.

———. 2011. *Elements of the Philosophy of Right*, ed. Allen W. Wood, trans. Hugh Barr Nisbet. Cambridge: Cambridge University Press.

———. 2013. *Phenomenology of Spirit*, trans. A. V. Miller, reprint edition. Oxford: Oxford University Press.

Heidegger, Martin. 2008. *Being and Time*, trans. John Macquarrie and Edward S. Robinson. New York: Harper Perennial.

Helander, Sofia. 2016. 'Movement and Empowerment: Explaining the Political Consequences of Activism'. *Revista Internacional de Sociología* 74(4): e049.

Hewitt, Martin. 1993. 'Social Movements and Social Need: Problems with Postmodern Political Theory'. *Critical Social Policy* 13(37): 52–74.

Hobbes, Thomas. 1998. *Leviathan*, ed. J. C. A. Gaskin. Oxford; New York: Oxford University Press.

Honig, Bonnie. 1993. *Political Theory and the Displacement of Politics*. Ithaca, NY: Cornell University Press.

Honneth, Axel. 1996. *The Struggle for Recognition: The Moral Grammar of Social Conflicts*. Cambridge, MA: MIT Press.

———. 2008. *Reification: A New Look at an Old Idea*. Oxford: Oxford University Press.

———. 2014. *Freedom's Right: The Social Foundations of Democratic Life*. New York: Columbia University Press.

———. 2017. *The Idea of Socialism: Towards a Renewal*. Cambridge; Malden, MA: Polity Press.

Howarth, David. 2004. 'Hegemony, Political Subjectivity, and Radical Democracy'. In *Laclau: A Critical Reader*, eds. Simon Critchley and Oliver Marchart, 256–76. London: Routledge.

Howarth, David R., ed. 2015. *Ernesto Laclau: Post-Marxism, Populism, and Critique*. London; New York: Routledge.

Hwang, Tzung-Jeng, Kiran Rabheru, Carmelle Peisah, William Reichman, and Manabu Ikeda. 2020. 'Loneliness and Social Isolation during the COVID-19 Pandemic'. *International Psychogeriatrics* 32(10): 1217–20.

Inwood, Michael. 1983. *Hegel*. London; Boston: Routledge & Kegan Paul.

Jaeggi, Rahel. 2014. *Alienation*, trans. Frederick Neuhouser and Alan E. Smith, ed. Frederick Neuhouser. New York: Columbia University Press.

———. 2018. *Critique of Forms of Life*, trans. Ciaran Cronin. Cambridge, MA: Harvard University Press.

Jansson, Jenny. 2012. *Manufacturing Consensus: The Making of the Swedish Reformist Working Class*. Uppsala: Uppsala University.

———. 2016. 'Class Formation in Sweden and Britain: Educating Workers'. *International Labor and Working-Class History* 90: 52–69.

Jasper, James M. 2010. 'Strategic Marginalizations and Emotional Marginalities: The Dilemma of Stigmatized Identities'. In *Surviving Against Odds: The Marginalized in a Globalizing World*, ed. Debal K. SinghaRoy, 29–37. New Delhi: Manohar.

———. 2011. 'Emotions and Social Movements: Twenty Years of Theory and Research'. *Annual Review of Sociology* 37(1): 285–303.

Kalleberg, Arne L. 2009. 'Precarious Work, Insecure Workers: Employment Relations in Transition'. *American Sociological Review* 74(1): 1–22.

———. 2011. *Good Jobs, Bad Jobs: The Rise of Polarized and Precarious Employment Systems in the United States, 1970s–2000s*. New York: Russell Sage Foundation.

Keucheyan, Razmig. 2013. *Left Hemisphere: Mapping Critical Theory Today*, trans. Gregory Elliott. London; New York: Verso.

Kohli, Ravi K. S., and Mervi Kaukko. 2018. 'The Management of Time and Waiting by Unaccompanied Asylum-Seeking Girls in Finland'. *Journal of Refugee Studies* 31(4): 488–506.

Korsch, Karl. 2012. *Marxism and Philosophy*. London; New York: Verso.

Kovan, Jessica T., and John M. Dirkx. 2003. '"Being Called Awake": The Role of Transformative Learning in the Lives of Environmental Activists'. *Adult Education Quarterly* 53(2): 99–118.

Kymlicka, Will. 1989. 'Liberal Individualism and Liberal Neutrality'. *Ethics* 99(4): 883–905.

Lacan, Jacques. 1991. *The Seminar of Jacques Lacan: Book II, The Ego in Freud's Theory and in the Technique of Psychoanalysis, 1954–1955*, ed. Jacques-Alain Miller, trans. Sylvana Tomaselli. New York: W. W. Norton.

Laclau, Ernesto. 1990. *New Reflections on the Revolution of Our Time*. London; New York: Verso.

———. 1996a. 'Deconstruction, Pragmatism, Hegemony'. In Simon Critchley, Jacques Derrida, Ernesto Laclau, and Richard Rorty, *Deconstruction and Pragmatism*, ed. Chantal Mouffe, 47–67. London; New York: Routledge.

———. 1996b. 'Why Do Empty Signifiers Matter to Politics?' In *Emancipation(s)*, 36–46. London; New York: Verso.

———. 2004. 'Glimpsing the Future'. In *Laclau: A Critical Reader*, eds. Simon Critchley and Oliver Marchart, 279–328. London: Routledge.

———. 2005. *On Populist Reason*. London; New York: Verso.

Laclau, Ernesto, and Chantal Mouffe. [1985] 2001. *Hegemony and Socialist Strategy: Towards a Radical Democratic Politics*, 2nd edition. London; New York: Verso.

Laclau, Ernesto, and Lilian Zac. 1994. 'Minding the Gap: The Subject of Politics'. In *The Making of Political Identities*, ed. Ernesto Laclau, 11–40. London; New York: Verso.

Lamont, Michèle. 1992. *Money, Morals, and Manners: The Culture of the French and the American Upper-Middle Class*. Chicago: University of Chicago Press.

———. 2009. *The Dignity of Working Men: Morality and the Boundaries of Race, Class, and Immigration*. Cambridge, MA: Harvard University Press.

Lefort, Claude. 1986. *The Political Forms of Modern Society: Bureaucracy, Democracy, Totalitarianism*. Cambridge, MA: MIT Press.

———. 1988. *Democracy and Political Theory*. Cambridge: Polity Press.

Lempiäinen, Kirsti. 2015. 'Precariousness in academia: Prospects for university employment'. In *The New Social Division: Making and Unmaking Precariousness*, eds. Donatella della Porta, Sakari Hänninen, Martti Siisiäinen, and Tiina Silvasti, 123–38. London: Palgrave Macmillan.

Lukács, Georg. 1972. *History and Class Consciousness: Studies in Marxist Dialectics*. Cambridge, MA: MIT Press.

McNay, Lois. 2014. *The Misguided Search for the Political: Social Weightlessness in Radical Democratic Theory*. Cambridge: Polity Press.

Maeckelbergh, Marianne. 2011. 'Doing is Believing: Prefiguration as Strategic Practice in the Alterglobalization Movement'. *Social Movement Studies* 10(1): 1–20.

———. 2012. 'Horizontal Democracy Now: From Alterglobalization to Occupation'. *Interface* 4(1): 207–34.

Marchart, Oliver. 2007. *Post-Foundational Political Thought: Political Difference in Nancy, Lefort, Badiou and Laclau*. Edinburgh: Edinburgh University Press.

———. 2018. *Thinking Antagonism: Political Ontology after Laclau*. Edinburgh: Edinburgh University Press.

Marcuse, Herbert. 2005. *Heideggerian Marxism*. Lincoln: University of Nebraska Press.

———. 2013. *One-Dimensional Man: Studies in the Ideology of Advanced Industrial Society*. Abingdon: Routledge.

Marx, Karl. 1972a. 'Capital (Volume One)' [1867]. In *The Marx–Engels Reader*, ed. Robert C. Tucker. New York: W. W. Norton.

——— 1972b. 'Wage Labour and Capital' [1849]. In *The Marx–Engels Reader*, ed. Robert C. Tucker. New York: W. W. Norton.

——— 1972c. 'The Coming Upheaval' [1847]. In *The Marx–Engels Reader*, ed. Robert C. Tucker. New York: W. W. Norton.

———. 1972d. 'A Contribution to the Critique of Political Economy' [1859]. In *The Marx–Engels Reader*, ed. Robert C. Tucker. New York: W. W. Norton.

———. 1975a. 'Economic and Philosophical Manuscripts of 1844' [1844]. In *Karl Marx and Friedrich Engels: Collected Works* (Volume 3), 229–347. London: Lawrence & Wishart.

———. 1975b. 'Contribution to the Critique of Hegel's Philosophy of Law' [1843]. In *Karl Marx and Friedrich Engels: Collected Works* (Volume 3), 3–130. London: Lawrence & Wishart.

———. 1986. 'Gründrisse' [1857–61]. In *Karl Marx and Friedrich Engels: Collected Works* (Volume 28), London: Lawrence & Wishart.

———. 2000. 'Capital (Volume One)' [1867]. In *Karl Marx: Selected Writings*, 2nd edition, ed. David McLellan. Oxford: Oxford University Press.

Marx, Karl, and Friedrich Engels. 2000a. 'The German Ideology' [1932]. In *Karl Marx: Selected Writings*, 2nd edition, ed. David McLellan. Oxford: Oxford University Press.

———. 2000b. 'The Communist Manifesto' [1848]. In *Karl Marx: Selected Writings*, 2nd edition, ed. David McLellan. Oxford: Oxford University Press.

———. 2000c. 'Theses on Feuerbach' [1845]. In *Karl Marx: Selected Writings*, 2nd edition, ed. David McLellan. Oxford: Oxford University Press.

Maslach, Christina, and Mary Gomes. 2006. 'Overcoming Burnout'. In *Working for Peace: A Handbook of Practical Psychology and Other Tools*, ed. Rachel M. MacNair, 43–59. Atascadero, CA: Impact.

Medearis, John. 2015. *Why Democracy Is Oppositional*. Cambridge, MA: Harvard University Press.

Mihai, Mihaela, Lois McNay, Oliver Marchart, Aletta Norval, Vassilios Paipais, Sergei Prozorov, and Mathias Thaler. 2017. 'Democracy, Critique and the Ontological Turn'. *Contemporary Political Theory* 16: 501–31.

Milner, Rich. 2013. 'Policy Reforms and De-professionalization of Teaching'. National Education Policy Center, 28 February. https://nepc .colorado.edu/publication/policy-reforms-deprofessionalization.

Monod, Jean-Claude. 2016. *Penser l'ennemi, affronter l'exception*. Paris: La Découverte.

Mouffe, Chantal. 1989. 'Radical Democracy: Modern or Postmodern?' *Social Text* 21: 31–45.

———. 1993. *The Return of the Political*. London; New York: Verso.

———. 2000a. 'For an Agonistic Model of Democracy'. In *Political Theory in Transition*, ed. Noël O'Sullivan, 113–30. London; New York: Routledge.

———. 2000b. *The Democratic Paradox*. London; New York: Verso.

———. 2005a. *On the Political*. London; New York: Routledge.

———. 2005b. *The Return of the Political*. London; New York: Verso.

———. 2013. *Agonistics: Thinking the World Politically*. London; New York: Verso.

———. 2019. *For a Left Populism*. London; New York: Verso.

Mountz, Alison. 2011. 'Where Asylum-Seekers Wait: Feminist Counter-Topographies of Sites between States'. *Gender, Place & Culture* 18(3): 381–99.

Mouvement Sol. 2021. *Monnaies locales: monnaies d'intérêt général. Étude sur l'utilité sociale des monnaies locales complémentaires*. https://base. socioeco.org/docs/monnaies_locales_-_monnaies_d_interet_general.pdf.

———. 2022, January 10. 'Pourquoi une monnaie locale?' https://sol-mon naies-locales.org/pourquoi-une-monnaie-locale.

Neuhouser, Frederick. 2009. *Foundations of Hegel's Social Theory: Actualizing Freedom*. Cambridge, MA: Harvard University Press.

———. 2014. 'Translator's Introduction'. In Rahel Jaeggi, *Alienation*, trans. Frederick Neuhouser and Alan E. Smith, ed. Frederick Neuhouser, xi–xvii. New York: Columbia University Press.

Norval, Aletta J. 2004. 'Democratic Decisions and the Question of Universality'. In *Laclau: A Critical Reader*, eds. Simon Critchley and Oliver Marchart, 140–66. London: Routledge.

———. 2007. *Aversive Democracy: Inheritance and Originality in the Democratic Tradition*. Cambridge: Cambridge University Press.

Ollman, Bertell. 1976. *Alienation: Marx's Conception of Man in Capitalist Society*, 2nd edition. Cambridge: Cambridge University Press.

Osborne, Peter. 1991. 'Radicalism Without Limit? Discourse, Democracy and the Politics of Identity'. In *Socialism and the Limits of Liberalism*, ed. Peter Osborne, 201–25. London; New York: Verso.

Ostiguy, Pierre. 1999. 'Peronism and Anti-Peronism: Class-Cultural Cleavages and Political Identity in Argentina'. PhD diss. University of California.

———. 2009. 'The High and the Low in Politics: A Two-Dimensional Political Space for Comparative Analysis and Electoral Studies'. Kellogg Institute Working Paper 360.

———. 2017. 'Populism: A Socio-cultural Approach'. In *The Oxford Handbook of Populism*, eds. Cristóbal Rovira Kaltwasser, Paul Taggart, Paulina Ochoa Espejo, and Pierre Ostiguy, 73–98. Oxford: Oxford University Press.

Ouassak, Fatima. 2020. *La puissance des mères: pour un nouveau sujet révolutionnaire*. Paris: La Découverte.

Paipais, Vassilios. 2017. *Political Ontology and International Political Thought: Voiding a Pluralist World*. London: Palgrave Macmillan.

Patten, Alan. 1999. *Hegel's Idea of Freedom*. Oxford; New York: Oxford University Press.

Pettit, Philip. 1999. *Republicanism: A Theory of Freedom and Government*. Oxford: Oxford University Press.

Pines, Ayala M. 1994. 'Burnout in Political Activism: An Existential Perspective'. *Journal of Health and Human Resources Administration* 16(4): 381–94.

Pinkard, Terry P. 1994. *Hegel's Phenomenology: The Sociality of Reason*. Cambridge; New York: Cambridge University Press.

Pippin, Robert B. 1997. *Idealism as Modernism: Hegelian Variations*. Cambridge: Cambridge University Press.

Plato. 1991. *The Republic of Plato*, 2nd edition, trans. Allan Bloom. New York: Basic Books.

Plyler, Jen. 2006. 'How to Keep On Keeping On: Sustaining Ourselves in Community Organizing and Social Justice Struggles'. *Upping the Anti* 3: 123–34.

Posner, Richard A. 1992. 'The Deprofessionalization of Legal Teaching and Scholarship'. *Michigan Law Review* 91(8): 1921–8.

Rancière, Jacques. 1976. 'The Concept of "Critique" and the "Critique of

Political Economy" (from the 1844 Manuscript to Capital)'. *Economy and Society* 5(3): 352–76.

———. 1999. *Disagreement: Politics and Philosophy*. Minneapolis: University of Minnesota Press.

———. 2009. *Hatred of Democracy*. London; New York: Verso.

Rawls, John. 1988. 'The Priority of Right and Ideas of the Good'. *Philosophy & Public Affairs* 17(4): 251–76.

Reed, Ralph R., and Daryl Evans. 1987. 'The Deprofessionalization of Medicine: Causes, Effects, and Responses'. *JAMA* 258(22): 3279–82.

Reich, Adam D., and Peter S. Bearman. 2018. *Working for Respect: Community and Conflict at Walmart*. New York: Columbia University Press.

Revers, Matthias. 2017. 'Digital Media and the Diversification of Professionalism'. In *Contemporary Journalism in the US and Germany: Agents of Accountability*, 197–217. New York: Palgrave Macmillan.

Riley, Dylan. 2017. 'Bourdieu's Class Theory'. *Catalyst* 1(2): 107–36.

Rosa, Hartmut. 2010. *Alienation and Acceleration: Towards a Critical Theory of Late-Modern Temporality*. Malmö: NSU Press.

———. 2019. *Resonance: A Sociology of Our Relationship to the World*, trans. James Wagner. Cambridge: Polity Press.

Rotter, Rebecca. 2016. 'Waiting in the Asylum Determination Process: Just an Empty Interlude?' *Time & Society* 25(1): 80–101.

Rousseau, Jean-Jacques. 1999. *Discourse on Political Economy; and, the Social Contract*. Oxford; New York: Oxford University Press.

Rummens, Stefan. 2009. 'Democracy as a non-hegemonic struggle? Disambiguating Chantal Mouffe's agonistic model of politics'. *Constellations* 16(3): 377–91.

Sandoval, Chela. 2000. *Methodology of the Oppressed*. Minneapolis: University of Minnesota Press.

Sartre, Jean-Paul. 2007. *Existentialism Is a Humanism*. New Haven, CT: Yale University Press.

Savage, Mike, Fiona Devine, Niall Cunningham, Mark Taylor, Yaojun Li, Johs. Hjellbrekke, Brigitte Le Roux, Sam Friedman, and Andrew Miles. 2013. 'A New Model of Social Class? Findings from the BBC's Great British Class Survey Experiment'. *Sociology* 47(2): 219–50.

Schaap, Andrew. 2009. 'Introduction'. In *Law and Agonistic Politics*, ed. Andrew Schaap, 1–13. Aldershot; Burlington, VT: Ashgate.

Schacht, Richard. 2013. 'Alienation'. In *International Encyclopedia of Ethics: Volume I, A–Bub*, ed. Hugh LaFollette, 198. Malden, MA; Oxford: Wiley-Blackwell.

Schmitt, Carl. 2008. *The Concept of the Political*. Chicago: University of Chicago Press.

Schrock, Douglas, Daphne Holden, and Lori Reid. 2004. 'Creating Emotional Resonance: Interpersonal Emotion Work and Motivational Framing in a Transgender Community'. *Social Problems* 51(1): 61–81.

Sennett, Richard. 1998. *The Corrosion of Character: The Personal Consequences of Work in the New Capitalism*. New York: W. W. Norton.

Shapiro, Ian, Rogers M. Smith, and Tarek E. Masoud. 2004. *Problems and Methods in the Study of Politics*. Cambridge: Cambridge University Press.

Sim, Stuart. 2000. *Post-Marxism: An Intellectual History*. London: Routledge.

Smith, Vicki. 2010. 'Enhancing Employability: Human, Cultural, and Social Capital in an Era of Turbulent Unpredictability'. *Human Relations* 63(2): 279–300.

Srnicek, Nick. 2017. *Platform Capitalism*. Cambridge; Malden, MA: Polity Press.

Staggenborg, Suzanne. 2013. 'Institutionalization of Social Movements'. In *The Wiley-Blackwell Encyclopedia of Social and Political Movements*, eds. David A. Snow, Donatella Della Porta, Doug McAdam, and Bert Klandermans, 613–20. Chichester: John Wiley & Sons.

Stahl, Titus. 2013. 'What Is Immanent Critique?' *SSRN Electronic Journal*, 21 November. https://ssrn.com/abstract=2357957.

Stavrakakis, Yannis. 2002. *Lacan and the Political*. London: Routledge.

Sutton, Rebecca, Darshan Vigneswaran, and Harry Wels. 2011. 'Waiting in Liminal Space: Migrants' Queuing for Home Affairs in South Africa'. *Anthropology Southern Africa* 34(1–2): 30–7.

Taylor, Charles. 1985. *Philosophical Papers: Volume 2, Philosophy and the Human Sciences*. Cambridge; New York: Cambridge University Press.

———. 2005. *Hegel*. Cambridge: Cambridge University Press.

Thomassen, Lasse. 2016. 'Hegemony, Populism and Democracy: Laclau and Mouffe Today'. *Revista Española de Ciencia Política* 40: 161–76.

Tilly, Charles, and Lesley J. Wood. 2020. *Social Movements, 1768–2008*. London: Routledge.

Tomšič, Samo. 2019. *The Labour of Enjoyment: Towards a Critique of Libidinal Economy*. Berlin: August Verlag.

Toren, Nina. 1975. 'Deprofessionalization and Its Sources: A Preliminary Analysis'. *Sociology of Work and Occupations* 2(4): 323–37.

Tralau, Johan. 2012. *Inbjudan till politisk teori*. Lund: Studentlitteratur.

Tsianos, Vassilis, and Dimitris Papadopoulos. 2006. 'Precarity: A Savage Journey to the Heart of Embodied Capitalism'. *Transversal Journal* 11(1): 1–12.

Tully, James. 1995. *Strange Multiplicity: Constitutionalism in an Age of Diversity*. Cambridge; New York: Cambridge University Press.

Tunick, Mark. 1994. 'Hegel's Nonfoundationalism: A Phenomenological

Account of the Structure of Philosophy of Right'. *History of Philosophy Quarterly* 11(3): 317–37.

Van der Linden, Marcel. 1997. '*Socialisme ou Barbarie*: A French Revolutionary Group (1949–65)'. *Left History: An Interdisciplinary Journal of Historical Inquiry and Debate* 5(1): 7–37.

Vitus, Kathrine. 2010. 'Waiting Time: The De-subjectification of Children in Danish Asylum Centres'. *Childhood* 17(1): 26–42.

Voss, Kim. 1996. 'The Collapse of a Social Movement: The Interplay of Mobilizing Structures, Framing, and Political Opportunities in the Knights of Labor'. In *Comparative Perspectives on Social Movements: Political Opportunities, Mobilizing Structures, and Cultural Framings*, eds. Doug McAdam, John D. McCarthy, and Mayer N. Zald, 227–58. Cambridge: Cambridge University Press.

Vrousalis, Nicholas. 2013. 'Exploitation, Vulnerability, and Social Domination'. *Philosophy & Public Affairs* 41(2): 131–57.

Walzer, Michael. 1989. 'Citizenship'. In *Political Innovation and Conceptual Change*, eds. Terence Ball, James Farr, and Russell L. Hanson, 211–20. Cambridge: Cambridge University Press.

Weininger, Elliot B. 2002. 'Pierre Bourdieu on Social Class and Symbolic Violence'. *Alternative Foundations of Class Analysis* 4: 119–71.

Westheuser, Linus. 2020. 'Populism as Symbolic Class Struggle. Homology, Metaphor, and English Ale'. *Partecipazione e Conflitto* 13(1): 256–83.

Wittgenstein, Ludwig. 1969. *On Certainty*, eds. G. E. M. Anscombe and G. H. von Wright, trans. G. E. M. Anscombe and D. Paul. Oxford: Blackwell.

Wolin, Sheldon S. 1994. 'Fugitive Democracy'. *Constellations* 1(1): 11–25.

Young, Iris Marion. 2011. *Justice and the Politics of Difference*. Princeton, NJ: Princeton University Press.

Žižek, Slavoj. 1990. 'Beyond Discourse-Analysis'. In Ernesto Laclau, *New Reflections on the Revolution of Our Time*, 249–60. London; New York: Verso.

———. 2001. 'What Can Lenin Tell Us about Freedom Today?' *Rethinking Marxism* 13(2): 1–9.

———. 2002. 'Postface: Georg Lukács as the Philosopher of Leninism'. In Georg Lukács, *A Defence of* History and Class Consciousness: *Tailism and the Dialectic*, trans. Esther Leslie, 151–82. London; New York: Verso.

# Index

EU representative:
Easy Access System Europe
Mustamäe tee 50, 10621 Tallinn, Estonia
Gpsr.requests@easproject.com

www.ingramcontent.com/pod-product-compliance
Lightning Source LLC
Chambersburg PA
CBHW070843300326
41935CB00039B/1390